Praise for **HOOK POINT**

"If you want to become a lasting, successful brand online and off, Hook Point *is a must-read. Brendan delivers proven strategies that are sure to help you stand out and grab people's attention."*
—Sally Newell Cohen, senior vice president of
global communications at ICANN;
former COO of Toastmasters International

"Wondering how you can stand out from the crowd in three seconds or less? Brendan Kane shows you how in his compelling, must-read book, Hook Point. *Brendan brings power with his approach and shows us how we do this with real-world, relatable examples. Be the hero that masters capturing people's attention and creates new opportunities for your enterprise by reading this book!"*
—Neil Sahota, United Nations A.I. adviser;
bestselling author of *Own the A.I. Revolution*

"An insightful read. I genuinely appreciate being a part of this book."
—John Kilcullen, creator and publisher of the iconic
For Dummies bestselling book series and brand

"In this new micro-attention world, it's becoming harder and harder to stand out. Hook Point *shares tried-and-true ways that get people to pay attention and is a must-read for anyone posting anything on social media today."*
—Cyrus Gorjipour, cofounder and CEO of Goalcast

"Do you want to create demand for your brand or business? Brendan shares methods that work in the 24/7 ubiquitous world we live in."

—Jonathan Skogmo, founder and CEO of Jukin Media

"The average American sees 4,000 ads a day, and who knows how many posts on social media. If you want to cut through the clutter and build a massive business or personal brand, Brendan Kane and Hook Point *are your secret weapons."*

—Craig Clemens, cofounder of Golden Hippo

"Today we are bombarded with so many messages, it's truly difficult to stand out. Luckily, Hook Point *gives you the tools to capture attention, maintain it, and grow a compelling brand."*

—Dorie Clark, author of *Stand Out*
and executive education faculty of the
Duke University Fuqua School of Business

"We are all looking for the biggest Hook to capture the market place. Hook Point *shows us how to get attention and build upon it. If you want people to pay attention to your brand, you need to pay attention to Brendan and* Hook Point.*"*

—Joivan Wade, founder of the Wall of Comedy,
actor in *The First Purge*, and the star of DC's *Doom Patrol*

"Brendan is relentless in his pursuit of finding new ways to help marketers do their job better."

—Latham Arneson, former VP of digital
marketing at Paramount Pictures

"*If you want to become a long-lasting, successful brand both online and off, look no further. Brendan helps you find the messages that get people to pay attention time and again.*"

—Melissa Ambrosini, bestselling author, speaker, podcaster, and entrepreneur

"*Brendan is a master at getting attention. If you feel you are in a crowded market and having a hard time standing out from the competition. His latest book,* Hook Point, *has tools and strategies you can use right away.*"

—Ajit Nawalkha, cofounder, Evercoach and Mindvalley

"*Hook Points are the essence of my success; without it I'm just another guy trying to get your attention, and we all know about how well that works these days!*"

—Michael Breus, PhD, best-selling author, internationally renowned as "The Sleep Doctor"

"*A must-read. In a world of constant transformation,* Hook Point *is the answer to standing out and growing your brand or business.*"

—Keith Ferrazzi, *New York Times* bestselling author of *Never Eat Alone*

HOOK POINT

ALSO BY BRENDAN KANE

One Million Followers:
How I Built a Massive Social Following in 30 Days

HOOK POINT

HOW TO STAND OUT IN A 3-SECOND WORLD

BRENDAN KANE

Waterside Productions

Cardiff-by-the-Sea, California

First Printing, 2020
Printed in the United States of America
ISBN-13: 978-1-949001-00-6 print edition
ISBN-13: 978-1-949001-01-3 ebook edition
ISBN-13: 978-1-949001-19-8 audiobook edition

Waterside Productions
2055 Oxford Avenue
Cardiff-by-the-Sea, CA 92007
www.waterside.com

To those with talent, intellect, and a pure heart whose voices are being suppressed or ignored. May this book be your guide to amplifying your voice, finding your power, and making a positive impact on the world.

CONTENTS

HOOK POINT

FOREWORD

GREEK AMERICAN ENGINEER, physician, and entrepreneur Peter Diamandis
(best known for being founder and chairman of the XPRIZE Foundation)
once famously said that if you're holding a smartphone in your hand today,
you have more access to information than the president of the United
States did in the late 1990s. The smartphone gives every single individual
on Earth the ability to make an impact through knowledge acquired by
research or through the sharing of messages that influence people, politics,
and business. In other words, the sum of human knowledge is now in the
palm of your hands.

Access to this vast amount of information is a gift, but it also creates a
problem—most people feel inundated, overwhelmed, and stressed out
because of the sheer magnitude of content flowing to them on a daily basis.
In 1970, 500 ads were seen by the average American per day;[1] today it's
between 4,000 and 10,000 ads per day.[2] This has led to a phenomenon
where human attention spans are getting shorter. These days, if you want

---

[1] Ryan Holmes, "We Now See 5,000 Ads a Day . . . and It's Getting Worse," LinkedIn,
Feb. 19, 2019, https://www.linkedin.com/pulse/have-we-reached-peak-ad-social-media
-ryan-holmes/.
[2] Ron Marshall, "How Many Ads Do You See in One Day?" Red Crow Marketing
Inc., Sept. 10, 2015, https://www.redcrowmarketing.com/2015/09/10/many-ads-see
-one-day/.

to get your message out to the world, you often have as little as three seconds to do so.

Think about it. The world's first contact with your brand or business is often on social media, where there are 147,000 photos uploaded, 54,000 shared links, and 317,000 status updates on Facebook every minute;[3] more than 95 million posts shared on Instagram every day;[4] and one billion hours of content watched on YouTube daily[5]—there's an incredible amount of distraction that prevents you from being seen. Whether you like it or not, if you want people to notice your brand or business—online or off—it's essential to master the art of grabbing attention quickly.

Luckily, Brendan Kane is a true expert in helping people stand out. Brendan's claim to fame happened when he decided to figure out how he could get one million fans in 30 days flat. After that achievement, he wrote a book about the process called *One Million Followers*. The book led to speaking opportunities, which is how I met Brendan, when I put him onstage at Mindvalley's A-Fest to share his knowledge about digital and social media. I was so impressed by what he had to share that I asked him to become an adviser for my company, Mindvalley.

In a matter of months, Brendan transformed the way my team and I communicate on the internet. He gave us the incredible ability to boost our company's revenue—as once you have a loyal following, you can get

[3] Salman Aslam, "Facebook by the Numbers: Stats, Demographics & Fun Facts," Omnicore, Feb. 10, 2020, https://www.omnicoreagency.com/facebook-statistics/.
[4] Dustin W. Stout, "Social Media Statistics 2020: Top Networks by the Numbers," Dustin Stout, 2020, https://dustinstout.com/social-media-statistics/#instagram-stats.
[5] Salman Aslam, "YouTube by the Numbers: Stats, Demographics & Fun Facts, Omnicore, Feb. 10, 2020, https://www.omnicoreagency.com/youtube-statistics/.

important messages out there, which ultimately helps you monetize that following. As a health advocate, one of the most important messages Brendan has helped us communicate to date was about the harmful effects and outlandish marketing claims of Coca-Cola. He guided us in launching a campaign with a video on the dangers of high-fructose corn syrup that amassed ten million views within a week (and it's still growing).

In short, not only did Brendan's ideas help our company thrive, but they also allowed us to disseminate important information, impact the consciousness of our audience, and become more effective activists. This is why it's so important to know how to stand out—you can have all the followers in the world, but to truly make a difference you need to know how to communicate with them.

This book will give you a process that helps you better communicate with potential audience members and business partners, as well as with current customers. You will learn how to make them loyal, engaged, core visionaries who support your visions, ideas, and mission. To get you started, here are some crucial tips about making an impact that I've learned as I've grown my following and reach for Mindvalley:

1. Be aware of whom you're talking to. Tailor your communication to your audience, whether it's millennials, baby boomers, or an ultraniche group of people such as auto mechanics.
2. Become your demographic. Mine comprises people who are passionate about transformation, health, and personal growth. Every single month I make it a point to read, attend a program or seminar, and work with a transformational leader. I put myself through experiences that make me wiser, healthier, and happier.

Then, I share these experiences with my audience so that I am not only a mentor and a thought leader but also a member of my demographic—a consumer of transformation.

3. Know your why—that is, know why you do what you do. I do what I do because of what I call the "Eve question." Eve is my six-year-old daughter, and before every action I take, I ask myself, "Will this make the world better for Eve?" This is why my communication is not just about spreading personal-growth information, but also about encouraging people to leave the world a better place for all the young children who will inherit this planet.

4. Be authentic and real. In my communication, I don't just share ideas from my business, I also openly share my difficulties and challenges. My most-commented-on and engaged posts over the last two years were the ones where I spoke about personal events—how my parents lost their home in a fire, how I was recovering from a serious injury and would have to go through a year of rehabilitation, and even a post where I shared why my partner and I were ending our marriage. People demand authenticity from leaders today and pay more attention when you're real and authentic.

Brendan covers all these tips in depth (and so many more) in this book. I bet you're eager to start reading, but before you embark on this journey to making an impact, I want to address one hurdle that may be in some of your minds: *Am I worthy of sharing? Am I unique or special? Do my thoughts really need to be heard?*

The answer is: *You won't know until you try.* So why not start today?

In 2008, when I first started my company, I only published other people's work. Even though I had considerable expertise in certain fields, I felt I was too young, too unworthy, and too unaccomplished to publish my own thoughts. I didn't feel good enough until a disaster struck several years later—I lost a deal with my biggest author. All of a sudden, there was a gap to fill, and I decided that perhaps it was a sign I should step up and become an author myself. When I did so, the universe seemed to support my choice. Not only did my book, *The Code of the Extraordinary Mind*, become a *New York Times* bestseller, but it hit the number-one spot on Amazon. Yet this was a book that I had put off writing for three years because I didn't think I had what it took!

All of us will face moments of insecurity and doubt—moments where we feel unworthy. Know that these moments are often nothing more than self-imposed limitations. So get out there and do your best. You will refine, grow, and enhance your ideas when you let them flow out to a world that will dissect, comment on, engage with, and mold them. Let public opinion and feedback become your friends. No matter where you are, put your insecurities aside, and *just do it*. You'll get better as you practice the tools that Brendan Kane shares right here in this book.

VISHEN LAKHIANI
FOUNDER, MINDVALLEY

INTRODUCTION:
LIVING IN A 3-SECOND WORLD

DIGITAL AND SOCIAL media have reshaped our world into one of micro-attention. With more than 60,000,000,000 messages sent out on digital platforms each day, we have an incredible amount of information being sent to us constantly. Whether it's a text, a push notification, an email, an advertisement, or a social media post, our brains have to adjust to processing larger amounts of content than ever before. In fact, the average person spends 11 hours a day interacting with digital media (including digital video, audio, TV, newspapers, magazines, etc.)[6] and scrolls through 300 feet of content.[7] People use their phones 1,500 times a week and check their email in-boxes 30 times an hour.[8] Every 60 seconds on Facebook, there are 400 new users, 317,000 status updates, 147,000 uploaded

---

[6] Joe Concha, "Adults spend more than 11 hours per day interacting with media: report," *The Hill, Aug. 1, 2018,* https://thehill.com/homenews/media/399819-adults-spend-more-than-11-hours-per-day-interacting-with-media-report.

[7] NetNewLedger, "Average Person Scrolls 300 Feet of Social Media Content Daily," NetNewsLedger, Jan. 1, 2018, http://www.netnewsledger.com/2018/01/01/average-person-scrolls-300-feet-social-media-content-daily/.

[8] Web Desk, "The Human Attention Span [INFOGRAPHIC], Digital Information World, Sept. 10, 2018, https://www.digitalinformationworld.com/2018/09/the-human-attention-span-infographic.html.

photos, and 54,000 shared links.[9] Approximately 95 million photos and videos are shared on Instagram on a daily basis.[10] More than 500 hours of content are uploaded to YouTube each minute,[11] and around 40,000 songs are uploaded to Spotify every single day.[12]

This bombardment of stimuli has changed the way we process information and communicate with each other, both online and off. New research from presentation software company Prezi says that we're becoming more selective about what we devote our attention to; and Latham Arneson, former vice president of digital marketing at Paramount Pictures, has been a close witness to this shift in communication. He says, "Before social media you had fewer sources for people to pay attention to. While there was still a lot of information being shared, today the inundation of platforms forces marketers to compete harder than ever before. There's a lot more distraction."

Erick Brownstein, president and chief strategy officer of Shareability, who's created digital content for soccer player Cristiano Ronaldo, the Olympics, Adobe, AT&T, and many other major corporations and celebrities, agrees, saying, "Now there's not only more content, but also better content. You have competition for limited time and attention, and many messages get lost in an avalanche of distraction."

---

[9] Salman Aslam, "Facebook by the Numbers: Stats, Demographics & Fun Facts," Omnicore, Feb. 10, 2020, https://www.omnicoreagency.com/facebook-statistics/.

[10] Mary Lister, "33 Mind-Boggling Instagram Stats & Facts for 2018," WordStream, Aug. 26, 2019, https://www.wordstream.com/blog/ws/2017/04/20/instagram-statistics.

[11] James Hale, "More Than 500 Hours of Content Are Now Being Uploaded to YouTube Every Minute," Tubefilter, May 7, 2019, https://www.tubefilter.com/2019/05/07/number-hours-video-uploaded-to-youtube-per-minute/.

[12] Brad Bennett, "Around 40,000 songs are uploaded to Spotify every day," mobilesyrup, May 1, 2019, https://mobilesyrup.com/2019/05/01/40000-songs-uploaded-spotify-every-day/.

Brownstein adds that today, even if you're planning on advertising on the side of a bus or on a billboard, it's important to think about what will make your marketing material shareable in a digital ecosystem. In your storytelling process, you need to think through a social media and digital-first lens as it influences the types of stories you'll tell and how you'll tell them. Doing so will make your messages more palatable to audiences that have higher expectations imposed by our new climate.

Serial entrepreneur Gary Vaynerchuk backs this up with his belief that we are grossly underestimating the power of the internet. He says, "If you don't adapt to the shifts in consumer attention, you'll lose. There are so many people who are wasting money in marketing every single day because they're chasing what 'used' to work. But the reality is, the tactic that used to work yesterday will put you out of business today."[13]

In response to all these changes in our behavior, Facebook started counting video views at three seconds instead of when it initially loads in the feed. They did so because advertisers were up in arms when they saw that they were being charged for views when most people were just scrolling past the feeds and not paying attention to their ads for more than a second. Facebook video product manager Matt Pakes believes that three seconds indicates a person's intent to watch a video, saying, "If you've stayed on a video for at least three seconds, it signals to us that you are not simply scrolling through [the] feed."

YouTube creator Hank Green has criticized Facebook's video view standard, saying that Facebook is "muddying the waters by calling something a

---

[13] "The Keys to Get Consumer's Attention in 2019," YouTube video posted by GaryVee TV, Nov. 26, 2018, https://www.youtube.com/watch?time_continue=1&v=b54bP5Nmz1c&feature=emb_logo.

view when it is in no way a measure of viewership."[14] But regardless of who's right in this debate, Facebook's choice affects the way we consume content on Facebook and Instagram, and it can't be ignored. Facebook's (and the majority of social platforms') algorithms are designed to push content that grabs and holds people's attention. Most videos don't get past the 3-second mark, so the algorithms help prioritize the best content that actually maintains people's attention.

By examining my own behavior and speaking with marketing professionals and friends during the research for this book, I have come to realize that the world has changed. My attention span is certainly shorter. Content, ideas—even people—have to work harder to stand out. If you can't capture people's attention in that first three seconds, or whatever short time period you have with them, then you can't get them to pay attention to the rest of your story, products, or services. And that's why this book is focused on how to develop Hook Points—a method to grab people's attention in the first three to five seconds, both online and off, so you can win the next 10, 15, 30, or 60 seconds to convey the rest of your message.

Learning how to capture attention successfully is the skill that people like Vaynerchuk most attribute their success to.[15] He explains that your ambition should always be to get the attention of the end consumer, and that building a real relationship with your audience is how you achieve lofty goals. For example, Kylie Jenner built a strong relationship with her

[14] Martin Beck, "Facebook Defends Its 3-Second Video View Standard," Marketing Land, Aug. 7, 2015, https://marketingland.com/facebook-defends-its-3-second-video-view-standard-137823.

[15] "The Keys to Get Consumer's Attention in 2019," YouTube video, posted by GaryVee TV, Nov. 26, 2018, https://www.youtube.com/watch?time_continue=1&v=b54bP5Nmz1c&feature=emb_logo.

social audience and leveraged that attention to sell 51 percent of her business for $600 million.[16] This happened because she knows how to capture attention and maintain relationships at scale.

A lot of people know who they are and what they do—a few even know *why* they do it (as concept author and motivational speaker Simon Sinek eloquently writes and teaches about, and which we'll discuss later on in this book). But even when brands or individuals have clarity in these areas, they often struggle to maintain a potential audience's attention long enough to get them to learn about the individual or brand. Many people have amazing products or services but fail to achieve great success because they don't know how to talk about what they do effectively. As Brownstein points out, people generally care about themselves, not *your* brand, product, or business. If you constantly put your brand in the spotlight of your marketing material, people will tune it out. Ever been on a date where the other person talks about him- or herself the whole time? *Boring!* Brands are doomed to fail if their main focus is on selling themselves. Instead, they need to think about how to bring value to their audiences.

This new reality presents marketers with serious challenges. How do you get past all the noise? In my first book, *One Million Followers: How I Built a Massive Social Audience in 30 Days* (www.OneMillionFollowers.com), I focused on teaching readers how to fight algorithms and how to create compelling content to drive massive scale and audiences on the various social platforms. In this book, I walk you through my Hook Point process, which helps you capture attention in the 3-second world in which we live

---

[16] Garyvee, "Kylie just sold 51% for $600m on attention arbitrage," Instagram, Nov. 18, 2019, https://www.instagram.com/tv/B5BvaBIgwe4/?igshid=1w9lqw3zd5d5j.

so you can generate new opportunities, innovate and scale your business, and create a compelling brand that works both online and off.

Knowing how to use Hook Points properly helps you become a more effective marketer and communicator. It gives you a nucleus upon which to scale your business and become a world-class brand. It's a critically important business tool that deserves marketers' time and attention.

Whether I'm talking to a young adult who's just graduated from college or a well-seasoned billionaire, I find that people at both ends of the spectrum struggle to identify how to package their messages in succinct, attention-grabbing ways that work in our 3-second world. Unfortunately, not knowing how to do so leads to missed opportunities.

I wrote this book because I truly believe that understanding how to use Hook Points can help individuals, businesses, and brands stand out and reach their goals more quickly and with more consistency. These are the first topic I address with clients, as they can largely enhance success.

A great Hook Point will not only allow you to capture people's attention in three seconds, but it will also help you hold that attention to get your audience to take specific actions for years to come.

I help people stand out with the Hook Point process every single day, so if at any point you'd like additional assistance in understanding how to stand out and innovate your company, or have a question about any topic in this book, feel free to email me at bkane@brendanjkane.com, or visit www.HookPoint.com.

CHAPTER 1

MEET HOOK POINT, YOUR NEW SECRET WEAPON

EVERY TIME YOU scroll through your phone, read the news, turn on your TV, listen to the radio, or look at a billboard, you're inundated with messages, content, and advertisements. To actually stand out and capture attention, you need an effective Hook Point or you'll get lost in the noise. So what is a Hook Point? A Hook Point can be comprised of **text** (e.g., a phrase, title, or piece of copy), **an insight** (from statistics or a professional's point of view, a philosophy, or a person's thought), **a concept/idea or a format** (e.g., an image or video), **a personality or performance** (e.g., music, sports, acting, or a cadence), **a product/service**, or a combination of some or all of these elements. It is used both online and/or offline to grab an audience's attention in the shortest possible amount of time. (If you wish to dive in deeper and see visual examples of some of the most common types of Hook Points, please visit: www.hookpoint.com/training.)

My team and I often aim for a Hook Point to capture a person's attention in three seconds or less, especially when designing content for digital and social platforms. A Hook Point's purpose is to help you get people interested in learning more about your content or business—it can help you generate new leads, launch products successfully, generate social followers at scale, drive massive revenue growth, create effective brand messaging, secure high-paying job interviews, perform well in important meetings, land A-list clients, and/or achieve other career-related goals and aspirations.

The term *Hook Point* is derived from many different concepts in advertising and branding over the past hundred years. I do not claim to have invented all the ideas connected to this concept. I've simply reframed and redefined what was once considered a hook line, a magazine headline, a "lead," or a "big idea" (among a variety of other terms in branding) to fit our current digital micro-attention culture.

Most great pieces of advertising start with a solid Hook Point. This is because they're designed to get people to lean in. Brand strategist Craig Clemens (follow him @Craig on Instagram), one of the top copywriters in the world (selling more than $1 billion in products) and the cofounder of Golden Hippo, a leader in direct-to-consumer marketing, grew up learning from some of the best copywriters in advertising. One of his favorites is the legendary Gary Halbert. Halbert's most famous campaign was created to launch a perfume line by Tova Borgnine, the wife of movie star Ernest Borgnine. Halbert wrote an ad in a newspaper to announce the launch party at the Century Plaza Hotel in Los Angeles. He used the headline: "Tova Borgnine Swears Under Oath That Her New Perfume Does Not Contain an Illegal Sexual Stimulant," with the subhead: "Wife of famous movie star agrees to give away 10,000 samples of her new fragrance just to prove it's safe to wear in public." More than 7,000 people showed up at the hotel, and more would have probably barged in had the fire marshals not stopped them.

The results that this hook produced were incredible—the campaign led to purchase orders from the biggest department-store chains, and the event was written up in *Time* magazine. As a result, the Borgnines went from grossing $20,000 a month to $800,000 a month (and this was back in 1977, so it was probably worth ten times that today due to inflation).[17] Clemens believes that this hook had such effective results because it tapped into the truth that people wear perfume to impress and attract the opposite sex. Halbert took that idea to the extreme to hook people with the concept that this perfume causes so much attraction that it's hard to believe it's not illegal.

Ernest Lupinacci, legendary copywriter, cofounder of ad agency Anomaly, and founder/chairman of the board of Ernest Industries, shares that one of his favorite Hook Points is from a long-copy ad for Timberland boots: "Your eyes are frozen. Your skin has turned black. You're technically dead. Let's talk boots." Lupinacci says that the writer apparently got the idea by looking up the definition of *hypothermia* and then wrote a headline that summarized the symptoms in a very dramatic way. Then he wrote an essay about hypothermia and wove in the various innovative features and design elements of the boots. The ad captured the attention of those who wanted to engage in outdoor activities but didn't want to freeze to death in the process. Lupinacci adds that the drama of the hook helped people understand the ad right away—they didn't even need to read the rest of the copy—which demonstrates just a bit of the power of a great Hook Point.

---

[17] Gary C. Halbert, "The Gary Halbert Letter," thegaryhalbertletter, 2005, http://www.thegaryhalbertletter.com/newsletters/2006/modesty_personified.htm.

Hooks have been an important part of copywriting for as long as I can remember, but now, in our 3-second world, they're even more essential. Lupinacci explains that for people who work in traditional advertising, "it's getting harder to make breakthrough TV commercials because brands are competing with a nearly inexhaustible amount of content, which includes viral videos, almost every film ever made available on streaming sites, and an unimaginable quantity of quality television programming. To make matters even more difficult, all of this content is on-demand."

Because of these realities, Lupinacci emphasizes that pulling off a commercial like Jeep's "Groundhog Day," which was created for the 2020 Super Bowl (which you can watch here: www.brendanjkane.com/Groundhog), was a remarkable accomplishment. Not only was the commercial charming, funny, flawlessly executed, and true to "the passion and irreverence of the Jeep brand," but viewers understood why Jeep was inserted into the *Groundhog Day* story—it worked. Although the Jeep Rubicon was not the star of the spot, it was (along with Bill Murray and the groundhog) the perfect costar, and a crucial part of the ad. To that end, Lupinacci commends Highdive, O PositiveFilms, and Jeep for delivering a great piece of branded content "that did what every piece of branded content should do, which is to focus on branded utility," and demonstrating how a brand can be useful or meaningful to a consumer's life.

At the end of the day, this ad worked because it had a great hook. Without the hook that the Super Bowl took place on Groundhog Day, and that Bill Murray was the star of a movie about this subject as well as the spot, the ad wouldn't have had as much success. Mike Jurkovac, Emmy Award–winning director/producer at TheBridge.co, believes that using these hooks helped Jeep "win the Super Bowl." He also adds that the hook was effective because Bill Murray embodies the Jeep brand—he's true to himself and a little bit quirky—he has the characteristics that connect the dots for someone who would buy a Jeep.

Great hooks need to be used regardless of where you distribute your marketing messages. When people scroll on Facebook, YouTube, or Instagram, so much more varied content bombards them than in the old world, where they only saw content in print or on television based on selected topics. This volume of content makes marketers' jobs harder, though the goal remains the same. Jurkovac agrees, saying, "There are literally thousands of different publishers and distribution points, whether it's the TV, your tablet, your phone, or a magazine stand—there's much more content, so breaking through is hard." Doug Scott, former president of Ogilvy Entertainment and current president of Big Block, adds, "Social media is causing marketers to reevaluate how they develop, produce, and deliver content that can be monetized through social engagements across multiple platforms."

Hook Points are especially helpful for standing out within the online clutter in today's world and are essential tools for helping you compete with clickbait. Clickbait captures attention but lacks substance. Using a Hook Point is a better and more powerful choice because it's always attached to an authentic and compelling story that provides value *and* builds trust and credibility (which I will cover in depth in later chapters). A Hook Point is not like the content that used to be featured on BuzzFeed, which, as Lupinacci points out, failed because "running clickbait about the world's largest rubber band ball wasn't actually content worth spending time with and didn't help build a brand." Instead, Lupinacci advises that when you create Hook Points, you should have Dr. Ian Malcolm's voice (from *Jurassic Park*) in your head, saying something along the lines of "scientists were so worried about whether or not they could create dinosaurs that they didn't consider if they *should*." To apply this concept to advertising in the age of clickbait, Lupinacci modifies the question, asking, "This copy will get people to click on our ad, so we *could* create it—but *should* we create it? Is this how we want to invest in our brand?"

Most important, knowing how to create effective Hook Points not only helps you grow your brand and stay relevant, but it can also help you survive. For example, perhaps if Blockbuster had known about and invested in Hook Points, they wouldn't have gone out of business. When Netflix first launched, Blockbuster was their biggest competition. Netflix was absolutely the David in this David-versus-Goliath situation but won the market because they had stronger hooks.

The first hook they used was the fact that they delivered DVDs to your door, and you could return them with no late fees. I discuss Netflix and their Hook Point genius more in depth in just a bit, but for now I want you to understand that Blockbuster failed because they didn't come up with any original hooks—they simply tried to copy Netflix's, did so with less finesse, and missed out on the most important hook, which was developing strong, original content and inventing binge-watching around their original content. In 2010, Blockbuster, a company once valued at $8.4 billion, filed for bankruptcy and left Netflix to grow into a company with a market cap of $140 billion (at the time of the writing of this book). The underdog start-up was able to beat the major corporation because they had more effective Hook Points.

We see a similar truth in Amazon's rise to power. Amazon took away market share from major stores like Borders, Radio Shack, Payless, Toys-R-Us, Circuit City, Sears, and so on, by coming up with a plethora of hooks, including the world's largest bookstore (their very first hook), one-click checkout, Amazon Prime, the Kindle, Sunday delivery services, Amazon Echo, and more. The point here is that learning how to come up with hooks through the Hook Point Framework can help you stay innovative and survive in today's market regardless of your current company's size or stature.

Remember, humans have always had short attention spans, and our new micro-attention world reflects that truth. It continues to evolve at an incredibly rapid pace because digital and social platforms have connected us all and made information more accessible. As mentioned in the introduction, we're inundated with more than 60,000,000,000 messages each day, making it more difficult for any of us to stand out. If you don't capture an audience's attention within the first three seconds—or whatever short period of time you're given—you won't get them to pay attention to the rest of your story about your brand, product, or service. Additionally, it's important to realize that to build a long-lasting brand, you can't just capture people's attention once—you have to do it consistently. The Hook Point Framework I will teach you in this book can help you grab people's attention to win the next 10, 15, 30, or 60 seconds (and beyond) to convey the rest of your message time and again so that you don't lose market share and can continue to compete at the top.

BATTLE ROYAL: HOOK POINT VS. USP VS. TAGLINE VS. POINT OF DIFFERENCE VS. MISSION STATEMENT

I've been asked if a Hook Point is the same thing as a unique selling proposition (USP), tagline, mission statement, or a brand's purpose. The answer is: "Sometimes." A USP "refers to the unique benefit exhibited by a company, service, product, or brand that enables it to stand out from competitors."[18] A tagline is "a short, memorable phrase that is used throughout your marketing. It should convey the main sentiment or feeling that you want people to associate with your brand."[19] Mission statements are the values of a company, and a brand's purpose is the reason it exists. In a marketing campaign, a Hook Point must grab attention. If using your USP, tagline, mission statement, or purpose works as your Hook Point by getting people to pay attention, they could be the same.

For example, as mentioned previously, when Netflix first launched, their biggest competition was Blockbuster, so the Hook Point that Netflix used was the fact that they delivered DVDs to your door and that you could return them with no late fees, which was also their USP. Then, later on, the fact that they started producing original content such as *House of Cards*, *Orange Is the New Black*, *Stranger Things*, and so on, also became their Hook Points and USP. Another USP that served as a Hook Point was the invention of binge-watching by releasing all of the episodes of a show at once. In all these cases, the USPs worked well as Hook Points.

There are times, however, when USPs (as well as taglines, mission statements, and a brand's purpose) will not be the best choice for Hook Points. A good example of a brand that has a different USP from their many Hook Points is Disney. Disney's USP is that they bring families together through experiences and content. But this is quite general and isn't the hook they use in their marketing campaigns. Instead, they constantly develop many different Hook Points to capture attention and to get people to watch

---

[18] Entrepreneur Media Inc., "Unique Selling Proposition," *Entrepreneur,* 2020, http://www.entrepreneur.com/encyclopedia/unique-selling-proposition-usp.

[19] Laura Lake, "What Is a Tagline?" the balance, Oct. 20, 2019, https://www.thebalancesmb.com/what-is-a-tagline-4017760.

their movies and cable channels, and return to their theme parks, again and again.

A Hook Point that Disney invested heavily in is Star Wars land. Few people know the tagline or name of Star Wars land (which happens to be Star Wars: Galaxy's Edge), but they do know that Disneyland and Disneyworld opened a *Star Wars*–themed section of the parks, which gets them excited about visiting. Disney had a bit of a rough start with this hook—some people thought that it was responsible for an increase in ticket prices, and others feared there would be longer lines for rides. (It will be interesting to see how this hook plays out in the long run.) Regardless, Disney has used entertainment content–related hooks for their theme parks many times—a lot of their attractions (especially the newer ones) are based on movies (e.g., *Finding Nemo*; *Guardians of the Galaxy*; *The Little Mermaid*; *Toy Story*; *Dumbo*; *Monsters, Inc.*, etc.) and characters dressed in costume roaming the park to meet fans (e.g., Elsa from *Frozen*, Mickey and Minnie Mouse, Snow White from well, *Snow White*, etc.). In fact, Disney is currently working on launching a section of their theme parks specifically around Marvel movies. This is probably because the largest amount of revenue for Disney, $26.23 billion in 2019, is generated from parks, experiences, and products. Disney's media networks fuel the theme parks, generating $24.83 billion in 2019; and studio entertainment (meaning their movies) only accounted for $11.13 billion of the $71.54 billion they generated in 2019.[20] Because theme parks have proven to be such a strong revenue driver, Disney is investing even further with acquisitions Pixar,

---

[20] Amy Watson, "Walt Disney revenue breakdown 2019," Statista, Nov. 11, 2019, https://www.statista.com/statistics/193140/revenue-of-the-walt-disney-company-by-operating-segment/.

Marvel, and Lucasfilm—all tremendously strong hooks for Disney's brand and business.[21]

Nike is a very clear example of how a brand's Hook Points can be different from their USPs, tagline, mission statement, and purpose. Nike's tagline is "Just Do It," and their shoes are their USP. Their mission statement is "to bring inspiration and innovation to every athlete in the world,"[22] while their purpose "is to unite the world through sport to create a healthy planet, active communities, and an equal playing field for all."[23] None of these elements reflect Nike's Hook Point. The Hook Points they use in their marketing campaigns are aligned with their tagline, USP, mission statement, and purpose, but the athletes and celebrities they sponsor, such as LeBron James, Serena Williams, Kevin Hart, and Michael Jordan, are the Hook Points that get people to pay attention to the brand in order to learn more about Nike's values. The connection to the athletes and celebrities helps Nike generate press and publicity and allows them to express their message in innovative ways. And it's part of the reason why they're one of the biggest athlete sponsors in the world, spending more than $6 billion a year on sponsorship/endorsements[24] . . . endorsements are an important part of their hook, and it pays off.

Copywriter Craig Clemens (whom I mentioned earlier) shared the evolution of Nike's Hook Points. He explains that when Nike first started out,

[21] Brooks Barnes, "Disney Is Spending More on Theme Parks Than It Did on Pixar, Marvel and Lucasfilm Combined," *New York Times, Nov. 16, 2018,* https://www.nytimes .com/interactive/2018/11/16/business/media/disney-invests-billions-in-theme-parks.html.

[22] Nike Inc., "What Is Nike's Mission?" Nike, 2020, https://www.nike.com/help/a/nikeinc -mission.

[23] Nike Inc., "Purpose Moves Us," Nike, 2020, https://purpose.nike.com/.

[24] BJ Enoch, "Top 15 Influential Nike Sponsored Athletes on Social," Opendorse, Feb. 14, 2020, https://opendorse.com/blog/top-nike-sponsored-athletes-on-social-media/.

their Hook Point was that they made the best running shoes. As that hook started to fade a little, they brilliantly started to use professional athletes (remember, this was back in 1972 before endorsement deals were a huge industry) as their Hook Points. Some of the first athletes Nike sponsored were Romanian tennis player Ilie Nastase, a breakout star in Olympic track and field named Steve Prefontaine, and basketball player Michael Jordan. Now, they have a plethora of athletes they sponsor and always have new Hook Points on the rise.

Most recently, the fact that the Olympics are considering banning Nike's Zoom Vaporfly running shoe has become an amazing Hook Point. Sports-science journalist Alex Hutchinson explains that "the five fastest men's marathons in history have all been run in the last 13 months, all by runners wearing Vaporflys." Scientists think that Vaporflys give runners an advantage by making them 4 percent more efficient, and that the shoe is seriously helping them break records never before thought humanly possible.[25] This controversy is a great hook that makes consumers desire the shoe.

With each new Hook Point, who Nike is and what they do doesn't change. Their Hook Points simply evolve to continually grab people's attention to bring them back to the foundation of the brand. Hook Points must evolve, because over time, culture and consumers change—Hook Points adapt to meet their needs, but the core of Nike stays the same, which is why their USP and tagline remain the same.

Another reason Hook Points change is because markets become saturated, and brands need to find new ways to capture attention. What works

---

[25] Delia Paunescu, "Nike's high-tech Vaporfly sneakers help athletes run 4 percent faster. Should they be banned for providing an unfair advantage?" *Vox*, Nov. 3, 2019, https://www.vox.com/recode/2019/11/3/20944257/marathon-nike-shoes-running-sneakers-vaporfly-reset-podcast.

today won't necessarily work six months from now, especially when competitors catch on to it and attempt to use a similar hook. Nike understands this fact and has become a master at evolving their Hook Points without losing the core focus of who they are and why they exist—they never create clickbait that captures people's attention without substance to back it up. All of their Hook Points are aligned with the core values of the brand; and bring people into the story or context where a tagline, USP, mission statement, or purpose can live and be provided with meaning.

GETTING IN THE DOOR WITH MTV, *VICE*, AND TAYLOR SWIFT

I've used the Hook Point process my entire career—it's been a major key to my success. Hook Points have helped me secure clients such as MTV, Taylor Swift, *Vice* magazine, and Paramount Pictures; obtain book deals, podcast interviews, television appearances; and allowed me to generate a million social media followers in 30 days.

Although I've always been good at creating Hook Points, I didn't realize the magnitude of their importance until I moved to Los Angeles in 2005 to pursue a career in film. I started at the bottom as a production assistant at Lakeshore Entertainment—a company responsible for producing movies such as the Academy Award–winning film *Million Dollar Baby*, the *Underworld* franchise, and *The Ugly Truth*, among countless other films. At the time, I felt like one in a million, lost in a sea of seekers; I thought it would take me forever to make my way up the ranks in the movie industry. But by following the process I outline in this book, in less than a year I was head of Lakeshore's first digital division. By listening and understanding how to craft Hook Points and stories, which is precisely what I teach you in this book, I communicated a strong hook and value proposition that led to this fast promotion.

But just because it happened fast doesn't mean it was easy. I was constantly looking for ways to innovate myself and stand out. Over time I realized that I wanted to forge a connection with Gary Lucchesi, the president of Lakeshore. I was dropping off scripts to his office and heard him speaking to his assistant one day: "I don't understand why people just starting out here don't come into the office and ask me more questions." He had previously been the head of Paramount Pictures and a successful talent agent for Kevin Costner, John Malkovich, and Michelle Pfeiffer. He knew a lot about the industry and seemed to want to mentor people.

Once I heard him express his desire to answer questions, I tried to schedule time with him, but his assistant wasn't interested in fitting me in. To bypass that obstacle, I started waiting outside of his office's entrance, which was located on the Paramount Pictures lot. I'd wait there at the close of business every single day. If he was on the phone or he looked busy, I didn't interrupt him. But on those days when he would look at me and say hello, I'd walk him back to his car and ask questions.

In the beginning, our conversations were focused on movie producing, because initially that was what I wanted to do. I listened to his pain points and tried to absorb everything I could. After a few weeks of listening intently, I realized how I could provide him with unique value.

I worked up a conversation about my background. The Hook Point that caught Lucchesi's eye was that I'd started a few internet companies while I was in college (which is rare), and also that I knew a lot about how digital platforms worked. I showed him that I could help him market the movies he was working on by using digital platforms effectively. Finding this insight and presenting the proper Hook Point took me from making coffee and copies as a personal assistant, to creating the first digital division of Lakeshore in less than a year. From there, I started getting called into marketing meetings and was brought into other studios that Lakeshore partnered with. Studios, directors, actors, and screenwriters started seeking my advice on how we could promote films through social media, and it all grew from there. I was even brought in to help rewrite parts of a script for a movie featuring Diane Lane called *Untraceable*—about a serial killer live-streaming deaths online—because of my knowledge of the digital field.

Eventually, I was ready to find a new Hook Point to launch me to another stage of my career at Lakeshore. Two years later, I came up with an idea for a type of advertising technology that stemmed from research I was doing on Myspace. At the time, Fox News Corporation had acquired Myspace for around $580 million, and I was trying to figure out how they would effectively monetize it. In my research, I noticed that they had a gold mine in front of them and were missing out on the most valuable form of advertising. Myspace users were posting movie trailers, music videos, and posters of their favorite brands on their Myspace profiles. Peers were sharing content with peers—word-of-mouth advertising at its finest, and influencer marketing in its earliest form (before social influencers existed). I believed that Myspace could monetize their network with the inherent peer-to-peer advertising that was already taking place. At the time, they were only getting bottom-basement cost per impression (CPM) rates from banner ads—it wasn't scaling or profitable, which was one of the main issues with their business model.

The Hook Point I presented in lieu of this insight was wrapped around the idea that people could make money off of this new digital behavior. In the story I told, I pointed out that users were posting movie trailers and brand posters on their Myspace profiles. I explained that this was the most valuable form of advertising—a friend telling a friend, "Check out this product or service"—and said that we should monetize it. Instead of getting one-dollar CPMs (cost per thousand impressions), you could charge companies one dollar per click (or possibly more). I shared the potential about where social media advertising could go with this concept.

Looking back on it now, the technology could be likened to the first-ever social media influencer advertising platform. Myspace users could choose a movie trailer, commercial, or banner from our library related to something that they were passionate about and put it on their Myspace pages. Then, anytime other users engaged with these advertisements, users who had it on their profiles would get paid. It was very similar to what an influencer platform is today, but again, since this was around 2007, influencers didn't really exist yet. Without even knowing it, I was laying the groundwork for what an influencer deal could look like, and for what social influencers would ultimately become.

Initially, I brought the idea to the president of Lakeshore and another business adviser. They both ended up investing in the technology. I built a prototype of the platform, and once it was done, we started to take it around and present it to different corporate partners.

During this time, I was forced to get really good at the process I share with you in this book. When you're just some kid at the beginning of his career, trying to get big corporations or partners to pay attention to yet another new start-up technology, you have to be articulate, different, and most important, you have to *stand out*. You need to figure out how to capture attention, as well as build trust and credibility, or big companies either won't take meetings with you or they do but they don't take you seriously.

We ended up meeting with Viacom, MTV, Yahoo!, Paramount, MGM, Fox, Myspace, and Facebook (back when it had fewer than 400 employees—so, yes, to this day I kick myself for not trying harder to land a deal with them). Eventually, we landed a licensing deal with MTV. Through this partnership, we created several iterations of the platform and had a lot of success testing it with Rock Band, *Vice* magazine, MTV, Country Music Television, VH1, and Viacom.

Not many people know that *Vice* magazine's video arm started out as a joint venture between MTV and Viacom. MTV invested a few million dollars to get them up and running; then *Vice* bought them out a few years later. Since they were partners during the time I was licensing technology to MTV, I got to meet with *Vice*'s founder, Shane Smith, and their head of creative, Eddy Moretti, who ended up licensing the technology as well.

Due to some complications—mainly the fact that it arrived too early to the digital scene—the technology never ended up launching out of private beta to the public. I don't see this as a failure; I learned a lot in the process and built solid relationships. And most important, for our purposes here, the Hook Point and the story around the platform was compelling enough to get people to buy in, and paved the way for the launch of my next Hook Point and product.

Shortly thereafter, I started developing a website technology that could dynamically write code, similar to the type of technology we now have access to through companies such as Wix and Squarespace. I brought a prototype of the platform to MTV and licensed it to them for another sizable check.

The Hook Point that got them interested in this website technology was developed from the fact that at the time, Viacom (the parent company of MTV, VH1, Comedy Central, BET, and Nickelodeon) was helping a lot of musicians and celebrities become big stars through MTV's network. But Viacom wasn't directly profiting off of anyone's leap to fame. My technology was an opportunity to start developing business relationships with some of these stars and celebrities. It was a tool that could help celebrities ramp up their digital business, and in turn, MTV could take a piece of the action.

Shortly after we closed the licensing deal, the lead executive asked me if I wanted to meet with Taylor Swift about the product. At the time I didn't know who she was. She was on the rise but wasn't the huge global superstar she is today. I took the meeting, which was primarily with Scott Borchetta—the founder of Big Machine Records (which was eventually sold to Scooter Braun)—which is the record label Taylor was under back then.

When I met with Borchetta the first time, it was backstage at a Grammy Awards rehearsal in LA. At some point Swift came into the room singing loudly, and we talked briefly, but the meeting was focused on showing Borchetta the value of the website technology for the growth of their digital business. It went well. That meeting led to several meetings with Swift's father, then her mother, and then eventually with Taylor Swift.

In each meeting I had to understand how each of the individuals perceived the situation. I had to listen to their concerns so that I could address them with a variant of the Hook Point and value proposition that met their needs and solved their specific pain points. Listening intently and crafting stories to address concerns was the key to my success.

Borchetta and Swift's father were concerned that they'd already spent six figures on a flash website. They were frustrated by how much they'd invested and that it had taken them two days to update any aspect of the site. To address those concerns, the Hook Point and subsequent conversations were centered around how much money they could save and make with our platform. Additionally, they were concerned about the current home-page bounce rate of 90 percent, which was causing them to lose e-commerce revenue from their merch store. I explained that with our technology, we could optimize the site on the fly, drop down the bounce rate, and keep people on the site for longer lengths of time. We could build a brand-new website in hours that any member of their team could dynamically change without having to know how to read and write code.

These Hook Points appealed to them, so I finally built up enough trust to earn a meeting directly with Taylor Swift. By then I'd learned a lot about what she wanted. From discussions with the various members of her team, I was aware that she was very hands-on. She loved to go on her social profiles, customize them, and actively engage with fans; she was frustrated by the fact that she couldn't modify the website herself in the same way she could modify her social media accounts.

When we met, I showed her the brand-new website that we'd built for her with our technology in less than six hours. I walked her through how she could change any aspect of it, in minutes, all by herself without modifying any code. I even had her use the mouse to change the backdrop of the entire site with different album artwork and showed her how she could change around the navigation system without writing any code. She experienced firsthand the fact that this technology would allow her to quickly express her creativity, which was what got her excited about it. After that meeting, we closed Taylor Swift as our first major client for the platform.

Knowing which Hook Points to use with specific audiences, and how to say it in a way that gets results, stemmed from the process you'll learn in this book. If you follow it, you'll have more access to the types of big meetings you've always dreamed about, and it will help you more effectively market your products and services, both online and off.

(If at any point you'd like extra assistance in understanding how to stand out and innovate your brand, feel free to email me at bkane@ brendanjkane.com, or visit www.brendanjkane.com/work-with-brendan.)

A GOOD HOOK POINT CAN CHANGE THE WORLD . . .

Early on in my career, I learned that understanding the effective use of a Hook Point was essential for marketing, branding, and positioning oneself for success. But it wasn't until I spoke with my copywriter friend Craig Clemens that it dawned on me that a great Hook Point doesn't just help foster success, it can actually change the world.

While we discussed Hook Points and their possible impact, Clemens shared that in the 1920s, there was a gentleman named Claude Hopkins— one of the great advertising pioneers and fathers of modern-day marketing— who created brands that are still around today, including Goodyear Tire and Quaker Oats.

. . . FOR BETTER

One of the most famous stories about Hopkins relates to how he got modern society to brush its teeth. Back in the 1920s, there was a toothpaste maker called Pepsodent. They approached Hopkins and asked him to help them sell more toothpaste. Hopkins said, "Well, as you know, that's kind of a small market. . . ." This was because, back then, only 5 percent of people brushed their teeth on a daily basis. It sounds pretty gross now, but our current health standards didn't exist. Apart from one or two days a week when people took the time to brush their teeth, everyone was walking around with very bad-smelling breath.

Hopkins realized that the best way to increase sales for Pepsodent toothpaste was to go after the 95 percent of the population that was rarely brushing their teeth. He came up with a brilliant advertising campaign that explained that using toothpaste to remove film from teeth would make people look cleaner and better-looking.

The campaign featured pinup girls and men in the service—they were like celebrities at the time—and were used as Hook Points to show that good-looking people brushed their teeth so they could keep them super white. The tagline for the product was: "Pepsodent Makes Teeth Far Brighter," and the magazine ad copy read: "FILM, a dangerous coating that robs teeth of their whiteness. Here's a way to remove it that quickly restores brilliance." The copy also explained that you needed to use Pepsodent every day, twice a day, as an inexpensive and quick method to improve yourself and look like a star—another strong hook for the product.

The campaign was a success. Soon, the 1957 jingle was everywhere: "You wonder where the yellow went, when you brush with Pepsodent."[26] Pepsodent suppliers couldn't keep up with the demand. Not only did it become one of the best-selling products of the decade, and the best-selling toothpaste for more than 30 years, but it also changed the number of people who brushed their teeth on a daily basis. Those who brushed their teeth went from 5 percent of the population to 65 percent within ten years.

It's fascinating how the right Hook Point can forever change the world. In Clemens's words, "If you've ever kissed someone with bad breath, then

---

[26] E. L. Hamilton, "Breakthrough: Over 100 years ago, an ingenious ad campaign for Pepsodent helped save the teeth of a nation," *The Vintage News*, Dec. 13, 2017, https://www.thevintagenews.com/2017/12/13/pepsodent-iconic-ad/.

you definitely understand how important Hook Points can be for the betterment of our lives."

. . . OR WORSE

Hook Points can also be used to change the world for worse. . . .

Clemens shared that back in 1962, a gentleman named Edward Bernays became the father of public relations and propaganda. He also happened to be Sigmund Freud's nephew. He studied Freud's psychological theories, such as crowd psychology and psychoanalysis, and applied them to *consumer public relations*—a term he invented and wrote a book about in 1945. Bernays started the first-ever public relations company and became an associate of very powerful people, including presidents and CEOs. With all his knowledge and power, he did a lot of amazing things; unfortunately, not all of them were good.

George Washington Hill, the president of the American Tobacco Company, asked Bernays how they could get more women to smoke.[27] Bernays contacted psychoanalyst Abraham Brill, who disclosed that to a feminist, a cigarette symbolized nonconformity, and freedom from male oppression. This insight is what the Hook Point for his campaign was founded upon.

Bernays decided to get media attention in a natural way that didn't look like advertising (an act that was revolutionary at the time). He chose to do it at the biggest social event of the season—the New York City Easter Day Parade of 1929. Various high-society people would have floats there,

---

[27] Wikipedia, "Public relations campaigns of Edward Bernays," Wikipedia, Jan. 20, 2020, https://en.wikipedia.org/wiki/Public_relations_campaigns_of_Edward_Bernays.

including one with a group of debutantes, who were equivalent to the Paris Hiltons and Kim Kardashians of our day.

Bernays contacted the press before the parade and told them that a group of women's-rights marchers would "light 'Torches of Freedom' at the parade."[28] He gave the debutantes and other women packs of Lucky Strike cigarettes. They were instructed not to light them until they crossed the street, where he had photographers eagerly waiting to take their pictures. On April 1, 1929, the *New York Times* reported on the event and wrote: "Group of Girls Puff at Cigarettes as a Gesture of 'Freedom.'"[29]

The news about how these debutantes declared independence and strength with their torches of freedom led to much higher rates of female smoking. That year alone, the percentage of female smokers rose by 7 percent,[30] and it created lasting effects on the way people perceive women who smoke. Even today, when people think about female smokers, they see someone like supermodel Kate Moss—a leather jacket–wearing badass chick who fires up. This long-lasting image is the product of a Hook Point.

Quick Tips and Recap

- A Hook Point can be composed of **text** (e.g., a phrase, title, or a piece of copy), **an insight** (e.g., from statistics, a professional's point of view, a philosophy, or a person's thought), **a concept/ idea or format** (e.g., an image or video), **a personality, a**

---

[28] Wikipedia, "Torches of Freedom," Wikipedia, Jan. 10, 2020, https://en.wikipedia.org /wiki/Torches_of_Freedom.

[29] Brandt, Allan M. (2007). *The Cigarette Century.* New York: Basic Books, pp. 84–85.

[30] O'Keefe, Anne Marie; Pollay, Richard W. (1996). "Deadly Targeting of Women in Promoting Cigarettes," *Journal of the American Medical Women's Association.* 51 (1–2).

performance (e.g., music, sports, acting, or a cadence), **a product/service**, or a combination of some or all of these elements.

- Hook Points are used both online and/or offline to grab an audience's attention in the shortest possible amount of time.
- Hook Points help you generate new leads and followers at scale, create powerful brand messaging, secure job interviews, and perform well in important meetings. They can also help you land A-list clients, drive massive revenue growth, and/or achieve other career-related goals and aspirations, including podcast interviews, speaking gigs, and television appearances.
- A Hook Point is not clickbait—it is attached to an authentic and compelling story that provides value *and* builds trust and credibility.
- A good Hook Point can help your business survive.
- We're inundated with more than 60,000,000,000 messages each day, which makes it difficult for any of us to stand out.
- The Hook Point Framework can help you grab people's attention to convey your messages so that you don't lose market share and continue to compete at the top.
- Hook Points need to constantly evolve as markets change and become saturated.
- A Hook Point should always remain true to who you are as a brand.
- Great Hook Points can literally change the world.

(If at any point you'd like extra assistance in understanding how to stand out and innovate your company, feel free to email me at bkane@ brendanjkane.com, or visit www.brendanjkane.com/work-with-brendan/.)

CHAPTER 2

TESLA, THE BLAIR WITCH, AND YOUR GUIDE TO CREATING A PERFECT HOOK POINT

WHEN DEVELOPING A Hook Point for a company, product, or piece of content, I typically base it on what I feel the audience may want or need. My first thoughts are, *How can I solve my audience's specific pain point or problem?* and *What is an outcome my audience has been seeking that they've yet to find?* For example, a Hook Point I've used in the past to grab attention at scale, "Zero to a Million Followers in 30 Days," attracts people because they're seeking the outcome of building a large, effective social following, but they don't know how. By tapping into people's desires to market themselves on social media, I get them to pay attention. Notice, however, that I don't say, "I'll help you grow fast on social media" or "Let me teach you how to grow fast on social media." I simply make a bold statement: "Zero to a Million Followers in 30 days." (We will get into the specifics of crafting a compelling Hook Point later on, but I want you to be aware of this distinction as you observe the Hook Points presented throughout this chapter.)

Even the Hook Point I use for the subtitle of this book, "How to Stand Out in a 3-Second World," fulfills a pain point. Brands and individuals are struggling to stand out among the competition and noise. They want to create or find better jobs, secure more prestigious clients, drive revenue growth, and close bigger deals. A large part of achieving these goals is simply getting someone to pay attention to you long enough to have the opportunity to express the value of your product line, service, and/or brand.

You want to appear unique, desirable, and different. Focusing on how you can position your value proposition to inspire your potential audience will help you go further, faster. Let's look in depth at some examples of people and companies who've developed great Hook Points.

ROPE-FREE SOLO

Free Solo, a film by documentary filmmakers Jimmy Chin and Elizabeth Chai Vasarhelyi, won the Academy Award for Best Documentary Feature in 2019. The Hook Point of this movie is the plot. It's about a professional rock climber named Alex Honnold who was the first person to climb El Capitan, a 900-meter vertical rock face in Yosemite National Park **without ropes**. The novelty of seeing the incredible feat of climbing a mountain that steep and that high **without ropes** draws audiences in. I put "without ropes" in bold because that is the hook—if Honnold had climbed El Capitan *with* ropes, the Hook Point wouldn't be as strong.

Proof of this point is that the same directors, Chin and Vasarhelyi, had previously made a film called *Meru* about the first ascent, *with* ropes, of the "Shark's Fin" route on Meru Peak in the Indian Himalayas. *Meru* has a good Hook Point in the trailer (you can watch it here:

www.brendanjkane.com/meru), showing how the filmmakers thought they were going to die while climbing Meru. It hooks you right away and makes you wonder if the climbers will survive, but the movie didn't achieve the critical acclaim and box-office success of *Free Solo*.

I personally feel that *Meru* is the better movie (keeping in mind that I'm someone who knows nothing about rock climbing), but the Hook Point in *Free Solo* is stronger because it's tied to the fight-or-flight response that it produces in viewers when they see Honnold's struggle to make it to the top **without a rope**. (You can experience this by watching the *Free Solo* trailer here: www.brendanjkane.com/free.) This trailer helps you realize that Honnold could die at any moment during this climb—it puts you on the edge of your seat as you watch, feeling as if you're up that high with him, **without a rope**. I want to be clear that I think *Free Solo* is a good movie, but I believe it did well at the box office and won an Academy Award because of its strong Hook Point. The Hook Point is what allowed the film to break through to mainstream audiences that have no interest in rock climbing.

Free Solo is a great example of how a product or an idea itself can be a Hook Point. You don't have to risk your life to have a good Hook Point, but you do need something story-worthy or different. You need something that can be packaged in a way that's concise, catchy, impactful, interesting, and true. You want to capture your audience's attention and leave them wanting more.

ONE FOR ONE®: WITH EVERY PRODUCT YOU PURCHASE, TOMS WILL HELP A PERSON IN NEED

When Blake Mycoskie started Toms Shoes, his initial hook was "one for one"—meaning that for every product consumers purchased, Toms would help a child in need on their behalf. Mycoskie had a strong story to back up his Hook Point. In 2006 he was visiting a small village in Argentina and noticed that the children there didn't have shoes. Wanting to help these kids, Mycoskie developed the "one for one" concept, which became his Hook Point and allowed the company to succeed and grow at a rapid rate. In fact, by 2014, Bain Capital invested $313 million in Toms, which led to its being valued at more than $600 million.[31]

Unfortunately, over the last few years, the company's growth has stalled significantly—there were negative credit ratings and bankruptcy rumors. A Moody's report said net sales for 2018 were around $336 million.[32] Former Starbucks and T-Mobile executive Jim Alling, who has been with Toms since 2015, admits that the brand struggled when they started to focus more on design than their mission. He says, "You have to be great at footwear, but what distinguishes us is our total story."[33] Also, the original hook has been copied many times by other brands because of how much it helped Toms stand out, receive funding, and grow at a rapid rate. In fact, this copying of the model is a contributing factor to why the original hook

---

[31] Eliza Ronalds-Hannon, and Kim Bhasin, "Even Wall Street Couldn't Protect Toms Shoes from Retail's Storm," *Bloomberg, May 3, 2018,* https://www.bloomberg.com/news/articles/2018-05-03/even-wall-street-couldn-t-protect-toms-shoes-from-retail-s-storm.

[32] Katie Abel, "Can Blake Mycoskie's Bold New Social Agenda Reboot Toms?" FN and Footwear News, Mar. 25, 2019, https://footwearnews.com/2019/business/retail/toms-blake-mycoskie-interview-business-sales-mission-1202764082/.

[33] Ibid.

lost steam and why new hooks have needed to be introduced to keep the company relevant and make it stand out among the competition.

Now, Toms is trying to tackle homelessness and support female empowerment and social entrepreneurship in the hopes of evolving into different Hook Points and expanding the brand. Regardless, to date, Toms has donated more than 35 million pairs of shoes to children and expanded the model to include sunglasses and coffee. Through that effort, the brand has given eyeglasses to 250,000 people in need, and clean water to five different countries.[34]

NO LATE FEES

As mentioned earlier, the initial Hook Point for Netflix was "No late fees." They knew that one of the frustrating aspects about renting movies from Blockbuster (their biggest competition) was that you always had to go to the store to rent and return movies. And if you returned a movie even one day late, you were charged late fees. Apparently, Netflix CEO Reed Hastings was not a fan.

One day Hastings checked out the movie *Apollo 13* from Blockbuster, lost the cassette for a few days, and was penalized with a late fee of $40. After he left the store frustrated and embarrassed (a pain point almost every Blockbuster customer could relate to—myself included), he drove to the gym. On the way there, he started to think about a better system for movie rentals. He wondered why it couldn't be more like, well, joining a gym. What if people paid a monthly fee and rented an unlimited number of

---

[34] TOMS, "96.5 million lives impacted—and counting," TOMS, 2020, https://www.toms.com/one-for-one-en/.

movies each month? Shortly thereafter, Netflix started mailing people DVDs, three at a time, and the company was born.[35]

Netflix has grown way beyond its initial beginnings (and into different hooks), but the initial Hook Point, "No late fees," is what attracted attention to a small start-up and paved the way for it to become the media giant it is today. Over time, this Hook Point allowed Netflix to dominate the market, kill off Blockbuster (who failed to come up with new Hook Points to keep their market share), and become one of the most valuable media-service providers in the world. Netflix generated $15.8 billion in revenue in 2018[36] and had approximately 125 million customers[37] (not too shabby).

ELON MUSK'S UGLY CYBERTRUCK

Tesla's Cybertruck doesn't look anything like any other truck on the road (or any other car, for that matter). Public opinion around the press launch for the Cybertruck was very polarized, but one thing is for sure—this vehicle quickly caught people's attention. Pickup trucks have had the same design for nearly a hundred years,[38] and most truck owners are very loyal. Tesla CEO and cofounder Elon Musk knew that if he wanted to make an

---

[35] Blake Morgan, "Netflix and Late Fees: How Consumer-Centric Companies Are Changing the Tide," *Forbes, Oct. 7, 2016,* https://www.forbes.com/sites/blakemorgan /2016/10/07/netflix-late-fees-and-consumer-centric-ideas/#463faedb13ec.

[36] Trefis Team, "A Closer Look at Netflix's Valuation," *Forbes, Mar. 26, 2019,* https://www .forbes.com/sites/greatspeculations/2019/03/26/a-closer-look-at-netflixs-valuation-2 /#731dd73328c7.

[37] David Bloom, "Is Netflix Really Worth More Than Disney or Comcast?" *Forbes, May 26, 2018,* https://www.forbes.com/sites/dbloom/2018/05/26/netflix-disney-comcast -market-capitalization-valuation/#3edefb415618.

[38] John Linden, "History of the Pickup Truck," Car Covers, 2020, https://www.carcovers .com/resources/history-of-the-pickup-truck.html.

impact in this industry, he had to do something very different, which is why he came up with a design that was unlike anything anyone had ever seen (or imagined).

The Hook Point of the Cybertruck is effective not only because it catches people's attention, but also because there's a method to its madness. The new design gives the truck superior utility offered at an affordable price. Marketing and brand strategist Mike Gastin calls the truck a "masterstroke" of branding—it truly aligns with Tesla's vision of "delivering the future, today." Time will tell if the Cybertruck outdoes Ford's F150, but generating more than 250,000 pre-orders of the Cybertruck right after it was announced is remarkable.[39]

ZERO TO A MILLION FOLLOWERS IN 30 DAYS

"Zero to a Million Followers in 30 Days" is the main Hook Point I initially used to scale my brand. What a lot of people don't know is that building this massive social following was for that exact purpose—to have a strong Hook Point to leverage for larger opportunities that could help expand my brand.

I set out to build a million followers in 30 days because I knew that the Hook Point would capture attention so that I could provide value to others. I was never trying to become an influencer or a celebrity—I just wanted to entice people to listen to the larger story that I had to tell. And that's why, before I built my following, I approached a renowned literary agent, who

---

[39] Justin Bariso, "Elin Musk Made the Cybertruck 'Ugly' on Purpose—and It May Be the Smartest Thing He's Ever Done," *Inc., Dec. 3, 2019,* https://www.inc.com/justin-bariso/elon-musk-made-cybertruck-ugly-on-purpose-and-its-smartest-thing-hes-ever-done.html.

currently represents me, and asked him if the topic of generating a million followers in 30 days would appeal to publishers. I knew that there was a big difference between proposing the book title *Zero to a Million Followers in 30 Days* versus something along the lines of *How to Grow Followers on Social Platforms*. The former is specific and catchy, while the latter is general, generic, and overused in a very crowded market. My knowledge about Hook Points helped me secure that publishing deal and sell a lot of books, which eventually led to the next deal for this book, and many other significant business opportunities that have resulted in millions of dollars in revenue.

When choosing Hook Points, it's important to keep specificity in mind. You can't tell a story that people have heard a hundred times or they'll get bored and become numb to it. The whole point of a Hook Point is to help yourself stand out. Think about what makes you, your brand, or your product unique—completely different from others in your field.

SUBVERTING EXPECTATIONS:
FLIPPING EVERYTHING YOU KNOW ON ITS HEAD

Many good Hook Points get people to think differently, which is why subverting expectations with your Hook Points is a good tactic for capturing people's attention. One way to do so is to take commonly held beliefs or phrases and flip them on their heads. For example, in a successful social video, my team and I created the Hook Point "WARNING!! Safety is Dangerous." This challenged the commonly held belief that playing it safe was a good approach to life—instead, it encouraged people to take risks and fight for their dreams.

Your beliefs don't necessarily have to be in agreement with the subverted phrases you come up with. For example, in one video that I recorded for my social accounts, I used the Hook Point "Meditation is a scam!" I've been meditating for ten years and think that it can provide huge benefits when done correctly. I use this hook to capture people's attention so that I can deliver the real message behind that hook, which is that because meditation is so popular, there's a lot of misinformation about what it is and how to do it properly. The goal isn't to try and trick people, but to grab their attention about a subject they may be interested in. By subverting expectations, you can share valuable insights that people may otherwise skip over if they aren't attracted to your initial hook.

Naveen Gowda, digital content strategist on my team and former VP of content at First Media, adds that the practice of subverting expectations is all about getting your audience to look at an idea or concept through a different lens or from a different angle. If you peer into a room from different windows located on various walls of a house, your perspective of that room will change. Subverting expectations with your Hook Points allows you to do the same thing—you can give people a new perspective or outlook on a familiar topic.

It's an especially useful tool when you work in a crowded market. If you're a yoga teacher, meditation teacher, chef, or the like, you won't stand out if you repeat the same information that everyone else does. And, unfortunately, this applies even when your underlying brand foundation or perspective is actually more useful than that of your competitors. That's why you need to switch up the conversation in a unique way. Otherwise, people will find your content boring and/or won't receive your messages, which never caught their attention in the first place.

Entrepreneur Gary Vaynerchuk (also known as Gary Vee) is an example of someone who subverts expectations all the time. In one of his social videos (which you can watch here: www.brendanjkane.com/gary), a woman comes up to his car and says, "Give me three words that'll give me inspiration for any day I'm feeling down." Gary Vee replies, "You're gonna die." He is an entrepreneur, like millions of others like him, who inspires people to hustle and work hard. This video is a perfect example of how he completely subverted this woman's expectations (and the viewers of the video) with his answer to her question.

When most motivational entrepreneurs are asked a question like this, they typically respond with common phrases such as "Work hard," "You'll make it," "Use your head," or "You'll be successful." Gary Vee's choice to say "You're gonna die" completely goes against the grain and definitely captures people's attention. Although Gowda thinks Gary Vee's choice is brilliant in the example above, he also warns that there's a delicate balance between subverting expectations and becoming a contrarian, so be conscious of this fact when coming up with hooks.

Another good example of a brand that knows how to subvert expectations is digital media company Yes Theory. The brand is built around the idea that "life can be as authentic and fulfilling as you wish if you seek discomfort." Their videos urge people to push themselves out of their comfort zones with hooks such as "Becoming Superman with the Ice Man, Wim Hof," "I Lived in a Luxury Airport for 4 Days. Nobody Noticed," "Asking Strangers to Go Skydiving on the Spot," "Traveling to the Least Visited Country in the World," and "Letting a Coin Flip Control Our Lives for 24hrs (Dubai)."

The idea of living outside of your comfort zone and pushing your boundaries has been spoken about many times, but Yes Theory presents the topic in a unique way by coming up with crazy adventures (that serve as powerful hooks) around this theme. By wrapping their messages in this format and context, they subvert expectations and grab more attention.

The video *Becoming Superman with the Iceman, Wim Hof* (which you can watch here: www.brendanjkane.com/superman) is a stand-out example—many other people have interviewed Wim Hoff (a Dutch extreme athlete noted for his ability to withstand freezing temperatures), but Yes Theory's video captured more attention, receiving more than eight million views with their strong hook for the interview.

HOOK POINTS DRAW PEOPLE INTO STORIES

Those of you who've read my book *One Million Followers* know that the underlying principles I teach are actually about content testing and optimization. The book is about so much more than simply how to gain followers quickly. If the book only covered one formula on how to hack follower growth, it wouldn't provide as much value to readers or help me become a thought leader in the digital space. Nevertheless, the Hook Point "Zero to a Million Followers in 30 Days" has gotten people to pay attention and has helped transform my career.

After finishing the book, I hired someone to film a short interview about the process and philosophy I used to generate a million followers in 30 days. Then, I used this video interview to create a few advertising campaigns on Facebook and Instagram that drove viewers to an application to work with me. As a result, I received 16,000 applications from people all around the world. That's how strong my Hook Point was—people wanted to know more about the story behind how I did it and how they could do it too. It tapped into a strong desire and need.

After that success, I leveraged the Hook Point and the book, not only to generate new clients, but also for speaking opportunities through companies and venues such as IKEA, Mindvalley, and Web Summit (which has an audience of more than 70,000 people); major podcasts like *Finding Mastery: High Performance Psychology with Michael Gervais*; TV and radio appearances on Fox Business, SiriusXM, KTLA, and Yahoo! Finance; and features in publications such as *Forbes, Entrepreneur,* and *Inc.* magazine, which gave me even more clout and exposed my brand to additional people.

The "Zero to a Million Followers in 30 Days" Hook Point allowed me to capture the attention of millions in order to tell a story that people needed to hear but may otherwise have skipped over or ignored. Also, the story behind my Hook Point was authentic (the importance of which I'll cover in chapter 5), so it allowed me to grow my business and help others worldwide achieve their goals.

The "Zero to a Million Followers in 30 Days" Hook Point wasn't my first hook and won't be my last. I've been constantly testing Hook Points over the course of my entire career. Whether it was while pitching one of the various technology companies I launched, a campaign idea for a movie, or an attempt to close a celebrity client, I'm always testing, learning, and refining hooks for myself and my clients.

I didn't become a true expert at developing Hook Points quickly and efficiently, however, until I worked with renowned broadcast journalist Katie Couric. That was when I started to test headlines, hooks, and content every single day for a year and a half. While working with her, I tested 75,000-plus variations of content (which I discuss in detail in the next chapter). It was during this time that I developed an innovative process to test headlines, topics, and themes at scale, and my Hook Point method started to conceptualize as I collected data.

THE FOUR-HOUR WORKWEEK

Tim Ferriss's book, *The 4-Hour Workweek*, is a great example of a solid Hook Point with a strong value proposition. Readers are drawn to it because most people would love to work fewer hours, spend more time with their families and loved ones, travel, and enjoy their hobbies whenever they wish. Ferriss's Hook Point offers a solution to a common dilemma. If you read his book, you'll see that there are many strategies that go beyond the concept of working fewer hours per week. But the hook is so effective that Ferriss is constantly asked if *he* really only works four hours a week. He has explained that this annoys him, because the question only comes from those who didn't read the book. Regardless, it's the idea (and hook) of only working four hours a week that allows Ferris to capture enough attention to share the rest of his story.

Ferriss's book is a bestseller because of this succinct, thought-provoking message. I personally love the book, and the interesting thing is that the concepts are nothing revolutionary—people have shared similar advice in the past—but *The 4-Hour Workweek* stands out and has sparked more interest than its competitors because the concepts are tied to a solid Hook Point in the title.

Ferriss was well aware of the importance of his title hook. In fact, he tested dozens of other titles in Google AdWords to find the best one. *The 4-Hour Workweek* beat out *This Sucks, How to Live Like a Druglord* and *The Wild Gooserace*[40] (are you surprised?). The specificity of working only four hours a week was catchy and fresh. It created a clear image of a lifestyle choice (that didn't involve drugs or geese).

---

[40] Tim Ferriss, "Feeling Stuck? Read This . . ." *The Tim Ferris Show (blog)*, https://tim .blog/2011/01/31/feeling-stuck-read-this/#more-4680.

Copywriter Craig Clemens adds that Hook Points can take an unoriginal idea and get audiences to take it more seriously or find it more interesting. It all depends on how you say it and the context in which you wrap your message. You can get people to think you're a genius by presenting a familiar concept in an original way.

It's not enough to simply talk about yourself and explain what you do. Many others have the same skill sets. To stand out in three seconds or less, you need to find what makes you and your product or information unique and relevant to other people's lives—that is, develop a succinct, attention-grabbing way to relay your information. People will stop and pay attention if you associate yourself with timely, interesting topics that meet your audience's needs.

WHAT KEEPS YOUR AUDIENCE UP AT NIGHT?

As I mentioned earlier, Craig Clemens is the founder of Golden Hippo, one of the largest direct consumer marketing and brand-building companies on the web, and has generated more than a billion dollars in sales. There are very few people on the planet who've reached his level of success. Clemens attributes this success to knowing how to craft Hook Points that solve his audience's pain points. With this knowledge, he grabs the attention of those who browse around on Facebook, *The Huffington Post*, or TMZ—reading about the Kardashians or Donald Trump—and he changes their focus. He gets them to pay attention to compelling Hook Points.

Eugene Schwartz, the legendary copywriter of the 1970s and '80s, advises entering the conversation that prospects have in their own minds. Clemens feels that today it's more important than ever to think about your prospects and their internal thoughts. In this micro-attention age, your

Hook Point needs to tap into the problems that keep your audience up at night. Perhaps your potential clients suffer from persistent stomach pains and you have a vitamin that could ease the digestive process. Or maybe they don't have enough storage space on their computer and your company has a solution. Whatever the product, you can use a Hook Point to show that you can help solve an important problem in your audience's life. Jump into their minds as a guide, and teach them something new.

Marketer and psychological teacher Wyatt Woodsmall taught Clemens that if you describe people's problems better than they can, they'll subconsciously believe that you have the solution. So use your Hook Points to show your prospects that you understand their issues. It may help them gravitate toward your products, which will lead to purchases.

THE SLEEP DOCTOR

Michael Breus, PhD, is known as "The Sleep Doctor," which serves as his Hook Point. It has helped him secure appearances on programs such as *The Dr. Oz Show* more than 35 times, and on the *Today* show multiple times. So how did Breus find this powerful Hook Point? Well, very early on in his career, he became board certified in clinical sleep disorders. And while there are terms for different types of doctors, such as *pulmonologist* for a lung doctor or *otolaryngologist* for an ear, nose, and throat surgeon, there was no term for doctors who deal with everything related to sleep.

In an attempt to find an effective way to market himself, Breus read a book by Peter Montoya and Tim Vandehey called *The Brand Called You*. It explained that your brand name should consist of what you do in three to five words. Breus started asking people what they thought his occupation was, and their answers always revolved around medicine and sleep. From there, he started looking at URL names and discovered that "sleep doctor" and "the sleep doctor" were taken. He got ahold of the URL holder and purchased them, which turned out to be one of the best expenditures he ever made. Ever since, "The Sleep Doctor" has been a powerful Hook Point for Breus's business.

HOOK POINTS GENERATE STRONG RESPONSES

Immediately after choosing "The Sleep Doctor," Breus developed strong, positive recognition from his consumers . . . but backlash from people in his field. Because he was calling himself "The Sleep Doctor," his colleagues thought he was implying that he was the best in the field, or the only one who did this type of work, so there was a lot of jealousy. Breus was pushed out of many professional circles and wasn't invited to many conferences in his area of expertise. It took somewhere between five and ten years before people stopped calling him a "charlatan" and a "sellout."

When Breus was invited to a scientific meeting as a panelist, some audience members would protest, "You have no credibility here. You're an internet doctor." Ironically, by the end of the conference, those exact same people would come up to him and ask, "Hey, how do you get so much media attention?" In the public forum, he was an outcast, but behind the scenes, everyone wanted his advice. His colleagues' duplicity only gave him the strength to stick with the use of his Hook Point. He knew that if they wanted what he had, he wasn't doing anything wrong. Breus stayed the course because when it came down to the facts, no one could fault him for the way he was using scientific research. "The Sleep Doctor" is one of the best hooks I've ever heard, so I'm glad Breus persevered.

When creating a Hook Point, it's positive if people have a strong response, even if some of those responses are negative. People have called Elon Musk's new Cybertruck "ugly," and yet it generated a lot of pre-orders. Sometimes I even receive backlash for the "Zero to a Million Followers in 30 Days" Hook Point. People will comment on my Instagram posts, saying, "One million followers means nothing if you have no engagement." I don't feel offended when people write these kinds of things—if they actually read my book, they'd see that I agree with them. When people leave these negative comments on my posts, they're actually just helping me gain more visibility. But don't get me wrong, I'm not saying that *any* press is good press—if the response is overwhelmingly negative, you probably do have a problem. My point is that some negative responses will come with the positive—you'll never receive 100 percent positive feedback for *anything* you do—but as long as the positive outweighs the negative, you're in a good spot. You only need to change gears and head in a new direction if you aren't getting a response, or again, if the vast majority of responses is negative.

HOOK POINTS HELP YOU PACKAGE INFORMATION

Using "The Sleep Doctor" as a hook makes Breus more accessible, and his communication style matches this fact. He avoids big, scary terms when speaking to audiences. He can have a discussion about neurochemistry but doesn't think it appeals to his consumers. In the 3-second world, audiences want complicated information brought down into bite-size, actionable chunks—Breus's ability to do just that has led to his appearance on *The Dr. Oz Show* more than 35 times. This fact has now become yet another Hook

Point. When people hear about a sleep doctor who's appeared on *Dr. Oz* that many times, their interest is sparked; they want to know how and why this guy is getting so much media attention, and they immediately see him as a more credible source.

And Breus's Hook Points don't stop there; he constantly packages the information he discusses into hooks such as "The exhausted executive," "What's the best mattress to sleep on?" or "When's the best time for sex before sleep?" All of these Hook Points get people to pay attention. They are relatable and address an inherent interest in common problems. Basically, they turn Breus into a walking Hook Point. He capitalizes off the simplicity of messages that draw people in and plays off of their curiosity and the need for credible solutions.

You can do this, too, by packaging your information in ways that help you become more accessible. Break down your facts and test different Hook Points. And then, who knows? Maybe I'll be seeing *you* on TV sometime soon.

FORTUNE 500 AND CELEBRITIES

When I meet people in person and they ask me what I do, sometimes (again, I'm always testing), I'll say, "I'm a digital and business strategist for **Fortune 500** companies, brands, and **celebrities**." "Fortune 500" and "celebrities" are the keywords that typically drive people's intrigue and interest. Overall, this hook is left a bit vague on purpose—because I'm doing this in person—so I can measure the response in real time, listening to the types of questions people ask, and observing the expressions on their faces. Then, based on that feedback, I modify my responses with appropriate stories and additional hooks.

When people ask, "Well, what does that mean? What do you do?" I say, "I look at my clients' short-term and long-term business objectives, and the obstacles they're running into, and I help them craft a strategy to reach their goals in the shortest possible amount of time." Then, again, I craft my next responses based off of *their* responses. I'm looking for their pain points so I can show them that what I do can provide them with the maximum amount of value. I go over this process a bit more in depth in later chapters, but for now, let's go back to that initial Hook Point.

If my Hook Point was, "I'm a digital and business strategist," it wouldn't be as strong. I anchor the fact that I've worked with Fortune 500 companies and celebrities to pique people's interest and make them want to hear more. I layer in the subjects "corporations, brands, and celebrities," because the people I'm speaking to may work for, or may be trying to become one of, these three entities, and it shows them that I specialize in those areas. Also, the Fortune 500 and celebrity aspects build validation, credibility, and intrigue.

With all of that said, I don't use this hook for public-facing content that's presented to the masses. If I rented billboard space or was given the cover of a magazine to advertise my brand and services, I'd use the Hook Points "Zero to a Million Followers in 30 Days" or "How to Stand Out in a 3-Second World."

THE IF/THEN FORMULA

Copywriter Craig Clemens explains that his Hook Point creation process is different for each company and product because they're all unique. However, he shares a basic formula that you can use as a starting point to discover yours. It's a simple if/then formula: Point out your prospects' problems or needs after the *if*, and use your product as the solution to their problems after the *then*. For example, if you have a product that could help improve a person's dating life, you could use this formula: "If you're looking to increase the amount of dates you get with attractive, high-quality, smart women/men who have it together, then this is going to be the most important thing you'll ever read." Or, if you're marketing to someone who wants to become a better golfer, an example could be: "If you're looking to improve your golf game by five or ten strokes by the next time you set foot on the golf course, then pay close attention to the four secrets I'm going to share with you next." Clemens suggests using the if/then formula as a starting point, and then A/B testing the Hook Points you come up with against other ideas that are a bit more off the wall (more on A/B testing at the end of this chapter).

CREATE FOR YOUR AUDIENCE, NOT FOR YOURSELF

One of the biggest mistakes people make when coming up with Hook Points—or any content, for that matter—is creating them for themselves instead of for their audience. People tend to create content by thinking about what makes *them* look good or what is trendy or cool in *their* industry. But thinking about yourself and following the status quo won't help you stand out.

Clemens's wife, Sarah Anne Stewart, works as a certified Integrative Health Coach. She spends a lot of time focusing on nutrition, exercise, mindfulness, and other health-related topics. She stands out by offering a unique heart-centered approach in these areas. Although the people in her circle do some really impactful and unique work, when you look at their websites and Instagram accounts, a lot of their content looks the same. The majority of these people post pretty pictures of themselves drinking green juice, meditating, doing yoga poses over a skyline, or preparing recipes. The imagery is beautiful, but when everyone is posting the same type of content, it becomes less effective and intriguing. That's not to say you shouldn't pay attention to successful formats and structures of content that others are using. You should, but just make sure you understand the type of content that's working to create an engaged audience so you can make it your own.

Stewart, for example, focuses on giving her prospects health-related advice so they can improve their lives. Recently, she posted a video about the dangers of going on fad diets and offered tips about what people should do instead. Also, she frequently posts information that teaches her audience actionable steps they can immediately take to improve their health. She creates content that adds instant value to people's lives.

If you find that the Hook Points you generate aren't working, be sure you're approaching your marketing tactics from a consumer-focused angle, especially if you're trying to sell products. In this case, the if/then formula where you point out your audience's problem or need after the *if* and use your product as the solution to their problem after the *then* (explained in the section above) can be of great use. Thinking about your audience's desires will work much better than thinking about your hook from your own point of view. If you're working off the equation, "I want X, so I'm going to try and get my consumers to do Y," you'll typically lose.

In the film industry, studios often make the mistake of putting out advertising with messaging that says, "Buy tickets." This does not motivate potential moviegoers to pay attention. In fact, it does quite the opposite. Movie studios are the ones that want people to buy tickets, but patrons just want to watch great films, which is why ads with this type of messaging often fall flat. Potential moviegoers don't go to a theater because a studio tells them to; they go because they're intrigued by a concept, story, or experience that gets them to see a film based on their own desires. I know it might sound like common sense, but you'd be surprised how often people miss this fact. When studios take this into account and focus their marketing on the customers, they come up with better solutions.

The next time you go to a movie, listen to the comments from the people around you after each trailer finishes. You'll typically hear people say, "That looks terrible" or "I definitely want to see that!" This is a fun exercise that will help you learn which trailers have the best Hook Points and stories.

Also, remember the adage "People love to buy, but hate to be sold to." When people get the sense that you're trying to sell them something, it turns them off—it's not a strong Hook Point. Instead, be customer focused. If you give customers what they want, this will fulfill their needs, which ultimately will fulfill yours. If you're sure that your Hook Point is consumer focused and it's still not working, you may need to simplify the message or play around with the words. Test and learn until you find the winning combination.

(We'll talk more about how to create Hook Points soon, but if at any point you wish my agency's help in developing your Hook Points, please visit: www.hookpoint.com/agency, and fill out the brief questionnaire telling us about your business and goals.)

NEW BRANDS HAVE TO WORK HARDER

Latham Arneson, the former vice president of digital marketing at Paramount Pictures, reminds us that unestablished brands have to work harder than established brands to stand out and create compelling Hook

Points. Promoting a new Marvel movie isn't the same as marketing an independent film. A Marvel movie is part of an existing brand that's clear in people's consciousness and high in their levels of interest. You must be realistic about how important your brand or the topic of your content is in people's minds before you present it to them.

There are very few people and products that have an interest level so high that they don't have to work to get others to pay attention to them. If consumers have no understanding of who you are or what you do, you need to educate them. Be flexible and open to trying different formats to discover the best ways to present your concepts. Test various Hook Points to learn what works (a process that we'll discuss later in this chapter).

PREDICTING THE FUTURE: HOW TO FIND THE NEW NEXT

In the film industry today, it's become standard to do a five-second trailer before the full trailer to capture an audience's attention in the first three seconds on social media. As effective as it may be *now*, it's not going to work in the same way after people have seen it hundreds of times. "Your job as a marketer is to figure out what's next," explains Arneson. I discuss the mini-trailer concept and how it's a result of our 3-second world in the next chapter because I think it's useful to understand, but I agree with Arneson's point. When a strategy works, people start to copy it (as I pointed out with Toms Shoes, earlier in the chapter), but as Arneson notes, it's smarter to be on the experimentation side, pushing forward, rather than waiting to catch up. Stay culturally aware so you can get ahead of the curve.

If you spend your time copying the exact Hook Points that everyone else creates, you won't stand out. You'll simply end up doing what is considered normal. Instead, push yourself to find ideas that are exceptional—that's where the magic lies for long-term brand awareness and growth.

THE BLAIR WITCH PROJECT: EVERYTHING YOU'VE HEARD IS TRUE

The movie *The Blair Witch Project* came up with a creative idea for its marketing campaign, which created a lot of buzz and left people captivated before the film was released. Artisan Entertainment, the studio that made the film, marketed it as though it were a true story made from real-life footage. Their taglines, which also served as their Hook Points, were: "In October of 1994, three student filmmakers disappeared in the woods near Burkittsville, Maryland, while shooting a documentary. . . . A year later their footage was found"; "The scariest movie of all time is a true story"; and "Everything you've heard is true." Even the trailer made the movie look like a documentary—the actors were speaking directly into the camera while crying in the woods.

During the release of the movie in 1999 at the Sundance Film Festival, Artisan Entertainment posted missing-persons posters of the three main stars—Michael Williams, Joshua Leonard, and Heather Donohue—all over town. None of the actors were famous at the time, so people started wondering if this was actually a real documentary about three kids who went missing in the woods.[41]

---

[41] Chris Miller and Alex Mann, "20 years later, some still think 'Blair Witch Project' real," *Las Vegas Review-Journal, Oct. 27, 2017*, https://www.reviewjournal.com/entertainment /movies/20-years-later-some-still-think-blair-witch-project-real/.

The marketing team was also very tech savvy (for the time), and as a result, *The Blair Witch Project* was one of the first movies to be marketed primarily through the internet. Although the campaign was a huge success back then, I'm not convinced that a similar ploy would work today. People are now more sophisticated and aware, which is another reason why it's critically important to constantly test, learn, and *innovate*.

YOU CAN'T SKIP THIS GEICO AD
BECAUSE IT'S ALREADY OVER

The Martin Agency created an exceptional advertising campaign for Geico Insurance in 2015. It was a skippable pre-roll ad (a promotional video message that plays before the content a user has selected that a viewer can skip but only after watching it for a minimum of five seconds[42]) on YouTube called "Family: Unskippable." This ad ended up being part of a campaign that won *Ad Age*'s first-ever Campaign of the Year award.[43] It made fun of the fact that people often skip past pre-roll ads as soon as they can.

One of the ads from the campaign featured a family sitting at a dinner table. The mother says, "Don't thank me, thank the savings." This dialogue is finished after two seconds of the video starting. Then suddenly a voice-over says, "You can't skip this Geico ad because it's already over." That dialogue is completed by the end of the five-second mark. Then, during

[42] Shawn Forno, "YouTube Pre-Roll Ad Length: Timing Is Everything," IdeaRocket, Oct. 17, 2019, https://idearocketanimation.com/15369-pre-roll-ad-length/.

[43] Ann-Christine Diaz, "Geico's 'Unskippable' from the Martin Agency Is Ad Age's 2016 Campaign of the Year," *Ad Age, Jan. 25, 2016,* https://adage.com/article/special-report -agency-alist-2016/geico-s-unskippable-ad-age-s-2016-campaign-year/302300.

the skippable part of the ad, the family stays frozen while a dog comes up and eats all the spaghetti from each of their plates.[44] This ad worked because it was innovative, pointed out the truth, caught people's attention, and made them laugh. (You can watch the video here: www.brendanjkane .com/skip.)

FIVE STEPS TO CREATING AN EFFECTIVE HOOK POINT

Below are some guidelines to help you understand the essence of a great Hook Point. Of course, not all great Hook Points follow every single one of these rules, but I've seen that most Hook Points include at least some, if not all, of the aspects below. Use this as a guide, especially when you're creating Hook Points for the first time. Once you learn the system and get good at it, you can start breaking the rules and create your own guidelines.

A great Hook Point:

1. Uses as few words as possible (envision a magazine-cover headline)—that is, "Zero to a Million Followers in 30 Days."
2. Remains true to who you are and why you exist as a brand. If it's unrelated, it will come across as clickbait and inauthentic.
3. Makes people think differently and subverts expectations. For example, in a successful social video I created, the Hook Point was "WARNING!! Safety is Dangerous." This challenges the

---

commonly held belief that acting safely is a good approach to life.

4. Doesn't make people think very hard—it's presented in a simple-to-understand manner.

5. Doesn't make people think too little—if someone doesn't think at all about your hook, then it's probably being ignored.

6. Has an element of curiosity that leaves audiences wanting to learn or view more—that is, "Elon Musk Made the Cybertruck Ugly on Purpose—and It's the Smartest Thing He's Ever Done."[45] This article's Hook Point makes you want to understand why creating an ugly car was a smart decision.

7. Stands out with originality. If you've seen your Hook Point used somewhere else, it probably won't work.

8. Combines a common/relatable element with something that is unique, and that draws your audience in. An example is the Away Travel suitcase with phone-charging capabilities. Suitcases have been around for decades, but a suitcase that can charge your phone is a novel idea.

9. Can be grasped quickly. Make sure your Hook Point can be understood in three seconds max.

10. Offers a solution to your audience's pain points. Legendary copywriter Eugene Schwartz used pain points in his headlines all the time. For example, "Begin your middle years at 70, 80, even 90!" which addresses the pain point of aging, or "How to Stroke

---

[45] Justin Bariso, "Elon Musk Made the Cybertruck 'Ugly' on Purpose—and It May Be the Smartest Thing He's Ever Done," *Inc., Dec. 3, 2019,* https://www.inc.com/justin-bariso/elon-musk-made-cybertruck-ugly-on-purpose-and-its-smartest-thing-hes-ever-done.html.

Wrinkles Right Out of Your Face," which again addresses another pain point related to beauty and aging.[46]

When developing a great Hook Point:

1. Expect it to be a process. You won't typically find the perfect Hook Point on the first attempt (or even the first few attempts).

2. Create more ideas and variations than you think possible. If you can, create 50 to 100 potential concepts. Doing so pushes your creative limits and helps you come up with better ideas in the long term.

3. Rework ideas—reword them, reshape them, turn them upside down, and mix variations together.

4. Remember that a Hook Point doesn't have to sell your product or service. It just needs to get your customers and/or prospective customers to take notice of you. Once you have their attention, you can begin the conversation about the sale of your product or service.

5. Make it for your audience. Figure out what will grab their interest.

6. Don't force it to be funny. Make sure you're confident in your ability to create effective Hook Points before tackling humor, or hire a great comedic talent to help you.

7. Be aware that a Hook Point doesn't have to be words; it can be a concept. For example, YouTube channel "Ten Second Songs"

---

[46] "Eugene Schwartz Headline Formula," YouTube video, posted by Copy Skillz, Aug. 4, 2019, https://www.youtube.com/watch?v=lvqtqQUa6Qo&feature=youtu.be.

creator Anthony Vincent takes famous songs and breaks them up into different music styles every ten seconds. In this video, he takes Katy Perry's song "Dark Horse" and changes the style of the song so it sounds like bands such as The Doors, John Mayer, Queen, and so on. Check it out here: https://www.youtube.com/watch?v=jus7S5vBJyU.

8. Be cognizant of the fact that a Hook Point is often different from a tagline or a USP. "Just Do It" is Nike's tagline, and their USP is their shoes. Today, their strongest Hook Points, which are found in their different campaigns, are the athletes they sponsor (as explained in chapter 1).

9. Don't confuse a Hook Point with branding. A Hook Point activates a brand by getting people to pay attention to their products, services, and values. Again, Nike demonstrates this concept. The fact that Nike is an athletic fashion brand is not the hook— the uniquely differentiated products they put out (such as the running shoe that's going to be banned from the Olympics because it's so effective) or the celebrities they sponsor are what grab people's attention.

10. Know that scarcity and exclusivity can be great tools. The fact that a private, members-only club like Soho House is exclusive makes it more desirable.

11. Know that your Hook Point can be in a content format. In the next chapter we discuss Buzzfeed's video cooking channel, Tasty, and how the format in which they present their content is their Hook Point.

12. Remember, above all else, that it needs to **grab people's attention**.

Now it's time for *you* to practice the art of creating Hook Points. To do so, follow the "Five Steps to Creating an Effective Hook Point" process below.

Step 1: Study What Works

Look for effective Hook Points used by successful brands, and put them in a list. You may be tempted to skip this step, but don't. Even copywriter Craig Clemens, whose words have sold over one billion dollars' worth of products, used this method when he first started creating headlines and Hook Points because his original hooks were horrible. Looking at other brands' Hook Points helps you refine your craft.

Hooks can be pulled from:

- Book titles
- Social content:
    - Meme cards (text caption boxes that appear at the top or bottom of a video on Facebook or Instagram—they're explained more in depth in the next chapter)
    - Headlines
    - Concepts
- Launch campaigns
- Article headlines
- TV commercials
- Social media ads (use the Facebook Ad Library to search for ads here: https://www.facebook.com/ads/library/)
- Print ads (billboards, magazine covers)

Now, take the best Hook Points from the list you've just created and replace their offers, words, businesses, or services with your own. Pay attention to how these hooks (which are modeled after other brands' hooks) help you stand out. Keep in mind, however, that you can't use these hooks for your brand (unless you substantially change them). The purpose of this exercise is not to steal (or replicate) other brands' hooks, but to practice and spark ideas for new, original Hook Points.

Step 2: Learn from What Doesn't Work

Research underperforming Hook Points and diagnose why you think they don't work. To do so, you can go to social channels, search for videos, and look at the ones that aren't performing well. You can also go on Amazon, Google Shopping, and Yelp, type the name of a product or service, and observe which listings come up that have the fewest number of reviews or the most negative reviews in a certain category. You can also search for companies, products, and services that have failed, underperformed, or closed down, and find the ads that they were using when they went under. Additionally, you can go to a magazine stand and see which magazine or book titles don't capture your attention immediately. Finally, study billboards, and analyze the ones that don't intrigue you and that don't stop you in your tracks.

Hooks are generally ineffective because they're:

1. Too wordy
2. Confusing
3. Vague
4. Overused: hooks that have been copied thousands of times by other individuals or companies
5. Not relevant to a specific audience

6. Outdated—not relevant to today's society/culture
7. Created with the assumption that people are already interested in a particular topic
8. Inauthentic
9. Not unique enough
10. Unappealing, or use language that doesn't catch the eye

Step 3: Create Your Own

Now it's your turn to practice creating your own original Hook Points. Imagine that you've been given the cover feature article in a major magazine or newspaper. The goal is that once it's gone to print, it sells a massive amount of copies and generates a significant number of customers for your business. To achieve this, put yourself in your customers' shoes.

Imagine a woman, a potential consumer, walking down a busy street. Cars are honking, attractive people are walking by, others are shouting, and your prospect is getting bumped into left and right. Now she's passing a magazine stand with 30 other magazines and newspapers that could grab her attention first.

In this scenario, which headline/Hook Point could you create to grab your prospect's attention enough to make her stop, actually buy the magazine or newspaper with *your* headline (as opposed to the other 30 magazines sitting right next to it), *and* read your article?

You can get some inspiration by going to an actual magazine stand or by searching for previous covers of a magazine in your niche online. Intently study the magazines or newspapers you'd like to be featured on. Whether it's *Vogue*, *Sports Illustrated*, or *Entrepreneur*, take the time to notice the headlines. Which ones are compelling to you? Which ones don't stand out and make you want to dive in and read the article? What makes you pick up (or not pick up) the magazine or newspaper and read it? Think in those terms to help you find the most effective Hook Points for your brand.

You can do this exercise with a digital ad or a piece of content in mind as well. Imagine a man scrolling on his Instagram, YouTube, or Facebook feed—what's the headline or opening of a video that's going to capture his attention and make him stop for three or more seconds?

To test this out, you can even do a Photoshop mock-up of the Instagram Explore page (a page composed of posts from people your potential customer has followed, posts from accounts similar to the ones they follow, and posts with high engagement). If you think your audience spends more time on YouTube, you can also create a mock-up of the "Suggested Videos" section. This section comprises the videos that YouTube suggests you watch after a video is complete.

Once you've created the mock-up, insert your thumbnails, titles, and headlines to see which ones stand out and grab people's attention, and which ones get lost in the fray. Again, choose a combination that can compete with the dozens of other options. Your Hook Point needs to capture people's attention enough to make them want to click on *your* content to see more, rather than others'.

In this exercise, create as many Hook Points as possible. Begin with a large list and pare it down. You'll often start with things that are in your comfort zone, but continue to push yourself beyond that, as this is often where the best Hook Points develop. Come up with as many ideas—especially those that are outside the box—as you can. Remember, just because you write it down doesn't mean you have to use it, so let yourself feel free to jot down all your ideas. Think big; think different.

Once you've completed your list, narrow it down to the **three best choices**. Then, repeat the process—that is, create, narrow down to three, and repeat.

Step 4: Compare Your Hook Points

Take the original Hook Points you've just created and compare them to the successful hooks from Step 1. To do so, create a combined list with all these Hook Points on the same page.

Now, rank the top Hook Points from this master list. You can also ask friends, family, and other people on your team to select the ones they like best. If your original Hook Points from Step 3 are not at the top of this new combined list and beating out the ones from Step 1, then it's time to revise your hooks until they outrank the most successful ones you've found from other brands. This process will help you push yourself to become the best Hook Point creator possible. It may take some time to become an expert, but the investment will pay dividends when you beat out the competition.

Remember, more than 60,000,000,000 messages are sent out online each day. Your Hook Point must get past this noise.

Step 5: Test, Reiterate, and Repeat

After you've come up with Hook Point options that you feel pass the test, show them to your friends and colleagues to discover which ones attract the most attention. You can also A/B test your Hook Points on social media, with your email list, and on search-engine advertising platforms.

Don't worry if you don't have immediate success—this process may take time. The most important thing is that you continue to modify, repeat, and improve your Hook Points so that you can find the most compelling ones for your brand or business.

A/B TEST YOUR HOOK POINTS

Craig Clemens says that no matter how experienced you are at creating strong marketing content, you'll still come up with a lot of Hook Point ideas that fail miserably. Furthermore, some of the concepts that are home runs are the ones you never would have expected. This is why it's essential to continually A/B test your ideas. A/B testing is the process of comparing two versions (or more) of something (e.g., a headline, a web page, an email, social content, or other marketing asset) and measuring the difference in performance between them.

Even when you find iterations that work, I suggest continuing to test and learn. You can find a lot of information about how to do this in my book *One Million Followers* (www.onemillionfollowers.com), and in a step-by-step guide on how to A/B test headlines and Hook Points at this URL: www.brendanjkane.com/test).

If you find Hook Points that perform well, you'll want to start investing advertising and media dollars in them so that your current and potential customers can see them. Eventually, you'll reach a point of dilution with your Hook Points. This will require you to continue to create new Hook Points, and test and refine them. Hence, the purpose of this book and the exercises above is to make you an expert in developing Hook Points consistently so that you can sustain long-term growth for your brand.

Quick Tips and Recap

1. When creating Hook Points, think about what makes you and your product or information unique and relevant to other people's lives: What pain points are being solved? What is the ultimate outcome your product or service is providing in someone's life?

2. Subverting expectations with your Hook Points is a good tactic for capturing people's attention. Take commonly held beliefs or phrases and flip them on their heads.

3. People will stop and pay attention if you associate your brand with timely, interesting topics that meet your audience's needs.

4. Think about your prospects and the conversations they may be having in their own minds—tap into the issues that keep

them up at night. Provide solutions to the problems they're try-ing to fix.

5. Find ways to package your information that makes you more accessible. Break down your information into bite-size chunks, and test it out in the form of Hook Points.

6. Figure out the new next. Be culturally aware, follow the latest trends, and try to stay ahead of them.

7. Refer to the "Five Steps to Creating an Effective Hook Point" in this chapter to help you create Hook Points.

8. Remember that if your audience has to think too hard or too little about your Hook Point, it's not a good choice. Make sure your concept doesn't take more than three seconds to grasp.

9. When creating Hook Points, start with a broad list and pare it down to the three best choices. Then repeat the process—that is, create, narrow down to three, and repeat.

10. Get Hook Point inspiration by going to a magazine stand or bookstore, looking on social media, or checking out other places with lots of hooks to study.

11. It's essential to continually test your Hook Points. It will help you get more clear about which ones are the absolute strongest. You can A/B test to your email list, on social media, or on search-engine advertising platforms.

(If you'd like help developing the best Hook Points for your brand or busi-ness, please visit: www.hookpoint.com/agency, and fill out the brief ques-tionnaire telling us about your business and goals.)

CHAPTER 3

60,000,000,000 MESSAGES A DAY: HOW TO FIGHT YOUR WAY THROUGH THE NOISE

Now THAT YOU understand the principles behind what makes Hook Points strong, let's look specifically at how to apply their power to the creation of digital content and videos. With more than 60,000,000,000 messages sent out on digital platforms each day, Hook Points are essential tools that help you stand out among the noise; and you can use them to more effectively package content for a better chance at having meaningful engagement, a strong viral presence, and growth.

In this section, I will also introduce you to the importance of images and visual storytelling tactics that capture and hold attention. Visual storytelling is vital—59 percent of senior executives would rather watch a video than read text if they have the option. It's a new phenomenon called the "picture superiority effect," where information presented with visuals is learned and remembered more easily than information without. Including an image in your social media posts delivers 180 percent more engagement and increases content retention up to 65 percent.[47]

USE HOOK POINTS TO PACKAGE YOUR INFORMATION

Back when I was working with journalist Katie Couric, we interviewed some of world's biggest celebrities, including Jessica Chastain, Joe Biden, Chance the Rapper, and DJ Khaled, among many others. By testing all this content, I discovered that the popularity of the celebrity at the time had little correlation to how well the content performed. The simple fact that someone is famous doesn't provide enough incentive to get people to stop and pay attention to content in today's world. What truly captures attention is the way information is packaged, presented, and communicated on digital platforms. The topic the celebrity discussed, and the way the topic was presented to the audience, was often more responsible for the content's success than the fact that a celebrity was featured. In other words, leveraging fame wasn't enough; celebrities needed to be discussing topics that had a strong hook to get audiences to stop scrolling through their feed, watch, and engage.

We set out to innovate the standard interview for digital platforms so we could help Couric's content stand out among the noise. When we first started working together, she had just made the jump from TV to a digital-first distribution partnership with Yahoo!, and the algorithms were not

---

[47] Web Desk, "The Human Attention Span [INFOGRAPHIC], Digital Information World, Sept. 10, 2018, https://www.digitalinformationworld.com/2018/09/the-human -attention-span-infographic.html.

favoring her content. In other words, her content was getting suppressed and wasn't being shown to her fans or the fans of the celebrities she was interviewing. To fix this, wc had to completely change the way we produced, edited, and distributed her content across social media. So, instead of starting with what questions she would ask in an interview, we focused on what the final output of the interview would look like. More specifically, what were the potential Hook Points we could generate from the interview that would grab audience's attention at scale? We designed hooks for each interview based on its appeal to different audiences we felt would not only have an interest in the interview but also share it with everyone they knew.

When Couric first brought me into meetings with Yahoo!, the executives told me that her content had a very narrow audience. I understood that they wanted to hit that specific demographic to stay relevant and deliver for their current advertisers, but I also knew that if we were going to achieve scale and gain favor with the algorithms, we needed to extend the appeal of her content beyond that audience and do it fast.

I knew that the best strategy to achieve this was to identify core advocates for each interview based on the person we were interviewing and/or the topic being covered. To accomplish this, we would develop different hooks for each interview, designed to statistically increase the chances of getting these core advocates to share the interview with everyone they knew. The idea was that if we could get more people sharing each interview, it would trigger the algorithms to give the content more reach and increase the overall viral potential. In doing so, we were scaling Yahoo!'s advertiser target audience and opening up Couric's and Yahoo!'s brand to new audiences at the same time. Effectively, we were getting friends to share with friends, sons and daughters to share with their parents, and siblings to share with siblings. By leveraging Hook Points, we engineered hitting any audience we desired at scale.

The first interview Couric and I tested together was with actress Elizabeth Banks. The interview was structured with three major Hook Points in mind. Again, we started with the Hook Points rather than the questions Couric would ask. Since Banks was in the movie franchises *The Hunger Games* and *Pitch Perfect* and was a strong feminist advocate, we designed Hook Points that would resonate with each of these audiences.

As mentioned above, we made all our decisions with the final output in mind—which Hook Points about *The Hunger Games*, *Pitch Perfect*, or feminism could make people stop scrolling through their feeds and pay attention to what Couric and Banks were discussing? How would they be packaged to stop the never-ending scrolling? The fact that Banks spoke about popular subjects wasn't enough. The way the interview was packaged needed to have many unique hooks—something the audience didn't know and hadn't seen before.

When we were coming up with Hook Points, I used the magazine exercise (Step 3, shared at the end of the last chapter). I thought, *If Hunger Games fans were walking down the street, which headline would capture their attention enough to make them stop and check out the article?* The headline/hook that performed the best out of the content we created from the Banks interview was: "How I got a role in *The Hunger Games*." This hook appealed not only to fans of the movie, but also to those who aspired to be actors or were simply curious about what it takes to get a role in a major film. It's important to note that we created 30-plus Hook Points for this interview alone and tested hundreds of different variations of these hooks to find the winning variation.

Developing a high-performing Hook Point is not about guessing and putting all your eggs in one basket; it's about testing, iterating, and testing some more until you find the right answer that drives results.

(To learn more about the A/B testing process I used for all of the interviews I worked on with Couric, check out my first book, *One Million Followers*, and the step-by-step A/B testing guide here: www.brendanjkane .com/test.)

Although the Banks interview received a lot of engagement and views, the top-performing interview Couric and I worked on together was with Brandon Stanton, the founder of the photoblog "Humans of New York." The top clip from that interview generated more than 20 million views and was shared over 240,000 times. The headline we used was: "Creator of Humans of New York joined Yahoo News Global Anchor Katie Couric today to discuss his open letter addressed to Donald J. Trump on Facebook." The video touches on very political and emotional topics, and whether people are in support of President Trump or not, they often have strong opinions about him.

With this specific video, the Hook Point didn't come from the headline, but from Stanton's opening remarks: "I've watched you retweet racist images. . . ." And it wasn't just his words, but the intensity with which he delivered them, that drew people in—they wanted to hear what he would say next. The timing of the video also helped. It was released during the height of the 2016 election, when many people were on edge and feeling very emotional. Many Hillary Clinton supporters shared this interview with just about everyone they knew. This is a perfect example to demonstrate that success is not just tied to celebrity. We interviewed celebrities with 100 times the fame of Stanton, yet this interview outperformed them all because of the subject matter, the packaging of the clip, the pacing, Stanton's personality, and a polarizing hook.

MY VIDEO WENT VIRAL. HERE'S WHY.

Derek Muller, creator of the YouTube channel "Veritasium," which has nearly six million subscribers, made a video called *My Video Went Viral. Here's Why.* The video explains YouTube's algorithms and the importance of having a Hook Point to draw people to your content. (To watch the full video, you can check out: hookpoint.com/veritasium.)

In the early days of YouTube, subscriptions were king, meaning that if people subscribed to a channel, YouTube would show them that channel's content when they arrived on the site. This kept things fairly simple for creators—those who had a lot of subscribers had high amounts of watch time on their channels. But now that we live in a 3-second world, YouTube has had to adapt. To keep people on their platform, as opposed to Facebook, Instagram, and so on, they had to change their algorithms. YouTube quickly discovered that typically headlines with great Hook Points were capturing a significant amount of watch time, and that getting people to watch content was like selling newspapers on the street (I told you so!).

Muller worries that the algorithms push people to create sensational news items. He thinks they encourage the practice of yellow journalism— the sharing of news with little or no legitimate research—which uses eye-catching headlines for increased sales. He believes that social platforms can only serve up truthful stories when the algorithms favor channel subscriptions. That way, creators don't have to use tricks to help them fight for people's attention.

Nevertheless, YouTube, and the majority of other social platforms, cater to the 3-second world. YouTube has reduced the importance of subscribers and has increased the importance of what Muller describes "clickbaity thumbnails." I don't recommend being inauthentic or using clickbait. Besides, it isn't as effective as it used to be because the algorithms have caught on to clickbait. Currently, algorithms don't solely favor clicks, but also watch time and retention (discussed further below). I mention the importance of creating authentic Hook Points and stories more in depth in chapter 5, but for now, keep in mind that catchy headlines (not clickbaity headlines) are important, especially when it comes to being successful on YouTube.

Muller goes on to explain that one of his most viral videos, with more than 32 million views, was created with this headline theory in mind. He was in New York at the Creator Summit showing MrBeast (a YouTuber with more than 34.4 million subscribers) some video footage about the black plastic balls that were on the LA Reservoir to protect water quality. MrBeast knew that the footage would be popular, so the two discussed which headlines and thumbnails would provide the greatest hook. Muller was thinking about calling the video *Throwing Shade Balls*, but MrBeast steered him away from that title. Instead, he suggested *Why Are There 96 Million Black Balls on This Lake?* Muller changed the word *Lake* to *Reservoir* (because that's what it is), but the point is that Muller believes that the popularity of the video is highly linked to the hooky title and thumbnail. It created intrigue and sparked people's curiosity.

Muller explains that going viral and getting tens of millions of views on YouTube is dependent upon two metrics:

1. Watch time. You perform well in YouTube's algorithm when someone watches seven to eight minutes of your video. To reach

this amount of watch time, your videos should be no less than 15 minutes.

2. A high click-through rate. This is where Hook Points become especially important. A high click-through rate is composed of the total number of clicks on your titles and thumbnails, divided by the number of times the titles and thumbnails have been shown.

MrBeast told Muller that as you approach a 10-, 20-, or 30-plus percent click-through rate, the number of views and impressions your video will receive jumps up dramatically. In fact, it's such a dramatic increase that it turns YouTube into a site where the titles and thumbnails (which serve as the Hook Points for videos) have an overwhelming importance.

"You can have a great video, but unless you have a great hook to get people in, it's not going to go viral," states Muller. So, there you have it—proof that this book is genius! Just kidding (sort of). In all seriousness, though, Hook Points matter. YouTube may adapt and change again, but it doesn't take away from the fact that as these platforms become more inundated with content, standing out is critical.

Muller goes on to explain how you can use thumbnails to stand out. They are some of the first visual elements of Hook Points. To find the most optimal thumbnail choice, many YouTubers will Photoshop various options into a screenshot of their current YouTube home page. They experiment with various thumbnails in different positions to see which ones are the most eye-catching. Top performers on YouTube test various thumbnails because they know that effective ones can help them stand out and receive more views.

This is going to be even more important in the near future, because YouTube is adapting the platform to show click-through rates in real time. Muller hypothesizes that this change will lead to the practice of launching videos and then immediately testing variants of thumbnails in real time to achieve the highest click-through rates. In fact, Muller thinks that if creators don't do this, they'll be left behind, and their videos won't be seen. Video topics, titles, and thumbnails need to hook viewers if they don't want their content to be buried and lost. He says, "The truth is, the audience only knows you're there if they see your titles and thumbnails."

There is limited real estate in which to show people videos of interest. All social channels need to use their real estate, aka their feeds, to show people the videos they want to see. Audiences on YouTube communicate what they like through actions such as watch time and clicks. And although algorithms are always shifting, for now, YouTube is optimizing for long-term watch time. So, use the power of Hook Points and good storytelling techniques that you learn in this book to satisfy audiences and beat algorithms on all social channels.

ALGORITHMS

Let's briefly discuss algorithms. People get very frustrated when algorithms don't work in their favor, but they're designed to do one thing really well: make sure people keep coming back to a social platform. Imagine if you opened up Facebook, Instagram, or YouTube and the content that loaded on your screen was boring, uninteresting, and unamusing. What would you do? You would close the application and move on to something else. And if this kept happening every time you opened up the app, you would slowly change your behavior and start allocating time to another platform. To avoid losing users' attention, algorithms are designed to find content that will engage unique users each time they come to the platform. With so much content being uploaded every second, and with most users following hundreds, if not thousands, of accounts, the algorithms have to decide which content rises to the top of the feed and which content gets stuck at the bottom.

When you see accounts with huge followings but low engagement, it's typically not because the audience isn't engaged or because they have fake followers. It's usually because the algorithms have deemed that there is more engaging content on the platform and is prioritizing that content to the followers of the account. When this happens, they don't get high engagement because most of their followers don't even see their content.

Let's say you have an account with 100,000 followers, and each time you post a piece of content, the algorithm will send it out to 500 of those followers and measure core metrics (for example, views-to-reach ratio, share-to-views ratio, engagement to reach ratio, etc.). If the ratio and engagement match up with what the algorithm is looking for, it will extend the reach of that piece of content to 500 more people. If the ratios are good again, then another 1,000 people will see it, then another 2,000, and so forth. The algorithm will keep pushing your content further beyond your audience if it's deemed effective. On the other hand, if the ratios are not good, when your content is sent to the first 500 followers, your reach stops right there— the algorithm sees that the content is not resonating with the people to whom it was released. And to make matters worse, if you keep putting out content that doesn't engage your audience, your account as a whole gets recognized as ineffective, and your reach is very limited from the onset each time you post. Essentially, the algorithm will stop giving your account a chance.

That's why it's important to continually push out content that is designed not only to engage audiences but also that matches what the algorithms are searching for. When the algorithms recognize that you're an effective content creator, you get more reach each time you post. It sets you up to experience dramatic growth like content creators Jay Shetty or Prince Ea, who get massive reach and scale and generate billions of views each time they share a piece of content.

(To learn more and stay up-to-date on this subject, visit my blog: www .brendanjkane.com/bkblog.)

THE 3-SECOND RULE

When I was a kid, we often talked about the "3-Second Rule." It meant that if you dropped a piece of food on the floor, you had three seconds to pick it up and eat it before it was considered contaminated. Well, now the same principle applies to social media video consumption. Within three seconds, viewers have determined if they'll continue to watch or scroll past a video in their social channel's feed (and oftentimes they've already decided within one second).

Where does the 3-second rule come from? As pointed out in the introduction, video product team manager Matt Pakes explains that three seconds is the metric Facebook uses to register video views in the news feed. He says, "If you have stayed on a video for at least three seconds, it signals to us that you are not simply scrolling through the feed, and you've shown intent to watch that video."

The more people you can get to watch the first three seconds of your video, the better. It raises your chance for a high number of views, and for a longer length of view time. In turn, the algorithms will work in your favor and push your content to more people.

Capturing attention within one second to generate the 3-second view is difficult, as it's a short amount of time. That's why having a solid Hook Point for your content is so essential. Let's explore how you can use your knowledge about Hook Points to structure your videos to significantly increase the number of views.

GIVE THE GAG AWAY

As I mentioned earlier, Erick Brownstein is the president and chief strategy officer of Shareability (and has created digital content for Cristiano Ronaldo, the Olympics, Adobe, AT&T, and many other major corporations and celebrities). He explains that linear storytelling doesn't apply to social videos—it doesn't help you capture attention within the first three seconds. Instead, he advises social-content creators to consider giving away the gags at the beginning of their videos. Shareability's videos will often give away the punch line or the emotional reveal within the first ten seconds. They do so because it gives the videos a better chance of being more engaging and even going viral. When coupled with more obvious visual storytelling tactics—including optimizing content for mobile phones, using close-up images, and shooting with proper lighting—putting the most interesting or emotional parts of your content in the beginning helps you capture attention quickly.

HOW TO DESIGN THE PERFECT PROMISE

Naveen Gowda, whom I mentioned earlier is the digital content strategist on my team and former VP of content at First Media, brought First Media's social media content's performance up to nearly three billion views a month. The social channels he managed catered to millennial women and mothers with content in the do-it-yourself (DIY) crafts and life hack–related spaces on Blossom: https://www.facebook.com/FirstMediaBlossom/; content related to food on So Yummy: https://www.facebook.com/firstmediasoyummy/; and content related to beauty on Blusher: https://www.facebook.com/firstmediablusher/. Typical content concepts included videos that taught viewers how to make picture frames out of baby-food jars, unique and interesting recipes, or special ways to clean and repurpose everyday household items.

When Gowda started at BabyFirst (a brand within First Media), the content was barely achieving 1,000 likes a post. He was frustrated because he noticed that other publishers in the digital space were getting millions of views on a regular basis. He set out to discover their secrets.

He started by analyzing the high-performing content of his competitors from a communication and design perspective. Gowda studied successful channels such as Tasty, a social channel created by BuzzFeed that shares videos related to cooking, recipes, and food. He deconstructed how Tasty approached content creation and replicated it through the lens of the BabyFirst brand. He chose Tasty as his model because it was revolutionary in the food space. In 2016, they had 3.7 million subscribers and more than 190 million video views in less than a month.[48] To date, Tasty's

---

[48] Erin Griffith, "BuzzFeed's Foodie Channels Are Blowing Up in Facebook," *Fortune, Jan. 19, 2016,* https://fortune.com/2016/01/19/buzzfeed-tasty-proper-tasty/.

most-viewed YouTube video is *I Made a Giant 30-Pound Burger*, with more than 33 million views. (You can watch that video here: www.brendanjkane .com/tasty, or at https://www.youtube.com/watch?v=z4L2E6_Gmkk.)

Gowda's most important finding was that the first three seconds of digital videos should be used to make a promise to their viewers—a promise as to what the content is about and how the message will be delivered. You don't have time to communicate your entire brand's concept or summarize it within three seconds—viewers are barely getting prepared for what you're about to say. A better way to use this time is to set expectations for how your message will be delivered. Is it going to be clear and engaging, or messy and difficult to follow? You want your viewers to enjoy watching the first three seconds so they give you more of their time.

In fact, every time you put out a video on social media, or anywhere for that matter, it would be helpful to imagine that you're applying for a position in your viewer's world. The job is your audience's time, and you're applying for some of this precious resource. Viewers can be doing a myriad of other things, so unless you present your case in a way that appeals to what *they* need in this moment, you aren't going to get the job.

Viewers and the algorithms will trust you if you have a strong method of delivery. If you lose your audience's trust from the get-go, your video won't be shared widely, which is what makes those first three seconds so critically important.

THE EFFECT IS THE HERO

When approaching video creation and communication design for social platforms, the effect you have on viewers is the hero. Some of the most desired effects include getting people to have gut reactions that make them feel, "Oh my gosh, that was so smart," "Wow, I can really relate to that," or "This is really satisfying to watch." You want your audience to have gut reactions to your content rather than thoughts or a desire to analyze the video from a logical point of view. Virality stems from your viewers receiving feelings of value, not from thoughts about you, your products, or your ideals.

Once you know the gut reaction you want to produce in your viewers, be sure all of your other decisions related to messaging, visual style, pacing, actors, music, and so on, support that choice. For example, luxury brand Gucci is an expert at getting people to feel a certain way about their products. They create entire marketing campaigns to make you feel that if you wear their products, you'll have status, power, sophistication, and desirability. All of their messaging supports the effect they choose for the season. As soon as you walk into their retail locations, you're presented with a very different experience from that of a traditional retail store with stacks of folded shirts and a sales rack. Gucci promises to offer you luxury and exclusivity, which you feel as soon as you arrive or even pass by one of their store windows. The understanding of how to produce an effect is why Gucci can get away with selling a T-shirt for $450 that most likely only costs them $20 to produce. Well-designed content does the same thing—it offers $450 of value, while other content on that medium (Facebook, Instagram, YouTube) only provides $20 of value or less.

Choose your Hook Point knowing the effect you want to have on your viewers. For example, In-N-Out Burger is more successful than many of their competitors because they know the effect they want to have on their customers. Their hook is not the fact that they're a burger place, but that when you leave their restaurant, you'll feel satisfied and think about them the next time you're hungry. Gowda believes that all of In-N-Out's choices support this effect, including having a limited number of options on the menu. That way you don't get distracted or overwhelmed, and simply focus on the quality of their food. Reducing and simplifying is hard work, but it ensures a controlled consumer experience—consumers end up getting exactly what In-N-Out wants them to, and they can focus their efforts into making those specific elements excellent so that they can stay true to their tagline: "Quality you can taste."

Each time you create a piece of content, ask yourself, "What effect will this will have on my viewer?" and "What do I want the effect to be?" Once you've answered those questions, do research to determine if other content creators have set a precedent—that is, they already reach your audience successfully. Become a student of the vertical in which you want to create content. Otherwise, six months down the line, you may realize that you could have saved a ton of time and money by learning from other people's successes and failures.

Creating Hook Points—and the first three seconds of videos—with your desired goal in mind will help you design more effective content. Draw your audience in to your content so they want to watch it in its entirety, and so the algorithms keep showing your content to new, potential viewers.

(If you want to learn how to design videos effectively from our team of expert content creators who have generated billions of views online, you can see a few options here: www.brendanjkane.com/work-with-brendan/.)

HOW TO NOT BE BORING:
COMMUNICATING AT THE RIGHT PACE

Deliver your value at a quick and satisfying pace, rather than a slow and methodical one. Naveen Gowda reminds us that you have three seconds to present the structure and establish a promise about the effect the video will have on the viewer. Don't go slow, but also don't jump into things too quickly or rush. Instead, use the first three seconds to establish the scene. Create some kind of action or an unresolved situation. Then, when the three seconds are up, you can begin to act on the idea you want to present.

A lot of people try to communicate too much information too quickly, leaving viewers in a position where they fall behind. Once viewers fall behind, they start to feel like they need to play catch-up—it's as though they've come into a movie theater 20 minutes after the film has already started—which is a very unsatisfying feeling. If people feel lost, they won't want to finish watching the rest of the video. Additionally, videos that share too much information at once give viewers the feeling that every-thing has been smooshed together, which makes them lose interest.

Gowda adds that your videos don't necessarily have to be exciting, but they do need to be easy to follow and fun. It's not about incorporating spectacle, but about keeping the video engaging all the way through. "Boring" or unengaging sections of videos hurt video performance more than people think. Be honest with yourself about how captivating your content is, and think creatively about how to deliver segments that are not as engaging (and also decide if they're truly even necessary).

When creating DIY videos, where you walk viewers through the process of creating or learning how to do a task or an activity, Gowda found that a good way to set up the pacing in the first three seconds is to start with a static scene where the camera doesn't move or change angles. Then, an item is introduced to the scene and something happens to it. For example, Gowda's team created a video that began with a red plastic cup. The first three seconds were:

1. A red cup is introduced.
2. The cup is being crushed in the hand that holds it.
3. The smashed cup is put down.

After this intro, the actual content of the video starts. It may seem very primitive and simple, but the simplicity made it easy to follow and drew people in. Viewers stopped scrolling through the feed and watched the next ten seconds of the video. In fact, the video gained more than 2.2 million views: https://www.facebook.com/watch/?v=10155697878679586.

Make sure people can follow the steps or the information in the video you produce in the same way a person would speak about it. Gowda says the visuals should follow the rhythm of "First do this, then this, and then that." This easy-to-understand format sets the stage. It makes audiences believe, *I'm going to be able to follow this*. It starts the chain of thinking, *Okay, what's next?* Also, he adds that this linear form of communication doesn't solely apply to instructional videos—in fact, *all* videos should be structured linearly.

An example of a video that has good pacing and that shows how individual brands can deliver their first three seconds, is *If It Doesn't Hurt, It Doesn't Count*, which you can watch on my Instagram account here: www.brendanjkane.com/count. The first three seconds are effective because the video gives the viewer time to read the burned-in headline, also known as a meme card (which serves as the Hook Point) before the subtitles and voiceover start. Also, the visuals progress slowly enough so that you don't need to focus on them while you absorb the headline and voiceover.

The video's structure is set up to take viewers through the following process: First, read the headline; then, glance at the visuals and understand the context I'm offering. Now, listen to what I have to say. The later dynamic of cutting to footage of me speaking from the initial visuals gives the viewer the expectation that this isn't going to be a series of bland found footage, but rather, thought-out, conversational communication with the viewers. The footage of me conversing is a nonverbal storytelling cue that helps viewers follow me seamlessly.

SET THE STAGE WITH SATISFACTION

As a general rule, you don't want to start too much action until after the three seconds are up. Until that point your goal is to set the stage and spark interest. However, although the story doesn't need to develop just yet, you do need to show viewers that the video has good pacing and that it won't be slow, boring, and static.

In the first three seconds, you also need to communicate that the visual experience of the video will be satisfying to watch. This concept can't always be defined in logical terms. One way to think about it is through rhythm. The rhythm of the visuals in the first three seconds should feel satisfying and hold your audience's attention. It's very similar to how you feel when you hear the first few seconds of a great dance song in a club. If it can get you moving, you're excited about hearing the rest.

This doesn't mean your videos need high production value or that some-thing impressive needs to happen. You could open your video with a bowl and then pour a can of Coke into it in an interesting way. One may assume that watching that would be boring, but that's too logical of an analysis. Sequences like this work because they're visually appealing. It's the type of sequence Gowda has used to generate billions of views online.

DON'T MAKE YOUR AUDIENCE THINK

Don't make your audience think during the first three seconds. In fact, don't try to force them to think too much throughout most of the video. If you ask viewers to think, it needs to be impactful. That said, contrary to traditional clickbait and headline theology, this effect is not always designed in terms of shock or surprise. Sometimes you can create just as much of an impact and genuine interest in a video through satisfying pacing and good composition. Then, once you've established the right overall feel, finding places to drop in more technical, heady, or thought-provoking messages becomes easier and more palatable to your viewers. Gowda adds that establishing the right overall feel helps you avoid becoming the super-intelligent yet boring professor who drops fact after fact for two hours, versus the one who ties in stories and practical applications to make you feel excited to learn more about the technical elements behind those applications.

How to Get Satisfaction in Three Seconds

The first three seconds of an effective social video are:

1. Satisfying to watch. They hook the audience and convince them to invest their time in watching the rest of your content.

2. Moving at the right pace. Viewers need to know they can follow the video.

3. Linear in delivery (that is, don't make viewers work for you).

Gowda cites three examples of videos with great composition so you can get a visual of what he's been talking about:

    a. *Brighten up your day with these 5 surprising hacks!*: www.brendanjkane.com/bright

    b. *You Are Who You've Been Looking For*, by Adam Roa: www.brendanjkane.com/adam

    c. *When someone you love doesn't support your dreams*: www.brendanjkane.com/dreams

WHY MOVIE TRAILERS START WITH FIVE-SECOND ADS FOR THEMSELVES

"Jason Bourne takes off his jacket, punches a man unconscious, looks forlornly off camera, and then a title card appears." This is the first five-second teaser for the *Jason Bourne* trailer that immediately follows. Teasers before trailers have become the norm. The trailers for *The Two Popes*, *The Irishman*, *Once Upon a Time in Hollywood*, and *Hobbs and Shaw* are also structured in the same way. These micro-teaser openings act as Hook Points in an attempt to buy viewers' time to watch the full trailer.

Teasers within trailers exist for the sole purpose of capturing viewers' attention within the first three seconds. One of the trailers for *Independence Day: Resurgence* starts with loud and spectacular images that don't explain what's going on, but they stand out and spark intrigue. The actual trailer takes the time to explain what's happening in the footage that was shown during the first three to five seconds. Movie studios have started doing this because these trailers are shared on social media, giving marketers only a few seconds to convince viewers to stop scrolling and pay attention.

Latham Arneson, the former vice president of digital marketing at Paramount Pictures, believes that there are good and bad ways to execute the design of these trailers. He warns that just because the images are loud and bright doesn't necessarily mean they'll capture the audience's attention. The images need some level of intrigue. Get the audience to ask themselves, "Oh, what's this?" Elicit their desire to see more. If people are inundated with bright and loud images over and over again, those tactics will become ineffective. "Pay attention to what's out there so you're not copying everyone else," advises Arneson. Find new ways to create a high level of intrigue.

What's interesting is that even movie studios that invest millions of dollars, into a single piece of content have to work hard to find tactics to capture people's attention. The fact that they need to create a trailer before a trailer is a reflection of the heavy level of competition that exists to get views on social media.

WHAT HAPPENS WHEN YOU SLEEP?

Arneson worked on the marketing campaign for the movie *Paranormal Activity*, which had two really strong tag lines/Hook Points. They were: "What Happens When You Sleep?" and "Don't See It Alone." The visual hook of the trailer was that you were watching people's fearful reactions to the movie while watching it in a theater. The trailer barely shows any of the movie; the images mostly show the audience reacting in fear, shock, and surprise. Choosing to structure the trailer like this made viewers wonder what could be scary enough to get people that freaked out.

The trailer was structured in this way because *Paranormal Activity* was a low-budget film that built slowly; the movie wasn't intriguing in a short-content format. In fact, Arneson feels that if the trailer had simply shown clips of the film, it would have been boring. It wasn't a high-budget, catchy-at-first-glance or visually impressive action movie. It didn't have a budget like *Avengers* or *Star Wars*, so it wouldn't make sense to compete with trailers for films in that league. By filming the people watching the movie in a theater instead (showing them scared out of their minds), it created a situation where viewers of the trailer were excited because they wanted to experience similar reactions.

In summary, be conscious of what your product's strengths are, and present your content in a way that highlights those features. There are an infinite number of forms in which you can package your content. Use trial and error to find the methods that make the most sense for your product or brand.

200,000 INSTAGRAM FOLLOWERS IN A MONTH

I've spent a great deal of time developing strategies to grow quickly on Instagram. The fastest way I've found to grow, with an increase of about 150,000 to 300,000 new followers in a single month, is to test and distribute content on other accounts with large followings. This is the strategy I used to help me gain one million followers on Instagram and several million followers for other clients and partners.

The types of accounts where I've had the most success distributing content are memes. A meme account is one that isn't an individual person, influencer, brand, or corporation, but rather an account focused on a specific niche. There are meme accounts for almost every major niche: inspiration, fashion, food, sports, comedy, and so on. A more formal definition of the term *meme* is "something such as a video, picture, or phrase that a lot of people send to each other on the internet." Some popular examples of meme accounts include @thegoodquote, @noteforself, and @thefatjewish.

Meme-account creators have to be amazing content aggregators to capture the attention of millions of viewers and followers. One method my team leveraged to grow quickly on Instagram was posting my content on meme-account pages to drive people back to *my* accounts. There are two ways you can achieve this:

1. Organically, by structuring a share for share (meaning that meme-account creators will share your content if you share theirs), or some other form of distribution partnership where they're willing to post your content for free. This typically only works if your content is highly engaging or you're providing some other form of value to the account and its owner.

2. You can achieve this placement by buying what is called a *shout-out*, which is another term for buying an advertising placement on someone else's account. (For more information on how advertising on meme accounts works, check out my Rapid Audience Growth Course: https://www.rapidaudiencegrowth.com/.)

When you buy a shout-out with a meme account, you want to provide content that creates interest in your account. Essentially, you're creating an advertisement for your account with a strong hook. Often, it's in the form of a photo, along with messaging that inspires others to follow you.

To be successful, you have to figure out the type of content and hook that drives people to follow your account. That sounds simple, but it's really not. It's of the utmost importance to create a strong Hook Point, because otherwise, this process doesn't work. For example, one of our meme-distribution partners has more than 19 million followers. When we've posted content with an ineffective hook on their account, it can result in fewer than 200 followers, while a shout-out with a strong hook could result in gaining 5,000 to 20,000 followers in a 24-hour period. In both scenarios, the content is posted to the same account and is exposed to the exact same audience, but the content that has the more effective Hook Point grabs people's attention and generates enough motivation for viewers to want to learn more about the account promoted and to ultimately click on the "Follow" button.

About 99 percent of the people reading this book need to package their content with extreme creativity and effective Hook Points—I personally practice this with my brand and clients every day. To stand out in a 3-second world, think about the reactions you want people to have when viewing your content. Clearly define and test what will motivate them to go and follow your account. Like Hook Points, it's important to note that what works is constantly changing and evolving. The examples above may have evolved into a different format because the old one stopped working.

MEME CARDS: WHAT THEY ARE AND HOW TO USE THEM

By testing hundreds of thousands of variations of content over the past few years, I've learned that setting a clear and unique expectation about the information you're about to deliver (which can be expressed through a headline, meme card, or burned-in captions) is incredibly important in getting people to watch, click, buy, and/or share your videos.

A meme card, which is a text caption box that appears at the top or bottom of a video on Facebook or Instagram, can help you communicate your Hook Points quickly and clearly to those scrolling on social media. If you use social media, you've probably seen a meme card. It looks like this:

Gowda explains that meme cards are an important structure in Instagram's and Facebook's language—if you don't integrate them into your communication style, you'll probably have a harder time attracting attention on the platform. This is because meme cards set the expectation for communication delivery and act as initial impressions or introductions to your viewers. When you walk up to a checkout register and the person behind the counter doesn't smile, or is rude right off the bat, it sets the expectation that you're going to have an unpleasant interaction; whereas if the person is friendly, smiling, and patient, before saying anything else this individual has set the expectation that you're going to enjoy the interaction. Meme cards also help you set expectations—they help you make the promise that you'll deliver your interaction (aka content) in a certain way.

Gowda explains that oftentimes people create vague meme cards with phrases like, "You have to watch this till the end." A meme card providing this little value is basically telling its viewers that they have to work extra hard for the creator, as opposed to receiving something intriguing and clear from that creator.

Recently, copywriter Craig Clemens posted a video with a meme card that reads: "Impress her by eating healthy." This sentence is the beginning of a story about how he impressed his wife by eating healthy and then goes on to talk about the importance of a nutritious diet. By delivering the Hook Point through the meme card, Clemens gives his viewers enough value to know that their time won't be wasted by watching, and that they won't be forced to do any extra thinking—they can consume the content passively. Eventually, he can translate that attention into action, but not right off the bat. This is because you can't ask your viewers to do something for you in each piece of content you produce. Viewers have tons of other options and will choose to watch other videos that provide them with more value without asking them to work hard for it.

An effective Hook Point for a meme card creates intrigue. Gowda clarifies that the intrigue doesn't have to act as an all-encompassing summary of the story in the post; you can start out with a very controversial or outlandish statement while the story you tell is completely motivational or inspirational—as long as the communication is authentic. This means: don't create meme cards that are clickbait, and make sure the phrase you choose makes sense and is in line with the overall content of the post.

An example of a post that does this effectively is this clip of Adam Roa giving a motivational speech on Mindvalley's Instagram account. (You can view the video here: www.brendanjkane.com/roa.) The burned-in caption (which acts as the meme card in this case) starts with a statement that's a little bit shocking: "Buy this car, you'll get girls. Buy this bra, you'll get guys." Then Roa tells a story that promotes the opposite of that Hook Point. The story is motivational and explains why you shouldn't listen to a consumerist society that tries to make you feel like you need material goods to attract mates. Mindvalley chose those shocking sentences as the opening Hook Point because they attract attention and because the true intent behind the statement can be understood by viewers once they watch the rest of the story. It's not simply a shocking clickbait headline—it has a purpose that's backed up by the story.

Mindvalley only started using Hook Points in their videos recently. By using Hook Points in the form of meme cards, Mindvalley's video performance has tripled. Their top-performing videos were receiving around 20,000 or 30,000 views before the use of Hook Points, and now they're able to reach 100,000-plus views on Instagram for most videos. In fact, some of their top performers on Facebook are generating millions of views.

By front-loading the videos with this packaging and communication design, the promise they make is clear, and viewers are responding by giving them more of their time and attention.

(If you want to dive deeper into understanding meme cards and other viral formats we use with our private clients, we have a detailed report available here: www.brendanjkane.com/viralreport.)

TESTING MEME CARDS

To help you find the best phrases for your meme cards, Gowda recommends testing multiple versions. Remember, your meme card needs to support your message, not necessarily reiterate it. If the messaging or the video is covering a complex topic, use a meme card to give your concept a baseline or a floor on which to ground itself. Only when the visual action starts at a slower pace can you use a more complex and punchy meme-card phrase.

For example, the meme card "Laugh at yourself, or other people will" (www.brendanjkane.com/laugh) features a phrase that's a pretty big thought—it's a lot to process—which is why we chose to match it with uncomplicated visuals of a lady sliding down a snowy hill. This keeps the visual development minimal during the first three seconds, which gives viewers time to process the meme card. Gowda notes that if you try to communicate a complex thought in the meme card and show complex visuals at the same time, this tends to overwhelm viewers. Keep that in mind, and be sure to establish a nice balance between the text and visuals in your communication design.

You can discover the right balance for your communication design by testing granularly. Gowda and I A/B test different meme cards and

3-second intros to find the right balance. Perhaps option A will delay the start of the voiceover by half a second, so that we know, by viewers' responses, exactly where to edit the video to balance perfectly with the meme card. And in subsequent options, we may test different text headlines in the meme card and/or open the first three seconds with different found-footage clips. As you can see, there are many nuanced details that go into generating highly viral social clips. We've spent years testing and refining this process. With that said, here are a few simple tips to start you on the path of testing and learning:

Three Tips for Creating Effective Meme Cards

1. Do a competitive analysis. Look at your competitors' successful videos and see what kinds of meme cards they use. Put your ideas next to theirs, and make sure yours stand out. (Refer to the Hook Point exercise from the end of chapter 1.)

2. Provide value. It's easy to create meme cards with text along the lines of "Watch this till the end," "This will inspire you," or "You won't believe what happens next," but those phrases don't provide value. Audiences generally tune out these vague messages. Instead, try to incorporate a tangible element of value in your meme cards.

3. Be mindful of your typography design. Identify the key phrase or keywords within the sentence or phrase in your meme card. If possible, highlight them, and separate your phrase or sentence where you want to break the line. You'll see this in the meme card for "Laugh at yourself, or other people will." (You can view this video again at: www.brendanjkane.com/laugh.)

You'll see that my team brought out "Laugh at yourself" as a key part of that sentence. We chose to distinguish one line from the other. Also, notice that we put the first line in bold. By doing so, we're subconsciously communicating how to read this sentence, which helps make it easier for viewers to digest. We could have chosen to bold "Laugh" as the keyword, but in this case, it would have been a mistake because it's not enough of a complete thought. Gowda recommends providing tangible value right away, whenever possible. On its own, "Laugh" doesn't tell the audience anything—it's just a word—whereas "Laugh at yourself" is a complete thought that provides value.

(We break down our typography-design principles for meme cards in our viral video and framework report, which is available here: www .brendanjkane.com/viralreport.)

USE SOCIAL ANALYTICS AND SEARCH TO TEST AND FIND HOOK POINTS

While working at Paramount Pictures, Arneson tested his Hook Points with social analytics. Whenever his team released a piece of content, they would get tens of thousands, or sometimes even hundreds of thousands, of comments on social channels. From this data they could evaluate how people perceived the messages they sent out. They would learn which themes and ideas people most cared about and responded to.

For example, when Arneson's team released horror films, they knew they were on track if people commented, "I'm scared out of my mind!" That was an obvious signal that the content or trailer was working. There were moments during the *Paranormal Activity* campaign when people would comment that the commercials were keeping them up at night. This is the exact effect his team wanted—they wanted viewers to be so scared that they couldn't sleep. The conversations Arneson's team saw on social media were some of the biggest markers of success.

Gowda cautions, however, to be wary about how you listen to comments from your audience. Generally, he feels that analytics such as views, retention, or shares trump comments. He agrees that you can get cues from comments and need to be aware of the effect your videos are having on viewers, but it's dangerous to listen to comments too literally. Doing so can stifle growth or lead you in the wrong direction. Instead, look at people's reactions in terms of scale and ratios rather than one-off pieces of advice. Read the analytics and make inferences before you look at comments, to help you judge them more astutely. Use comments to support your analytics, not as a guide on their own.

For example, if your analytics are showing that the content is strong, and perhaps you're getting an incredibly high ratio of shares to views, you can look at the comments with the knowledge that the campaign worked. That way, if a commenter criticizes the video, it won't affect your future decisions. Instead, you'll know to pay attention to the positive comments to glean additional, perhaps nuanced, insights about why the content is performing well. Look at the data before you heavily weigh the comments from your audience.

SEARCH DATA

Another indicator of success for Arneson's team was search volume within Google and other search engines. When the first *Cloverfield* movie trailer was released, the film didn't have a title. Paramount decided to use the release date at the end of the trailer in lieu of the title. Arneson ran the search department at Paramount, and he could see that after they released the trailer, there were search spikes on the internet for the release date of the movie. This showed that the intrigue for understanding what the movie was about was very strong. Therefore, his team put more money behind promoting the film to build off of that momentum and capture even more attention.

You, too, can use search data to help you identify effective angles for Hook Points in marketing campaigns. Gowda agrees that more people should be aware of the power of studying and searching across various platforms. Facebook, Instagram, YouTube, Reddit, and Google each have their own algorithms that function distinctly to find the most effective content. Use that to your advantage, but be aware of the pitfalls. One such pitfall is that the algorithms can make content creators and social media managers lazy—they let the algorithm do all the work for them, which limits their analysis to only the highest-performing content from the most well-known content creators in their vertical. Gowda warns that you need to look broader than solely at the content that exists in your space. In most cases, it's hard to come up with great ideas when you limit yourself. His secret is to find ideas from content across various platforms and from content that doesn't necessarily perform well (explained below).

Reddit

For Gowda, Reddit is one of the best platforms where you can find new ideas. He feels that Reddit gets a lot of the best content first because their algorithm has a lot less weight—content is pushed to the top from user engagements. This is because Reddit is an active-engagement platform—meaning that users aren't just shown content to swipe through; they actually have to click on posts, which forces them to work to curate content on their own. The platform trains viewers to be super intelligent in terms of how they respond to content, so when a GIF, video, or concept actually makes it to the top of the feed, it's much more powerful than when it does so on other platforms. Reddit is a place where the best content (regardless of the prestige of its creator) can be discovered.

You can usually find a subreddit (a specific online community, and the posts associated with it) for most broad categories. Gowda says that it's tricky to be super specific in your search, so he recommends subscribing to subreddits and getting suggested posts related to broad topics in your space. He also recommends using Google to search for topics with the word *Reddit* after your search query because Google's search tool is more effective than Reddit's. Then, once you find your subreddits, look through all the content and find what makes you say, "Wow that's cool." That's a foundation for building Hook Points and stories.

Tubular Labs

Gowda also recommends doing searches on Tubular Labs, which is an advanced tracking tool that tracks all video content on YouTube, Instagram, and Facebook. It lets you sort and search by views, shares, and likes, and allows you to export data organized by various metrics. It's a good way to find top-performing videos and content creators. Gowda pays the most attention to views within a certain time period or the ratio of shares to views. He does caution, however, that you have to be discerning about how you read the data. Sometimes paid media can spike a post's performance, and you don't want to walk away thinking that the video was a great idea, when in reality it just had an effective ad campaign behind it. Do your homework by clicking into each video, and decide (based on the metrics) if it looks like the views were a result of a paid campaign or not.

YouTube

The last tool Gowda recommends for coming up with content ideas and Hook Points is YouTube. By searching beyond the obvious keywords that most people in your space would use, you can take the extra step of digging in and finding content that didn't get a ton of views, and that may have poor production value but that nevertheless offers little nuggets of gold. By doing a granular search of this nature, Gowda has found ideas for some of the highest-performing videos he's ever made.

For example, one time he found a video of an older woman in China folding clothing. She had a very slick technique—a one, two, three approach that allowed her to fold a pile of T-shirts in seconds. Gowda's team took the concept, packaged the idea distinctively, promised good communication, and it generated more than 300 million views.

Alternatively, you can search for ideas to repurpose from videos on YouTube with high production value that also weren't packaged correctly. For example, Gowda once found a well-produced video of an April Fool's joke that only had 4,000 views. His team repurposed the idea, downgraded the production value pretty heavily, and got 150 million views. In this case, the lower production value felt more authentic for audiences and worked better.

There is no one-dimensional truth in this space. You need to search, test, and learn to come up with the best Hook Points and communication design for each piece of content. Be willing to continually learn and grow to find the best ways to share your message.

Quick Tips and Recap

- Choosing the right Hook Point and packaging content is highly important for getting people to watch, share, click, and purchase your content, products, and services.
- Set clear expectations for your content through the use of headlines, meme cards, or captions.
- The first three seconds of your digital videos make a promise to your viewers. Make sure that promise is clear and intriguing.
- Your desired audience can do a myriad of other things with their time, so present your content in a way that appeals to their needs and provides them with value.
- Each time you create a piece of content, ask yourself, "What effect is this going to have on my viewers?"

- Do a competitive analysis of other content creators in your space. Pay attention to what's out there so you can learn from other people's successes and failures.
- Make sure the first three seconds of your videos are satisfying to watch, move at the right pace, and are delivered in a way that doesn't make viewers think too hard or play catch-up.
- There are an infinite number of ways to package your content. Use trial and error through A/B testing to find the methods that make the most sense for your product or brand.
- Meme cards are important tools that help you set the expectation for how you're going to communicate with your viewers and help introduce your videos.
- Let social analytics guide you in monitoring your success and in deciding what to create next.
- Use Reddit, Tubular Labs, and YouTube to find content, Hook Points, and story ideas.

CHAPTER 4

BECOME PRESIDENT AND SAVE THE PLANET: MASTERING THE ART OF STORYTELLING

WHETHER IT'S A young adult who's just graduated from college or a billionaire who's had a tremendous amount of success, people across the board struggle to package their value propositions. They aren't sure what makes them unique and don't know how to come up with a captivating and succinct story that both captures and holds people's attention in our 3-second world. Telling stories that speak to audiences and that meet their communication styles and needs is one of the most important skills you can learn. When attempting to secure new business in a meeting, create a viral video for social channels, or write copy to market your brand, you need to know how to tell a story, quickly and efficiently, that shows people the value you or your product can offer.

Over the years I've crafted several stories about who I am and what I do, which include case studies about the clients I've worked with. While in meetings, I ask questions to get an understanding of my prospects' pain points. Then, based upon their responses, I strategically choose to tell them different variations of my stories based on their needs.

One time I was in a meeting with a gentleman named Michael Wright, who, at the time, was CEO of Steven Spielberg's film production company, Amblin Entertainment. A partner of mine had set up the meeting, and neither Wright nor I had any idea what the meeting was for—all we knew was that it would have to take less than 25 minutes because Wright was super busy.

We sat down, and I spent the first seven or eight minutes asking Wright questions about Amblin Entertainment's core focus. I asked what his goals were as CEO, what he viewed as his core obstacles and roadblocks to success, and the company's current strategy to overcome those challenges. I wanted to clearly understand how he operated, what his biggest pain points were, and what he deemed valuable.

Wright told me that Amblin Entertainment was investing a lot of money to launch a new brand initiative. They wanted to have the same level of brand recognition as Marvel—because even though people know who Steven Spielberg is, they don't often recognize that Amblin Entertainment produced movies such as *E.T. the Extraterrestrial, Jurassic Park*, or *Saving Private Ryan*. The team was investing a lot of money and time in launching a website where people could consume and engage with Amblin content, but because of this lack of brand recognition, Wright feared that once launched, the site would only receive a few thousand visits a month.

By asking the right questions and listening, I discovered that turning Amblin into a brand that receives the level of recognition that Marvel has was an important goal for Wright, and that the website was one of the key steps in making that happen. In that moment I realized that I had a solution to his problem, and even more important, a Hook Point and story to effectively communicate that solution. I knew I could help drive traffic to the site at scale to solve Wright's concern. The Hook Point was the fact that in one month, we pushed close to seven million people to Yahoo!'s website to consume Katie Couric's content. Then, in the story, I broke down the strategy we used for Couric and Yahoo! to drive traffic from Facebook to her interviews on Yahoo!'s website at scale.

Within 20 minutes, I provided a very clear idea of how to overcome the problem, and Wright was super excited about moving forward and finding a way to work together. Our strategy was to identify strong Hook Points within Amblin's film library, leverage specific film clips and interviews that best expressed those hooks, and A/B test them against each other to identify winning variations that would drive traffic at scale to their new website.

In the end, we never actually launched the project because we ran into a lot of politics with other parties involved, and Wright left Amblin Entertainment to become president of Epix. Regardless, the way I leveraged the initial hook and story worked. It caught Wright's attention, helped build a relationship, and got him excited about working with my partner and me.

Some meetings will go well and lead to more business, while others won't. What I want you to take away from this is the fact that even without previously knowing what the meeting would be about, I found the pain point, crafted a strategy in the moment, and wrapped it into a compelling story to prove my value.

BE FLEXIBLE: AN IMPORTANT LESSON
THEY DON'T TEACH YOU IN YOGA

Prepare for meetings by coming up with a story that matches the Hook Point that helped you get the meeting in the first place, but once in the meeting, be flexible. Or, as in my case with Amblin Entertainment, if you don't know the hook that got you into the room, go in with the intent to focus on listening, which helps you avoid one of the biggest mistakes people make, which is having a preconceived pitch. This type of pitch makes you say the same thing regardless of who's sitting on the other side of the table, which is not an effective strategy. Instead, it's smart to take a step back, think about the people you're talking to, and listen to what they have to say.

Take time to read body language and consider the mood of those in the room. How do they respond to your questions? Get an idea of who they are, and ease into the conversation. Thoroughly understanding them and their needs will help dictate how you package your information. Not every story will resonate with every person. Sometimes you need to tell a different story—or your current story in a slightly different way—to be effective.

I'M A SUPERHERO, NOT A COMEDIAN:
HOW TO PLAY TO YOUR STRENGTHS

When telling stories, it's important to play up your personality strengths. For example, I'm not a comedian. Generally, I don't crack jokes or tell funny stories; I'm a more serious and analytical person. My stories are structured to follow this truth. If you, on the other hand, are a big personality and can tell funny jokes, work that into your stories. As long as they don't become a distraction and you don't lose the trust and credibility of your listeners, humor can add value. Use your authentic strengths to get people to pay attention to you and want to work with you.

MIND THE TIME: SETTING A WORLD RECORD FOR THE SHORTEST MEETING

It's important to make sure you're articulate, clear, concise, and to the point. The stories I tell in meetings are typically anywhere from two to six minutes long. I don't go over that amount of time because the stories would then become too drawn out. You also want to leave time for feedback, questions, and to see how people are reacting. You don't want to do a 30-minute presentation only to find out that the way you're positioning your story is not of value to the people on the other side of the table. Besides, very important meetings are usually short, as important individuals have limited availability.

When creating content for social media, you don't have this immediate feedback loop and the ability to adjust on the fly. But you can measure the success of each piece of content; notice its length, format, and structure; and keep it in mind for the next video you produce. Remember to look at the analytics and let them guide you. Additionally, you can be aware of the consumption-behavior patterns on each platform. For example, Facebook and Instagram are known for short-form consumption behavior while YouTube can drive long-form consumption behavior, with some viewers watching videos that are an hour long or more. Test different platforms and various content formats to find what resonates most with your audience.

STORYTELLING FOR PUBLIC SPEAKING

As soon as Michael Breus, The Sleep Doctor, books a speaking engagement, he talks to the event promoter to understand the demographic of his audience. He wants to know the ratio of men to women, their net worth, their occupations, and where they live. Understanding these profiles is critically important because it helps Breus adapt his presentation to meet the audience's needs. I also apply this tactic and have found it to be effective for my speaking career as well.

If Breus is speaking to an audience composed of 90 percent men and 10 percent women, he makes sure he has three case studies about men. Even if men can identify with aspects of each woman in a case study, it makes more sense to choose slides that better match the audience's demographic and that speak to them directly.

Once he's in the room delivering a speech, Breus usually puts up a character profile and reads it to the audience. He then asks, "How many of you identify with this person? If you do, raise your hand." Usually half of the group raise their hands immediately. Then he'll add, "Okay, from those of you who didn't raise your hand, would three of you raise your hand right now?" After three people have raised their hands, he asks, "So what about this profile wasn't you?" He listens and is usually able to find another case study in his deck that meets their needs. He lets them know that they'll be included in the conversation by saying, "Oh, this is awesome, because later on I'm going to talk about someone just like you, so hold tight." This exercise allows him to better understand his audience and gear his communication toward them.

If your audience doesn't feel spoken to, they'll stop listening to what you have to say, which is why Breus gives himself the power to tailor his messages specifically to the people in the room. Knowing the audience's profiles helps him keep them more engaged during the presentation as he customizes each section to their needs.

I recently experienced the power of tailoring messages to meet the needs of an audience when I delivered a keynote speech to more than 7,000 dentists. I had never delivered my keynote to dentists, so I did as much research and due diligence about who was in the room as I could. Once I had this information, I reworked my entire speech, specific to the needs of this audience, addressing their pain points, challenges, and goals.

An additional trick Breus uses to keep audiences engaged is making eye contact with every single person in the room. At some point during the lecture, he looks at each individual, even if it's only for a half a second, because he wants each person to feel seen. It keeps audience members present and helps them feel more comfortable sharing their sleep-related issues.

The final storytelling technique Breus uses to make the most of speaking engagements is starting off Q&A sessions with questions related to his best Hook Points. For example, he'll open these sessions by saying, "One of the questions I get asked all the time is, 'Hey, Dr. Breus, what's the best mattress for sleep?' or 'Hey, Dr. Breus, when's the best time for sex before sleep?'" These Hook Point topics are interesting, risqué, and leave people wanting to learn more.

Find out who your audience is so that you can best match their needs. You'll be more helpful and have more engagement if you truly understand them.

THE PROCESS COMMUNICATION MODEL

The Process Communication Model (PCM) is a behavioral observational tool that allows you to communicate more effectively. It's been used by the likes of NASA, Bill Clinton, and Pixar to help them achieve their business and communication objectives. Jeff King, a PCM expert, gives us a brief overview of the best ways to reach and engage audiences through the use of this model.

King explains that when telling a story, you must think about your audience. If, instead, you tell stories that are focused solely on the way in which *you* perceive the world, you'll be on the wrong track. Unfortunately, that's what the majority of people do—subconsciously they gravitate toward the vocabulary or currency in which they speak and only tell stories in that vein.

In the PCM, there are six vocabularies that are related to the six PCM personality types, which include Thinkers, Persisters, Harmonizers, Imaginers, Rebels, and Promoters. Each personality type experiences the world in a different way. Thinkers perceive the world through thoughts, and logic is their currency. Persisters perceive the world through opinions, and value is their currency. Harmonizers perceive the world through emotions, and compassion is their currency. Imaginers perceive the world through inactions, and imagination is their currency. Rebels perceive the world through reactions, and humor is their currency. And Promoters perceive the world through actions, and charm is their currency. All of the personality types are in each of us, but we have a base personality type that we're born with that doesn't change over the course of our lives. This base personality dictates how we communicate to others, the preferred method of how people communicate with us, and how we perceive and interact with the world.

If you're a Thinker, for example, your preferred vocabulary is logic, and you'll tell stories with messages made up of 70 to 80 percent logic vocabulary. Unfortunately, if Thinkers structure their stories in this way, they'll miss 75 percent of the population who are not of the Thinker personality type. Effective storytellers, on the other hand, will use the logic, values, humor, imagination, action, and emotions vocabularies. They will insert messages for all six of the personality types so they can hook 100 percent of the audience. Some employees at Pixar Animation Studios are trained in the PCM and use the model successfully. When you watch a Pixar movie, you see all six of the PCM vocabularies used throughout the storytelling (generally represented by having a character that matches each personality type). The fact that they speak to all of the personality types is one of the reasons why their movies are so successful.

THE PCM COPY FOR ADS

Let's try an exercise where we create copy to advertise a car. Using the PCM, King explains how he would construct the content to make sure that he communicated the clearest message about the car, wrapping it in a way that makes sense for each of the personality types. King suggests writing something like this:

> Think of a car. This car model gets 50 miles per gallon. The car's miles per gallon are at the highest rate compared to other models in its class. We believe that this car provides more value to our customers in regard to what you're going to pay for. Bottom line—it's the best car on the market. It feels good, it looks nice, and you're going to be so comfortable driving this car. All your

friends are finally going to want to hang out with you, because this car is awesome.

Now let's break this down to see which personality type each sentence speaks to:

- These sentences use LOGIC and speak to Thinkers: "Think of a car. This car model gets 50 miles per gallon. The car's miles per gallon are at the highest rate compared to other models in its class."
- This sentence uses VALUE and speaks to Persisters: "We believe that this car provides more value to our customers in regard to what you're going to pay for."
- This sentence uses CHARM and speaks to Promoters: "Bottom line—it's the best car on the market."
- This sentence uses FEELINGS/COMPASSION and speaks to Harmonizers: "It feels good, it looks nice, and you're going to be so comfortable driving this car."
- This sentence uses HUMOR and speaks to Rebels: "All your friends are finally going to want to hang out with you, because this car is awesome."

This ad speaks to the majority of the population, whereas most ads don't—they're usually designed in the communication style of the person creating them, thus alienating a vast percentage of the population who perceive the world differently. This means that if a woman producing this car ad perceived the world through opinions, she would likely focus on the currency of value in her communication and she'd lose the attention of those that perceive the world through logic, action, reactions, and feelings.

THE PCM FOR MEETINGS AND JOB INTERVIEWS

Jeff King is the head of the MUSE School, and CEO of MUSE Global, where they teach students from early childhood through the 12th grade. All the teachers at the school are thoroughly trained in the PCM. That way, no matter what the student's preferred communication style is, MUSE teachers can assess, connect with, and motivate each student.

By high school, all the students are also thoroughly trained in the PCM. Campus visitors are often shocked by how well the students, whether two or 18 years old, communicate. By the time students have college or job interviews, they know how to effectively motivate the people in front of them based on how they perceive the world. In fact, many colleges and universities make comments about how well MUSE students communicate.

King believes that a lot of educational facilities do not prepare our youth for the working world. Often the focus is on memorizing and regurgitating information, but they aren't shown how to communicate, manage stress, or negotiate conflict, which is exactly what the PCM teaches them.

If a person is unaware of the PCM, they're more likely to disengage interviewers. For example, if an interviewer asks a question based in logic, such as, "How long did you work for Apple?" and the interviewee's preferred language is emotions, the person may respond with an emotional response such as, "I worked there for a few years and loved it. Apple is such an amazing place." Whereas, if someone is trained in the PCM and the interviewer opens with this logic-based question, the person will respond with a logic-based answer such as, "I worked there for four years and three months." Those trained in the PCM are more likely to stay in the same vocabulary so that the interviewer remains engaged and connected.

Effectiveness in interviews and meetings comes from understanding the perspective of those on the other side of the table. You want to meet their needs. It's not about going in and blurting out whatever is on your mind, so try to actually understand the people on the other side of the table, and communicate on their level so that you're on the same page.

HOW BILL CLINTON LEVERAGED THE PCM TO BECOME PRESIDENT

Bill Clinton is a great example of how the PCM can enhance your career. He constantly uses it to assess others and connect with them, and he consistently uses all six of the PCM vocabularies in his speeches. When Clinton ran for president, he engaged just about 100 percent of his audience. He had all ears on him—which is exactly what you want when you're a public speaker.

One of the key turning points during the 1996 presidential election was when Clinton won a critical debate against George Bush. King explains that during the debate, a woman asked a question about how each party would address the economic crisis and how it was affecting people's lives. She also stated that she felt the economic recession had negatively impacted her own life, as well as her friends' and family's. Bush responded to the question with thoughts and logic, as well as value and opinions. However, the woman perceived the world through feelings and emotions, so Bush's answer didn't connect with her.

On the other hand, Bill Clinton picked up on her communication style right away. He responded to her personally and shared that he felt her pain.

He also explained how he felt about the economic recession and how it had affected him and his life. He connected with her on a deep and feeling-based level because he saw that *she* was a feeling-based person (like 30 percent of the North American population). By using those words, he immediately gained the trust of the people in that group and made the woman (and those like her) feel understood and heard.

Hillary Clinton, on the other hand, did not follow in her husband's footsteps. One of the reasons she lost the election to Donald Trump was because she only spoke two vocabularies: logic and values. King thinks that Hillary Clinton may have been the most qualified person to ever run for president of the United States, but because she only spoke in logic and values, she wasn't accessible to a significant portion of the North American population.

The PCM teaches that when people are in a positive life position, we can speak from all six vocabularies and can effectively connect and appreciate the diversity of all six personality types. When we're in a negative life position, we're in what the PCM refers to as *distress*. When we're in distress, we behave in a way that is negative to those around us. Thus, we're not concerned about the well-being of others or about connecting with others to motivate them in a positive way.

Trump usually communicates in distress from his Promoter personality type. Promoters in distress are willing to say whatever it takes to appease their audience. Promoter distress behavior is to manipulate people and to get them to argue and fight with one another. King points out that Trump has said things like, "I'm going to turn my taxes over," or "I will sit down with Robert Mueller." King believes Trump never had any intention of doing either of those things—he only said them because he knew that it was what his audience wanted to hear.

Promoters can also be very skilled at manipulating people and setting groups up against each other. Over the past couple of years, and even while Trump was running for the election, he pinned groups against each other so he could step back and say, "Well, they're not getting along. I have to go in and save the day."

When promoters are not in distress, they can act in positive ways, just like any other personality type. Each personality has a positive and negative (distressed) side. The PCM teaches individuals how to keep *themselves* in a positive life position and how to help *others* move from distress to a more positive life position.

YOU WANT TO SAVE THE PLANET?

Unfortunately, King finds that environmentalists are often some of the worst communicators on the planet. In fact, the majority of people who tell stories with the intent to spark change run into a common problem. Although they're usually filled with wonderful passion for their cause, it often leads them astray. You very rarely see an environmentalist get up and speak to all six of the personality types, like Bill Clinton. Instead, they tend to speak in values or logic, which only hits a very narrow segment of the population. They don't engage a large portion of their audience, and therefore don't engage a large area of the country. King believes that failure to communicate effectively has slowed progress on solving environmental issues.

An example of failure to communicate effectively is when an environmentalist says, "You know, we should stop eating fish because the ocean is going to run out of fish, and besides, all the fish are filled with plastic. If you eat fish, something's wrong with you because you don't care about the oceans and you don't care about our environment."

Honestly, who's going to listen to that? From a fact perspective, the environmentalist may be 100 percent correct, but when speakers belittle and attack their audience, those who are listening get turned off and lose trust in those people. Words such as *should, ought,* and *need,* or statements like "Something's wrong with you if you don't do what I want you to do" don't inspire change.

Instead, environmentalists—or anyone for that matter—would benefit from trying to share a message that hits all six currencies. A better speech would be:

> We love the oceans and the fish so much. The data states that we're going to run out of fish by 2030. We strongly believe that we have to find some alternatives to fish because we want our oceans to be awesome for many generations. Imagine a future where we have an abundance of fish and where the waters are not polluted. Join me so we can take action now.

Each sentence in this speech speaks directly to one of the six PCM personality types.

THE PCM AND MOVIES

Only 5 percent of the North American population has the Promoter personality type (people who perceive the world through actions and use charm as their currency). They are unique because they take big risks and have a lot of charisma. What is fascinating about Promoters is that they inspire the other 95 percent of the population because non-Promoters wouldn't feel as comfortable taking those risks. King says that a lot of successful film trailers and movies have a main character with a Promoter personality type, which helps entice people to show up at the box office. When audiences watch a character such as Iron Man, James Bond, or even con man Frank Abagnale (played by Leonardo DiCaprio in *Catch Me If You Can),* they feel moved in some way and think, *I would love to be that character.* You'll also find that Promoters often find their way into major leadership roles because of this as well (i.e., Steve Jobs, Bill Clinton, and Donald Trump).

PCM FOR TV COMMERCIALS

Although movies and trailers tend to do better with Promoters as the lead characters in their stories, advertisers need to think more broadly when it comes to TV commercials. King explains that in these ads, it's beneficial for advertisers to play the numbers game, hitting emotions with 30 percent of their messaging, logic with 25 percent, humor with 20 percent, and perhaps values with 10 percent. Essentially, they need to use a wide range of the PCM languages in order to capture a larger audience.

The Dollar Shave Club created a video called *DollarShaveClub.com— Our Blades Are F***ing Great,* which spread the PCM language very effectively. The video went viral shortly after it was released in 2012 and currently has more than 26 million views. It helped the company launch, and led to their acquisition by Unilever for more than $1 billion.[49] King believes that the storytelling in this video worked because it used logic, emotion, and humor in its messaging, which reaches the largest percentage

[49] CNBC Make It Staff, "This CEO sold his company for $1 billion—here's how he finds work-life balance," CNBC Make it, Feb. 6, 2019, https://www.cnbc.com/2019/02/06 /dollar-shave-club-ceo-michael-dubin-work-life-balance.html.

of the population and helped them knock it out of the park in terms of capturing audiences' attention.

THE PCM FOR SOCIAL CONTENT DESIGN

When designing content for online distribution, the story you tell should hit all the different ways in which people perceive the world. Again, emotions, logic, and humor are the top three vocabularies in North America, so if that's your main audience, try to design content with those elements in videos, articles, and posts.

Unfortunately, most content designers focus too heavily on the way they perceive the world, alienating a huge percentage of the population. They end up subconsciously communicating to themselves when they should be communicating to their audience. If your preferred vocabulary is logic, don't tell a story using only this vocabulary. Remember that communication is never about *you*; it's always about those you're speaking to.

ONCE UPON A TIME IN A WORLD OF
HEROES AND DRAGONS . . .

Telling a story in a room where no one is listening is not effective. To avoid this, Erick Brownstein's team at Shareability begins story creation by discovering what makes people care about the brand they're creating content for. Mike Jurkovac, the Emmy Award–winning director/producer at TheBridge.co, does the same and says that if you don't find a way to connect emotionally with your consumers, you're wasting your time.

Brownstein explains that if you have a sneaker line, it's not enough to tell a story about the fact that your shoes have good support. There are a lot of sneakers with good support, which is why brands like Nike take risks. They get people to pay attention with Emmy Award–winning ads such as "Dream Big," featuring Colin Kaepernick, the former NFL quarterback. Kaepernick's protests against police brutality and racial inequality during the national anthem were controversial. Nike took a chance when they featured him in their commercials, but it shared their values and got people talking. There was a huge payoff when stock prices reached an all-time high immediately after the ad was released.[50]

Copywriter Ernest Lupinacci adds this tip to make stories more shareable: "Hypothetically, you could argue that every brand story, in regard to its proposition to the customer, could be structured like a fairy tale." For example, Lupinacci explains, we're all familiar with fairy tales that have been told for centuries that follow this three-act format: "Once upon a time, everything was fine, until a dragon showed up. Then a hero came along and killed the dragon, and then in the epilogue, we learn that everyone lived happily ever after in the new world."

Lupinacci suggests that structuring your brand's story like a fairy tale makes it more shareable. If he were to create a fairy tale for BMW, it would be:

> Once upon a time, everyone aspired to drive a good domestic car, right? You know, you dreamed of owning a Cadillac. And then along came a dragon called Too Much Choice. It included

---

[50] Jia Wertz, "Taking Risks Can Benefit Your Brand—Nike's Kaepernick Campaign Is a Perfect Example," *Forbes, Sept. 30, 2018,* https://www.forbes.com/sites/jiawertz/2018/09/30/taking-risks-can-benefit-your-brand-nikes-kaepernick-campaign-is-a-perfect-example/#71ec193e45aa.

inexpensive and expensive Japanese cars, super expensive European cars, and way too many domestic cars. All of a sudden none of the cars available seemed satisfying. Then a knight showed up named BMW—the Ultimate Driving Machine. Everyone who ended up driving that car lived happily ever after.

Essentially, if your product is the solution to your customer's "dragon," and you tell it in a shareable way, more people are likely to pay attention to what you have to say.

YOU KNOW HOW YOU WISH THERE WAS A SIMPLE FORMULA FOR SUCCESS?

Lupinacci's favorite phrase to help find concepts for Hook Points or copy for any brand, product, or service is: "You know how . . . ?" Essentially, you share your idea with people by beginning with the phrase "You know how . . ." in each sentence to see if they agree. For example, when Lupinacci relaunched the Dasani brand, he knew that the other bottled-water companies' selling points were focused on the premise that water is healthy and that it comes from a good source. But Lupinacci was intuitively aware that when people drink the beverages they like, they aren't so much driven by how healthy they are or where they come from as much as whether or not they like the taste. In addition, while a lot of people don't think water *has* a taste, Lupinacci knew that this simply wasn't the case. Most people can absolutely tell the difference between tap water and bottled water, and each bottled water has a different taste.

So, Lupinacci capitalized on all these insights and truths and used the following "You know how . . . ?" logic to see if other people would agree with his theory. He structured his thinking as follows:

> **You know how** there are 75,000 water brands in the market, and we're supposed to drink eight glasses of water a day? "Yeah, I do know that. I hear it all the time. People repeat that to me. There's one of those giant water coolers in my office. Water, water, water, water." **Well, you know how** you can't figure out if one is better than the other? "Yeah." **Well, you know how** at the end of the day, whatever you drink or eat still needs to appeal to you? It's got to taste good; otherwise, it's medicine, right? "Yeah, I do know that." Well, you should try some Dasani. "What makes it so special?" Dasani is the water that makes your mouth water.

By doing this exercise, Lupinacci can quickly tell how effective his campaign ideas actually are.

The next time you come up with a hook, a story, or a new business plan, tell your concept to someone with the "You know how . . . ?" structure and see if it passes the test. If the majority of people do not resonate with your message, you'll know you're off track. And if people nod their heads yes to what you have to say, you'll be closer to knowing your next Hook Point.

IS THIS THE KIND OF ATTENTION YOU WANT?

When marketing any product or service, your job is to get people to pay attention. However, it's important to be wary of what kind of attention you elicit. Attention doesn't always translate to success, especially when your messages aren't properly aligned with the theme of your products.

For example, to digitally market the movie *Rings*, the third movie in *The Ring* trilogy, Paramount's team developed a hook that made their promotional videos go viral. The digital team filmed customers' reactions to the main character of *Rings* scaring them at various electronic stores. Customers are seen shopping for TVs and then screaming out of fear as the creepy girl from the movie walks toward them out of the TV. (You can watch the customer reactions in the video: *Rings (2017)–TV Store Prank*: www .brendanjkane.com/rings.)

Rings (2017)–TV Store Prank received around ten million views. However, while the content promoting the film went viral, the movie itself didn't. The video made people laugh, and that was part of its hook, but *Rings* is in the horror genre, so telling a story that produced laughter wasn't in line with the overall theme or reaction that a viewer would have to the movie itself. To attract the right audience, it probably would have been more effective to elicit fear instead of laughter in the video.

Creating something that hooks people doesn't matter if it's not the right kind of hook. Make sure your stories grab attention that are aligned with the overall message/theme of your products. If you fail to do so, you may produce a buzz, but ultimately you won't reach the people who want what you have to offer.

YOUR BRAND IS NOT THE HERO OF YOUR STORY

Erick Brownstein of Shareability explains that when we tell stories, the brand should not be positioned as the hero. For example, Shareability has created several videos for Adobe that tell stories related to sensitive issues.

One video called *Students Help Victims of Hurricane Harvey Restore Lost Memories | Adobe Creative Cloud* shows how students helped restore family photos destroyed in the hurricane. If the stories in these videos weren't authentic, and/or were exploitative, people would have quickly noticed. To avoid that situation, the Adobe brand needed to position itself in the background. The heroes in the videos are the victims, the students, and the local nonprofits that helped them. Adobe does not try to steal the spotlight, but rather acts as the theater or stage where a light is shined on these issues and heroes. The more a brand takes a back seat to the heroic characters, the more trust and credibility they can build with their audience.

Red Bull has leveraged a similar marketing tactic. On their website and in social content, they feature athletes from every sport. Whether it's a climbing, basketball, or cricket star, they create the stage on which to tell a story about these accomplished individuals. Again, they don't talk about their sports drinks; instead, they make the athletes the heroes of the stories.

In fact, in 2012 Red Bull invested more than $60 million to stage, film, and promote its Stratos event, which featured supersonic skydiver Felix Baumgartner's jump from a helium balloon in the stratosphere more than 24 miles above earth's surface.[51] Baumgartner reached speeds of up to 725 miles per hour and broke three world records, including breaking the sound barrier at Mach 1.24.[52] Red Bull staged the event and used its

---

[51] "Red Bull Invests $65M on Space Jump As More Than 8 Million Watch on YouTube," *Sports Business Daily Global*, Oct. 16, 2012, https://www.sportsbusinessdaily.com/Global /Issues/2012/10/16/Marketing-and-Sponsorship/Red-Bull.aspx.

[52] Dominic Rushe, "Skydiver Baumgartner lands safely on Earth after supersonic record," *The Guardian*, Oct. 15, 2012, https://www.theguardian.com/sport/2012/oct/14/felix -baumgartner-lands-safely-record.

production company, Red Bull Media House; and TV channel, ServusTV; to distribute images to various other media outlets. Additionally, YouTube's live stream "recorded more than 340 million site views before the actual jump." At the time, the event helped YouTube set a new record, with more than eight million viewers watching simultaneously.[53] Owen Gibson of *The Guardian* reported that major brands "have been talking for years about becoming content producers rather than simply paying media and rights owners to advertise or slap their logos on shirts and hoardings. But none have taken it as seriously as Red Bull."[54] The amount of time and money that Red Bull invested in this event proves that they value the impact of making athletes the heroes of their stories—not to mention, "skydiving from space" is a crazy-good Hook Point.

Brownstein explains that even when creating business-to-business (B2B) videos, they don't put the business they're creating the video for in the spotlight. For example, they made a B2B video for the Adobe Experience Cloud. One of Adobe's clients that uses this product is St. Jude Children's Research Hospital. In the content Shareability created for Adobe, they told the story of how the hospital uses Adobe's technology to be more effective in their work. St. Jude's and its customers are the heroes of the story, while Adobe, like Red Bull, acts as the stage.

Another company that knows how to stay in the background of their marketing efforts is Nike. When they created the aforementioned

---

[53] "Reb Bull Invests $65M on Space Jump As More Than 8 Million Watch on YouTube," *Sports Business Daily Global, Oct. 16, 2012,* https://www.sportsbusinessdaily.com/Global/Issues/2012/10/16/Marketing-and-Sponsorship/Red-Bull.aspx.
[54] Owen Gibson, "Red Bull and Felix Baumgartner take sponsorship to new heights," *The Guardian, Oct. 15, 2012,* https://www.theguardian.com/sport/blog/2012/oct/15/red-bull-felix-baumgartner-sponsorship.

campaign with former quarterback Colin Kaepernick, they didn't focus the content around Nike at all. Kaepernick and his activism were the heroes of the story. People thought that taking a stand like that would kill the company, but instead, as noted, it drove their stock price through the roof.

Another stand-out example of great storytelling from Nike is their *Dream Crazier* video. It intercuts images of female athletes and coaches yelling and crying in different sports-related scenarios, explaining that people often label women's emotions or forthrightness as "crazy." Then it shows images of the first time a woman boxed or became a sports coach and explains that when they were first starting out, these women were also considered crazy. The message is that when seemingly crazy women take a stand, they become powerful and debunk myths about how women should act. Nike urges women to "dare to be crazy" so they can show people what crazy can accomplish.

Again, the video doesn't center around Nike. It simply tells a compelling story about the strength and power of women. Nike is only present because many of the athletes are wearing their clothing, we can see their logos at the end of the video, and they're the ones setting the stage.

Brownstein reminds us that storytelling is not primarily rational—it's emotional—which is one good reason why it's wise to get people to fall in love with your brand. He advises that to do so, you should take some hints from how actual loving relationships are formed. For example, they're not built through manipulation or by constantly asking others to take actions for you. To receive love, you have to give love. When you're generous, you receive. With brands and their audiences, the best way to earn people's attention and gain the right to ask for their business is by giving them value. By choosing to focus on building loving relationships with your audience, you'll tell better stories and touch more people's hearts.

Besides, people care more about themselves than your brand. If your brand is in the spotlight, people will tune you out. Instead, focus on the reactions you can elicit from your audience and on providing them with value.

WHERE BRANDS GO WRONG

Brownstein points out that oftentimes the metrics by which content is measured don't line up with telling good brand stories. Return on investment doesn't necessarily fit into brand building, and return on ad spend doesn't always relate to the value you can receive from content that builds up your brand. When you create content that's focused on storytelling, brand building, and driving engagement, you're not necessarily trying to get people to click and buy products or services. Engagement-and-conversion campaigns can go hand in hand, but they're not necessarily one and the same. Brownstein sees a lot of brands trying to achieve two different results with one piece of content, which can be ineffective, inefficient, and perceived as inauthentic. Trying to mix two different objectives can make audiences feel like they're watching a commercial as opposed to receiving content that has value.

It's essential to understand the difference between a piece of content or message that serves to tell a story to build a brand, versus a piece of content or message that's created to sell a product. When trying to achieve both objectives, Brownstein's team at Shareability uses a "full-funnel activation" strategy. First, they will often start with big, viral, shareable content; then they move on to content that causes additional engagement but still doesn't necessarily push a strong call to action; and finally, they'll often push content to people who engaged with the first two pieces of content, asking them to take an action (for example a click, download, or purchase) related to their clients' goals.

The Cricket Wireless campaign with John Cena in 2016, *The Unexpected John Cena Prank* video, brought an internet meme to life when Cena surprised fans who thought they were auditioning to be in a Cricket Wireless commercial. When the fans pretended to introduce John Cena, he actually burst through a poster of himself. The fans' reactions were priceless—you can see them here: www.brendanjkane.com/cena. Shareability launched this video on Facebook and YouTube and generated more than 235 million views overall! Then they produced a second, follow-up video, *John Cena Reacts*, which was actually part of a bigger campaign that Shareability launched called "John Cena Loves the Internet."

John Cena Reacts flipped the script of the original video. It was the reverse of the original *Unexpected John Cena*. In the second video, fans surprised Cena instead of Cena surprising the fans. He was opening fan mail thanking him for his "Never give up" motto that helped them bounce back from injuries and heartache. Then, as the video progresses, Cena gets emotional watching a clip of a young boy thanking him for helping his mother battle cancer. After the clip finishes, the son surprises Cena by coming through the same poster from the first video with his mother to thank Cena in person. He gets extremely emotional, and we see a beautiful exchange of gratitude between all involved.

One of the reasons these campaigns were highly successful was because they didn't ask for anything—their only purpose was to provide value to the audience, from making them laugh in the first Cena video to touching their hearts in the second. The second video became the most shared ad in the world in 2017 and was number three on YouTube's trending videos. On Facebook, it drove more than 2.5 million shares and 110 million views on the original upload and more than 175 million total views, including audience re-uploads. The entire "John Cena Loves the Internet" campaign gained nearly three million total shares and ten million engagements across platforms.

After the success of the first two videos, Shareability's team continued to bring value to the campaign by creating video ads to retarget the people who'd engaged with the content. They followed up with messages from Cena encouraging viewers to visit the Cricket Wireless website. The people who saw these more traditional ads were those who already felt a strong connection to Cena (and by extension, Cricket) because the original content was emotional and engaging. Fans are more likely to take notice, pay attention, and take action when they feel an authentic connection.

Brownstein adds that when you focus on providing value, you can end up with great, and sometimes unexpectedly wonderful, results. One time, for a major pet-products company, Shareability had 800,000 people click through to a website from two videos that were not primarily intended to be traffic drivers. This happened because the content was so compelling that it increased the effectiveness of the call to action at the end of the video: "If you want to learn more about how you can make the world a better place for pets, go here."

I also agree with entrepreneur Gary Vaynerchuk, who believes that info-product people are just out to make a buck and sell products—although they *do* make money, they're not looking at the longer-term vision of building a brand, which ultimately causes them to struggle. Instead, Vaynerchuk and I urge people to focus on giving away value in content to build a brand that attracts larger clients. With that in mind, a lot of value *can* be driven from direct-response advertising content. The majority of people simply make the mistake of taking a brand-building piece of content and turning it into a direct-response piece of content, and vice versa. However, I've been experimenting, researching, and testing how both brand-building and direct-response content can play off of each other, and thus far the results have been remarkable. Again, you have to come from an authentic and value-driven place, but if you interchange brand-building with direct-response content, both can drive results.

DIGITAL STORYTELLING VISUAL DESIGN TIPS

Digital content strategist Naveen Gowda spent a lot of time studying how people become top performers on YouTube, which is a long-form consumption-behavior platform that you can get people to tune in to for long periods of time. Gowda studied vloggers and individual brands on the platform and found that those who are successful share similar communication styles.

Effective communication design came down to factors such as the colors, pacing, and lighting in a video—a lot of seemingly smaller details had a huge impact on a video's success. For example, Gowda discovered that a disproportionately high ratio of the top performers, who were averaging four or five million views on a single video, were overenunciating their words. YouTubers who didn't overenunciate weren't receiving high numbers of views, regardless of the similarities in the messaging of their content. After studying all the details that made videos successful, Gowda has developed a deep understanding of communication design. These days, he can take video concepts that aren't necessarily strong and get them to receive hundreds of millions of views.

Remember, it's important to consider the visual and auditory aspects of your stories, because concepts presented with visuals are learned more easily and are more frequently recalled. Using this fact to your advantage keeps people interested in watching your content. And don't forget to study your competitors for shortcuts to making the right visual choices. If you take the time to see how they're handling the communication design of their videos, you could save hours of time and achieve better results more quickly.

(If you're struggling to get your social content to perform and would like assistance from Naveen Gowda and me, we have several different options for you to work with us here: www.brendanjkane.com /work-with-brendan/.)

SATISFYING TO WATCH

Gowda believes that the most important part of storytelling on digital platforms is creating videos that are satisfying to watch. Luckily, there are myriad ways to generate satisfying visual effects. He cites the example of watching a video of a person putting his or her fingers in goop—"it's enjoyable to watch, even if no one can truly explain why." Satisfaction can also come from watching a person speed-paint or fill in a whiteboard—as you follow along, you want to continue watching to reach the sense of completion you'll receive at the end. This is especially effective when you watch videos of plants growing in super-sped-up time—they tend to be visually satisfying because you see the whole thing develop in a way you'd never get to in real life. You get the full picture and, again, a sense of completion.

Think about your audience's viewing satisfaction while creating content, and it will lead to more viewers. Visual surprises and delights can enhance your marketing materials and social videos.

TELLING STORIES VIA EMAIL:
CRAFTING COLD OUTREACH EMAILS

Sales come out of relationships, which is why referrals are the best way to connect with the potential companies you'd like to work with. There are times, however, when you don't have connections to the people you'd like to meet. In that case, you need to find a way to forge those relationships. Tools such as LinkedIn can help you make these types of connections, but with the bombardment of messages that people receive on this platform, email is still king.

Email is more effective than direct messaging on LinkedIn because fewer people have access to email addresses of people they don't know—it's still the standard way to proposition your products and services to others. Besides, people on LinkedIn rarely check their in-boxes; they aren't managed as diligently as with email. Also, when you don't know someone, cold emails are more effective than cold calls. It's usually best to wait until you've been introduced or have had at least one in-person meeting before calling a cold target, which is why your ability to get people to pay attention to emails can greatly enhance your career, and perhaps even help you close your biggest deals.

One time a friend of mine closed a deal worth tens of millions of dollars that started with a cold outreach email. He did some research on LinkedIn to find the key players at the company he wanted to target. When he found the president of the department he wanted to reach, he figured out the person's email address by testing various email formats (a process described later in this chapter). Once he found that email address, he sent a message that said, "Hey, I have a couple of friends who've started a company. It would be great to learn what you think about it because I'm considering taking a job there."

This person got back to my friend fairly quickly and offered to meet up for coffee. At the end of the meeting, the president of the department said, "Take the job and tell them to come into town. I think there's a lot we can do together." That meeting led to a new job for my friend, and again, a deal worth tens of millions of dollars that all started with a cold outreach email. Most people never get responses from those types of emails, but if you can finesse your approach through the art of A/B testing, it can lead to something big.

Cold Outreach Email Headlines

The first trick to writing successful cold outreach emails is to use the subject lines to state your Hook Points. For example, in the email my friend sent to the president of the department, the subject line was: "Hey, can I get your advice on something?" He was not trying to sell this person anything. Let me say that again: *He was not trying to sell this person anything.* And yet, it led to one of the biggest sales of his career.

I emphasize this point because generally people do cold outreach all wrong (especially on LinkedIn). They try to sell people their products or services right off the bat. I'll talk more about why this approach doesn't work in chapter 7, but for now, just realize that especially in your first batch of cold outreach emails, you should *not* be trying to sell anyone anything.

The Body of a Cold Outreach Email

In the body of my friend's email, he created copy that stood out and that didn't come across as pushy. He simply asked for the person's thoughts:

"We don't know each other, but this opportunity seems really interesting. I'm considering working here, and I'd like your opinion about it." Taking this approach allowed his target to think, *Hey, okay, the guy's not trying to sell me anything,* which was also authentic—in the moment my friend sent the first email, he truly wasn't trying to sell that person anything; he simply wanted his advice and perspective. The honest desire to learn opened the door to what later became a highly lucrative deal.

A/B Test Cold Outreach Emails

I recommend that you A/B test both your headlines and your email copy to learn which variations are most effective at reaching your target audience. First, build an email target list through research on LinkedIn. For example, if you want to reach out to entertainment companies in Los Angeles, identify 100 of them and search for their founders or management teams. Then, work to uncover their email addresses.

Finding email addresses is usually the most tedious and time-consuming part of the process. There are some online tools that can help you get a high probability of what the email address may be, such as hunter.io, Findthat.email, or Clearbit, or you can search a proposed email address and look for a match on Google. Another strategy is to see if that person has written an article, because oftentimes their email address is mentioned in those articles.

Once you've found the email addresses you wish to target, put your list into customer relationship management (CRM) software such as HubSpot, Salesforce, or Freshsales. Then build out an email cadence with up to five emails. I don't recommend building out more than four or five emails, because more than that is overkill. If your target doesn't respond after four or five emails, it's time to change the copy and move on to another person at the company.

An example of a four-email sequence structure is as follows:

Email 1: Top-line overview of how you can solve a specific pain point of the target's business through your services and products.

Email 2: Restate your services and products and see if they're interested. Possibly add an example, or list relevant clients you've worked with.

Email 3: Apologize for following up, and ask a question to see if the person's goals/objectives align with your services.

Email 4: Send a simple email asking if the person has time to connect.

Email 1 goes out on day one, email 2 goes out on day three, email 3 on day five, and email 4 on day seven. From there, measure the responses to different versions of each email. Test three versions of email 1 by changing the copy in the first paragraph of version 2; then change the subject line of version 3. Try to keep the changed variable simple so it's easy to identify the change that causes a successful response.

For example, in a sequence, you may try two different value points in email 1 to see which picks up more interest. The first email from Group A could have a subject line that says: "Stimulating [targeted company's name] growth with social media marketing," while the subject line in the first email of Group B's could say: "Social media marketing and how it can stimulate [targeted company's name] consumers in Los Angeles."

When sending out these two different emails, split the leads, meaning send 50 different companies the Group A emails, and then 50 more people at different companies the Group B emails. Then review which emails get a response. In case you don't get a response from any of the Group A emails, email another person at the same company using the Group B emails. Make sure to continue to A/B test until you find the absolute best email copy.

HOW TO WRITE COPY THAT QUADRUPLES YOUR SALES

Writing captivating copy is an essential skill. If you can't communicate your hooks effectively, you won't be seen or heard. To help you become a better copywriter, I recommend reading a book by Michael Masterson and John Forde called *Great Leads: The Six Easiest Ways to Start Any Sales Message*. In the book, they talk about the six best openers for copy, which include "The Offer Lead," "The Problem-Solution Lead," "The Big Secret Lead," "The Proclamation Lead," and "The Story Lead." For our purposes, I'm going to focus on the Proclamation Lead, as I believe it's a tool that can help you write effective hooks and stories.

A Proclamation Lead begins with an emotionally compelling statement in the form of a headline. It is bold, makes a promise about an imagined benefit, and is of a relevant subject to the prospect. Also, it's often based on a prediction about a future outcome that catches people by surprise. The goal is to raise curiosity with a promise that can "push the envelope of the incredible." However, for the bold statement to work, the copy that follows must provide information that proves the validity of that claim/promise. Additionally, a good Proclamation Lead does not reveal the most important aspect of the product or service until the end of the copy.

Great Leads explains that one of the most successful sales letters ever, written in order to sell the *Journal of Alternatives*, started with the headline "Read This or Die." This text grabs the attention of prospects, making readers wonder what information could be so important that they would die if they didn't have it. Then, once that hook grabs their attention, the following copy makes a bold prediction: "Today you have a 95 percent chance of eventually dying from a disease or condition for which there is already a known cure somewhere on the planet. The editor of *Alternatives* would like to free you from that destiny." The lead gets people to think, *Gee, if the statement about having a 95 percent chance of dying from a curable disease is really true, I better find out more about this.* Someone who is interested in health-related information will want to read on.

Another example of a Proclamation Lead in the form of a prediction is: "Countdown to Crisis! Three Shocking Events will wipe out *millions* of American investors by Dec. 31, 2006. . . ." Readers immediately wonder what three events could happen to cause this effect by the end of the year—their curiosity is piqued. The copy that follows then provides credibility for the prediction, explaining that it comes from a "famous market analyst." The emotionally compelling statement hooks readers into the story that follows. Masterson and Forde add that a great Proclamation Lead "can't be written, it must be found," and the best way to find one is through research. You need to come across proof that backs up your proclamation so that it can truly stand out and be disruptive in a credible way.

To find a great Proclamation Lead (or any type of lead/hook, for that matter) for your brand, copywriter Craig Clemens suggests writing a paragraph about your prospect's fears, desires, and needs. Then, think about how your product or brand can improve your prospect's life. (If you have data that proves exactly how bad your prospect's problem is or how good your solution is, even better.) Finally, find the intersection of where your prospect's problem and your solution meet, and create copy (or a social media video script) using that intersection as the main message.

A GOLDEN FORMULA TO MAKE YOUR MESSAGE RESONATE

On the podcast *Business Lunch with Roland Frasier*, Clemens outlines a four-step copywriting formula called "Impact Arcs" that gets your audience's attention. The process is as follows:

1. A(sk) a "Yes" question, one your potential customer would answer yes to—that is, "Do you want to make maximum return on your money that is just sitting in the bank? *'Yes.'* Then consider buying art."

2. R(eveal) that you've been in your audience's position—a place that is usually as far from successful as they would like to be in this area. Set the stage to show that through experience, you've learned critical information that can help them get there. Reveal something that is true and that made you strive to learn more—for example, "I used to look for places to invest my money, but I didn't know I could get a large return by buying art," or "I wanted to do it, but I didn't know where to start."

3. C(all) out the discovery that brought you out of the fog. Here, you explain what you learned that helped you get where you are now, which will help your audience arrive there too—that is, "I discovered a book by J Paul Getty, *How to Get Rich*, where he explains how he made wealth through art. It was really interesting, but I wasn't sure if these principles would apply to the current art world. I decided to meet with a prominent art investor who's made tens of millions of dollars from art. I showed him the book, and he explained how to apply the information to today's art world. I started using the principles, and over the last

five years I've averaged a 30 percent return annually, which is larger than my return from the stock market."

4. S(end) them to *do* something. This is your call to action, and the desired impact of your communication. This is where you get them to sign up for your email list, buy your book, or follow your account—for example, "I put the strategies up on a web page that is totally free that you can check out here," or "Sign up for my email list, where I'll reveal these tips one by one."

The formula can be used in one sentence, paragraph, video, or in an hour-long presentation. Listen to Clemens discuss the technique here: https:// podcasts.apple.com/us/podcast/business-lunch/id1442654104?i =1000429481263.[55]

Quick Tips and Recap

1. Try to thoroughly understand your prospect's needs. This will help dictate how you package your information and how you connect with your audience.

2. Use the PCM to reach your audience and to ensure that you're speaking the same language. Effective storytellers will use the vocabularies of logic, values, humor, imagination, action, and emotions. They will insert messages for all six of the personality

---

[55] *Business Lunch with Roland Frasier, "A Golden Formula to Make Your Message Resonate, Craig Clemens," Apple Podcasts, 2020,* https://podcasts.apple.com/us/podcast/business -lunch/id1442654104?i=1000429481263.

types so they can engage 100 percent of the audience with their stories.

3. Test your hooks, stories, and business plans with the "You know how . . . ?" structure to see if people resonate with your ideas.

4. Don't make your brand the hero of the stories you tell. Instead, focus on the reactions you can elicit from your audience and on providing them with value.

5. Tell a story that gets your audience to feel connected, fall in love, and take ownership of the story you're telling. If you focus on building a loving relationship with your audience, you'll have more loyal customers.

6. To generate significant views on your videos, think about communication design, including the visual and auditory aspects of your videos, as well as your audience's viewing-satisfaction level.

7. If used properly, cold outreach emails can be a gold mine in connecting with high-value prospects.

8. Use the subject line of cold outreach emails to state your Hook Point. Then A/B test your copy to see which emails get the best responses.

9. When writing copy to sell products or services, find the intersection of where your prospect's problem and your solution meet, and create copy (or a social media video script) using that intersection as the main message.

10. Use the "Impact Arcs" four-step copywriting formula to arc-in prospects.

CHAPTER 5

HOW TO AVOID PRISON TIME: A MASTER CLASS IN AUTHENTICITY, TRUST, AND CREDIBILITY

WHITNEY WOLFE, FOUNDER of the dating app Bumble, set out on a mission to empower women. She wanted to change the double standard in the dating world, which expects females to act coy and refrain from going after what they want. She hoped to change these dynamics by getting women to make the first move, so she created a dating app that requires females to send the initial messages to men they're interested in on the platform.

As a graduate of Southern Methodist University, Wolfe went to the various sorority houses on campus and spoke about how women have the right to get what they want. She explained that relationships don't have to be male dominated and that men appreciate being relieved from the pressure to pursue. By transmitting her excitement about changing social norms, Wolfe inspired these women to download the app. Then she went over to the frat houses and told the guys that there were hundreds of girls waiting to go out with them. Additionally, she gave the men a slice of pizza and cookies in exchange for downloading the app.

The Hook Point of creating a platform that was built to change dating dynamics and empower women led to a current 52 million downloads and $335 million in revenue.[56] This was quite an accomplishment, especially considering how crowded the dating-app space was when Wolfe launched back in December of 2014.[57]

Part of what has made Bumble so successful is Wolfe's authenticity. The brand is connected to her mission in life and was created with purpose. This authentic desire to create change has set her apart, made her stand out, and helped her company rise to success.

WHY DO YOU GET OUT OF BED IN THE MORNING?

Authenticity supports your ability to make a mark in our 3-second world because it helps your Hook Points stick. Without authenticity and purpose behind your hooks, stories, and products/services, they will lack substance and fall flat. If you're familiar with Simon Sinek's book *Start With Why*, you know that he urges brands to "clearly articulate why they do what they do." A brand's "why" is their "purpose, cause, or belief." Sinek urges brands to ask themselves, "Why does your company exist? Why do you get out of bed in the morning? And why should anyone care?" The answer to these

---

[56] Ingrid Lunden, "Andrey Andreev sells stake in Bumble owner to Blackstone, Whitney Wolfe Herd now CEO of $3B dating apps business," Extra Crunch, Nov. 8, 2019, https://techcrunch.com/2019/11/08/badoos-andrey-andreev-sells-his-stake-in-bumble-to-blackstone-valuing-the-dating-app-at-3b/.

[57] NPR How I Built This with Guy Raz, "Bumble: Whitney Wolfe," Apple Podcasts, Oct. 16, 2017, https://podcasts.apple.com/us/podcast/how-i-built-this-with-guy-raz/id1150510297?i=1000436036734.

questions has nothing to do with what you make, how much your products or services cost, or where you're sold. Understanding your "why" helps guide you in maintaining authenticity and building trust with your customers.

Many companies focus on making money and never stop to ask themselves why consumers would want to invest their precious time and money into a product or service in the first place. Consumers don't want to pay your salary—they want to receive something of value. When they see purpose behind what you do, it heightens your value and inspires them to become a part of your world.

Brands like Apple and Nike have mastered the authentic communication of their "why." You see it in the media related to their brands, in the design and packaging of their products, as well as in the layout of their stores. Each decision these companies make supports their overall brand visions. For example, Sinek explains that Apple communicates with its customers in a very specific fashion by basically using this philosophy: "Everything we do, we believe in challenging the status quo. We believe in thinking differently. The way we challenge the status quo is by making our products beautifully designed, simple to use, and user-friendly. And we happen to make great computers. Wanna buy one?" Apple's clear understanding and communication of its "why" helps us view their products as authentic expressions of their ideals.

Sinek adds, "Apple believed that its original Apple computer and its Macintosh challenged the dominant IBM DOS platforms. Apple believes its iPod and iTunes products are challenging the status quo and the music industry. And we all understand why Apple does what it does."

Legendary copywriter Ernest Lupinacci is a major proponent of the notion that people "don't buy what you make, they buy what you believe."

While working for advertising agency Wieden+Kennedy, Lupinacci went to Europe to help develop a campaign for Nike's entrance into the European soccer market. This happened at a time when soccer was going through a huge change—as you may know, France and England have always had a long-standing rivalry, for various historical reasons dating back to September of 1066 when the Battle of Hastings took place. But in 1992, to many people's surprise, a French superstar soccer player named Eric Cantona became the *captain* of the Manchester United soccer team in England. It was a historic event. But while Nike was already sponsoring Cantona, they didn't know how to leverage this fact into their marketing strategy—they didn't feel they had the credibility or authenticity to speak about European soccer because they were so new to the sport. When Lupinacci talked to Nike about how he felt they should present the brand to European soccer fans, he explained that the company had an incredible opportunity because of their history of being a brand that *just does it*. Lupinacci said, "Listen, if Nike had been around when Jackie Robinson broke the color barrier in the major leagues, they would have sponsored him. That's the kind of thing that Nike is all about. That's why this brand gets out of bed in the morning."

In the presentation to Nike, Lupinacci's team put a Che Guevara–inspired piece of imagery on a slide with all the great Nike footballers they'd signed, and the statement, "Nike, Inc. Dismantling the establishment since 1971." Then Lupinacci went on to share that the genius of the new European soccer pillar of the brand was that not only did they have the right to contribute to the conversation in the world of professional soccer, but they could say things about current events that their competitors couldn't. The conversation wasn't about equipment innovation—it was actually about "a revolution in the social fabric of the sport itself." The presentation struck home and set a tone for how the team could credibly and authentically demonstrate their point of view to the masses.

Lupinacci adds that credibility and authenticity are essential when trying to attach timely events (or what he likes to refer to as "inciting incidents") to campaigns. This is important because "imagine a TV show or a movie franchise that you love. If a character suddenly does something strange or out of character in an episode or in a sequel, you'll find it inauthentic and unsatisfying. The marketing analogy for that is every once in a while, a brand will do an extension, or it will create a message that seems inauthentic. Oftentimes this happens because the brand hasn't made a link between what they believe and what they make."

That link, again, is why Lupinacci believes that Nike had the right to enter the European soccer conversation: "Not because of their history in regard to making shoes, but because of the power and continuity of their message. Soccer may have been a new sport for Nike, but the belief system of the brand—and how it resonates with athletes—successfully transcends the various individual sports. The power of a brand isn't rooted in the quality of their products. The power of a brand is rooted in its *own* beliefs."

Another brand that understands its values is the *For Dummies* series, which also tells a story about being unconventional and challenging the status quo. John Kilcullen, founding member and chairman/CEO of IDG Books Worldwide, and creator of the *For Dummies* book series, shares that these works were created to provide a fun and easy reference to understand just what you need to know about a particular subject and get on with your life. Fans of the *For Dummies* series appreciated the comic relief, cartoons, and graphic devices throughout each book that made the learning experience more engaging.

The "why" of challenging the status quo went into the design of each element of the books and their marketing strategies. The series made sure to use humor in the writing, which was also often found in the packaging of the products themselves. For example, when the company released the French version of *Sex for Dummies*, they put a condom on the inside back cover with an arrow to text that said, "This way up." They used this type of respectful humor to engage people, stand out, and make the topics more approachable. If the idea, again, had not been in line with the soul of the brand, it would have come across as cheesy or inappropriate. But because this marketing stunt (and truly amazing Hook Point) did mesh with the company's messaging, *Sex for Dummies* ended up becoming the most popular *For Dummies* title sold outside of the United States.

For help in finding your "why," read Simon Sinek's book *Start With Why*. It will guide you as an individual or company in discovering what makes you tick. Knowing this will be a compass that helps you develop more authentic Hook Points and stories.

GILLETTE VS. NIKE

Knowing your "why" is imperative for coming up with Hook Points and telling stories. If you aren't clear about your "why," you can actually end up offending people. Recently, Gillette got a lot of pushback on its "We Believe" commercial that addresses "toxic masculinity," including sexual harassment, the #MeToo movement, and bullying. (You can watch the commercial here: https://time.com/5503156 /gillette-razors-toxic-masculinity/.) Although the message in the ad is great—of course, men and women should treat others with respect—it also makes sense that audiences have been put off.

As a brand, Gillette had not talked about social responsibility prior to this campaign. They'd always focused on hair removal, which is why when they suddenly came out with an ad telling men they need to behave differently, many consumers felt that they were trying to insert themselves in a conversation they had no permission entering because that's not who they are as a company. To some in the audience, the ad came across as gratuitous and opportunistic. Again, this is because Gillette generally talked about what it does—making razors with five blades and lubrication that cuts hair—they'd never been a company that told you *why* they made razors. So, although Gillette did attract lots of attention from this ad, it isn't clear whether or not it has actually helped build new connections and affinity. Jane Zupan, senior director of product marketing at Crimson Hexagon, believes that the campaign helped create new connections with women, but currently the ad has received 1.5 million dislikes and only 806,000 likes on YouTube.[58] Overall, I do not think the campaign has been a huge success.

These results are in stark contrast to those occasions when Nike takes a stand on a social issue. The company has experience in this arena and has done an amazing job of articulating their "why" over the years, so that's why the brand's controversial Colin Kaepernick campaign, which features Kaepernick's voice with the tagline "Believe

---

[58] Jane Zupan, "The Data Behind Gillette's Ad Shows It Had the Biggest Impact with Women," *Adweek, Jan. 22, 2019,* https://www.adweek.com/brand-marketing/the-data-behind-gillettes-ad-shows-it-had-the-biggest-impact-with-women/.

in something. Even if it means sacrificing everything." was a success. The tagline references the national-anthem protest against police brutality that may have cost Kaepernick his NFL career. The ad received mixed responses, but because Nike understood their core audience (Gen Z and millennial demographics) who support socially active brands, and because the ad appears to be aligned with the brand's core values (Nike said they would invest in those who sacrifice), the campaign was well received. After this ad was released, stock prices reached an all-time high, online sales grew by 31 percent the immediate weekend following the release, and they received more than 450,000 mentions on Twitter in a single day.[59]

The difference in the results between these two campaigns is a good lesson in making sure you choose a Hook Point that supports who you are and why you do what you do. You can't just go off and create random Hook Points and stories that don't support your underlying foundation, because it may backfire. If, on the other hand, you choose the right hooks—which are authentic to who you are—they can generate a lot of success.

GOOD HOOK POINTS ESTABLISH CREDIBILITY

Erick Brownstein of Shareability uses his Hook Points to quickly establish credibility for new business opportunities. When he's attending a

---

[59] Jia Wertz, "Taking Risks Can Benefit Your Brand—Nike's Kaepernick Campaign Is a Perfect Example," *Forbes, Sept. 30, 2018,* https://www.forbes.com/sites/jiawertz/2018/09/30/taking-risks-can-benefit-your-brand-nikes-kaepernick-campaign-is-a-perfect-example/#453918ef45aa.

conference and wants to connect with panel members, he only has seconds to grab their attention. After years of experience, he's learned that one of the best ways to establish immediate credibility is to use Hook Points. As soon as a speaker walks off the stage, he will often go up to the person and say, "Hey, that was awesome. I'd like to talk to you because **we're creating the most successful video content in the world right now**, and we can help you tell your story better and reach more people." The phrase in bold is the Hook Point that establishes the credibility and gets Brownstein into meetings. If he didn't include the information about creating the most successful content in the world right now, and left it at "I'd like to talk to you . . . ," he wouldn't stand out. He'd be like every other person vying for a speaker's attention.

PRESIDENTIAL CANDIDATES, TV GREEN ROOMS, AND A LESSON IN AUTHENTICITY

When I flew to New York to do some press interviews for my last book, I was featured on two shows. The first was *The David Webb Show*, which you can listen to here: www.brendanjkane.com/davidwebb/. After the interview, Webb asked if I was taking on new clients and if I could look at his social media presence. Although I went on his show with the sole intention of providing value, I ended up with a potential business opportunity. This happened because of my authentic desire to be helpful and do a good job, in addition to the use of the strong Hook Point of generating a million followers in 30 days (which was what got me invited on the show in the first place).

I had a similar experience when I was on the TV show *Kennedy* on the FOX Business network. While waiting in the green room, I met Democratic presidential candidate John Delaney. I didn't know who he was when we started talking; we were just having an authentic conversation about what I did and my viewpoint on social media, and then he asked if he could hire me to help him with his social media campaign. Meeting people organically, providing value, and connecting with them authentically builds enough trust and credibility to gain potential new business opportunities. (I didn't try to sell either John Delaney or David Webb anything, and I certainly didn't use a sales pitch.)

You can do this too! To build trust and credibility, start conversations with your strongest Hook Points and most compelling stories. If you follow the process I'm teaching throughout this book, it will open doors to more opportunities. The process works! It will require practice, however, so don't get frustrated if it takes time to get it down. Sometimes I spend months perfecting a hook and story before it really starts to land.

A MILLION DOLLARS AND THREE LESSONS IN FAILURE

Once you become a master at grabbing attention, you may generate more leads than you can handle. You'll get excited and want to say yes to everything, but don't make this mistake. I've found myself in situations where I've taken on projects that weren't actually the best fit. When I first started out, my strong Hook Points and stories led to generating deals even when I probably wasn't the best person for the job. This is a problem because when you land big projects and clients, you have to deliver.

Early on in my career, I raised millions of dollars for companies that didn't end up working out. I had a great Hook Point, told a compelling story, found investors, and ultimately the businesses failed. They failed for multiple reasons, but one of the main reasons is that my core expertise and skill set is not to run a company as a CEO or COO. Over time I realized that I am world class at providing strategy, clarity, innovation, and vision for companies—not at running the day-to-day operations.

The information in this book can help you close big deals, drive a significant increase in sales, and create more effective content, but you have to know what you're authentically good at to truly succeed. Authenticity is the glue that holds everything together. Although great hooks and stories can make people lean in and pay attention, your brand or company will fall apart if your stories don't ring true and you can't deliver.

Look at the scandal uncovered in the documentary *The Inventor: Out for Blood in Silicon Valley*. Elizabeth Holmes, who founded the now-defunct health-technology company Theranos, became the world's youngest self-made billionaire, but she couldn't maintain her success because, well, her product was fake. Her Hook Point made her great at finding investors and selling—I mean, who didn't want to believe that we could make blood testing cheaper and easier by running multiple tests off a single drop of blood? It would be amazing . . . if it were true. Unfortunately, Holmes was a better storyteller than product creator.

The same can be said about the people behind the Fyre Festival. The marketing behind this "luxury" musical event was amazing. But Billy McFarland, CEO of Fyre Media Inc., couldn't make it happen. Many people believe that McFarland was a con man, but I do feel that his team's intention was to pull off the festival they presented in their marketing material. I think they simply never imagined how hard it would be to organize a festival that had gained that much popularity.

SET CLEAR EXPECTATIONS

You can avoid the types of situations described above by being honest with yourself. If you do so, you'll be honest with all your clients. When I worked with Katie Couric and the producers of Yahoo!, there was always a constant line of dialogue about the need to optimize. I set the expectation with Couric that we would be continually testing a plethora of interviews. Very early on I cautioned, "Don't fall in love with any one interview. If an interview doesn't work, it's fine. We'll learn something from it and keep adjusting it until we find the interviews that go viral."

I set this expectation up front because it was the most realistic scenario. By speaking to Couric ahead of time, I kept us on the same page. From the beginning, we recognized that failure would be a part of the process.

WHAT TO DO WHEN YOU CAN'T DELIVER

In the Netflix documentary *Fyre*, you can see that even after the festival fell apart, McFarland didn't learn from his mistakes. In fact, while he was being sued, he created another scam around selling exclusive tickets for backstage passes to concerts he didn't have access to. We all make mistakes, of course—no one's perfect all the time—but you should try to learn from your experiences. Analyze which behaviors and strategies work and which don't so you can own your limitations, grow, move forward, and better set yourself up for success the next time around.

If, for whatever reason, you find yourself in a situation where you can't deliver, be open and communicate this fact to the client. The worst thing you can do is disappear. Get on the phone and explain why there are delays or setbacks. As difficult as this conversation may be, it's more effective than simply ignoring the fact that things aren't going as planned. Most people really appreciate and respect communication. If you try to hide problems and avoid communicating when things aren't going well, you'll most likely end up losing the client. And if that happens several times, you'll end up with a bad reputation. Instead, be honest and up front about what's going on, how you're trying to fix the situation, or even about needing to let the client go. Without a doubt, being honest will lead to better results in the long run.

THE POWER OF NO

When I decide to work with someone, I do so because I see an interesting and exciting opportunity. It's not that I go into meetings thinking, *Oh, this is a turning point in my career. This is a huge meeting. I'm going to make a lot of money.* Rather, I go in thinking, *I'm excited about this. I want to share this information with people. I feel that this Hook Point and story will deliver value to the person on the other side of the table.* If I don't feel that way, I turn the meeting or project down.

I believe that this mindset is critically important for success. If you're not authentically excited about what you're doing, it will show, which is why I never create a Hook Point or story about anything that doesn't excite me. I build trust and credibility in rooms with very high-profile people quickly because they can see my authentic passion for their projects. Again, if I don't believe in it, I don't do it.

Saying no to projects you don't believe in works in your favor. One time I had dinner with Hush, one of the top street artists in the world. Hush told me that he only creates a select number of high-end pieces a year and that he sells his work for tens of thousands of dollars because of that fact. When I asked him how he built demand for his work, he said that it was "by exercising the power of no." Oftentimes he'll get commissioned by groups or people who want his work, but if he isn't truly passionate about the project, he'll turn it down. He's found that the exclusivity of his work has created a higher demand.

So don't say yes to every opportunity. Only take on work that truly speaks to you. Doing so can increase your value.

"FAILING" IN LOVE WITH SUCCESS

To attain success in sales, you need to build relationships filled with trust. Your consumers, or potential partners, must believe that you'll deliver on your promise or they won't give you their money. And you should be building a good rapport even when people don't choose to work with you or purchase from you right away. You never know when potential consumers will change their minds, or when a new opportunity will appear that leads to your working together years down the road.

One time one of my colleagues failed in a meeting with an important client because he didn't do his homework to understand the company's needs. He pitched a service the company didn't want and realized immediately that the meeting hadn't gone well. Afterward, he took responsibility and apologized to the person who'd set up the meeting and who also happened to be in the room. My colleague was humble enough to admit that he'd messed up. Taking responsibility in this moment was the best choice he could have made. It helped him maintain his credibility with the person who'd set up the meeting, which turned out to be incredibly fruitful.

When you're young, you want everything to happen right away. But with experience you realize that you may have a conversation today that will lead to a company you create down the line. Don't be impatient and destroy future opportunities—always play the long game.

Also, when trying to close big deals, you have to be passionate and knowledgeable about the products or services you're selling. Know them inside and out so you can answer questions confidently, address your target's pain points, and eliminate doubts or concerns about the validity of your business.

However, in cases where you don't know the answer to a question, don't make up details to fill in the blanks. It's better to admit that you don't know, and tell clients that you'll get back to them when you have more answers. Remember, authenticity helps you maintain trust and credibility.

HOW TO CREATE GENUINE TRUST IN MEETINGS

In the article "How to Get People to Like You: 7 Ways From an FBI Behavior Expert" (a solid Hook Point for an article title, by the way), Eric Barker explains how to build rapport and create trust. He interviewed Robin K. Dreeke, the head of the FBI's Behavioral Analysis Program, who's studied interpersonal relations for more than 27 years. Dreeke's number-one piece of advice is to "seek someone else's thoughts and opinions without judging them." You don't have to agree with them, but you need to validate others by taking time to understand their dreams, desires, and needs.

Here's the full list of Dreeke's seven best ways to build trust and credibility:

1. Nonjudgmental validation. Seek the other person's opinions and thoughts without judging them.
2. Focus on the other person.
3. Listen with your full presence. Ask questions and actually hear the answers.
4. Ask the other person about their challenges.
5. Establish a time constraint early in the conversation. This puts strangers at ease.
6. Smile, and keep your palms open and facing up.
7. If you feel manipulated, clarify your goals. Don't get aggressive. Simply ask the other person to be honest about what they want.[60]

Some additional resources that can help you build trust and credibility with others include Dale Carnegie's *How to Win Friends and Influence People* and Marshall Rosenberg's *Nonviolent Communication: A Language of Life*. Both books teach you how to communicate effectively with others, and how to better understand their needs so you can build more trust and credibility.

---

[60] Eric Barker, "How to get people to like you: 7 ways from an FBI behavior expert," Ladders, May 22, 2019, https://www.theladders.com/career-advice/how-to-get-people-to-like-you-7-ways-from-an-fbi-behavior-expert.

AUTHENTICITY IN CONTENT CREATION:
WHAT THE HECK DOES THAT MEAN?

Authenticity helps establish trust with your audience and plays a huge factor in achieving success on digital platforms. Digital content strategist Naveen Gowda shares that most people are well accustomed to the tricks and practices of advertisers, which is why a lot of brands struggle to get meaningful engagement on social media. Rather than thinking about who they are and what they want to say, brands should be thinking about the needs of their viewers.

Stand-up comedian Joe Rogan has tremendous success in the 3-second world. He gets people to tune in to his channels for hours because he delivers strong content and makes no compromises on his quality standards. Gowda believes that although it may take longer, it's worth your time to establish a brand that is powerful and trustworthy—eventually, it helps you capture longer amounts of viewer time.

When you consistently create meaningful, quality content, you have a better chance of truly connecting with your audience and earning trust in our micro-attention world. Audiences will continue to watch your content for longer periods of time so they can receive the value it provides. Whereas, if you take shortcuts and post material just to keep up with metrics or timetables, the quality will suffer and you'll lose your audience's (and the algorithm's) trust. If you post a few bad videos in a row, the next video you post won't perform as well (regardless of how good it is). To avoid this scenario, Gowda often spends two or three times longer on research, ideation, and execution to create a single video than most other content creators would. He does this because he knows that if he gets it right, the video will perform 10 to 100 times better than it would otherwise.

Posting content is like showing up for a job. Simply showing up isn't enough. While there, you need to work hard, do the assigned tasks, and communicate effectively to maintain your clients' or bosses' trust. If, when you show up, you slack off or fail to fulfill the role you've been given for a few days, the trust will deteriorate. Gowda adds that with each video or piece of digital content, you should not only aim to do a good job, but to blow people away.

THE UNPOPULAR TRUTH ABOUT PRODUCTION VALUE

When viewers see highly polished and pristine content with fast cuts and fancy effects, they automatically assume they're watching ads. Gowda explains that when creating videos, you should try to be as real as possible. Production value doesn't dictate success on social platforms; success comes from telling an authentic and compelling story. For many of you, this is very good news. You could potentially shoot a video on your smartphone and reach millions of people with essentially no budget.

Quick Tips and Recap

1. Authenticity helps your Hook Points stick, and without it, they fall flat.
2. Let your "why" be a guide to building trust and authenticity with your consumers.
3. "People don't buy what you make, they buy what you believe." —Ernest Lupinacci
4. If your Hook Points don't support your underlying foundation, they can backfire.

5. Use Hook Points to quickly establish credibility with new businesses.

6. Be honest with yourself and your clients by setting clear expectations about what you can and cannot deliver.

7. Only take on work that truly speaks to you. Sometimes saying no can create more demand.

8. Success in sales comes from building trust-filled relationships.

9. Don't be impatient and destroy future opportunities—always play the long game, because important opportunities may come down the line.

10. Listen to your clients so you can truly understand their needs.

11. When you consistently create meaningful, quality content, you have a better chance of earning an audience's trust and viewer time.

12. Production value doesn't dictate success on social platforms; success comes from telling authentic and compelling stories.

CHAPTER 6

LEARN TO LISTEN; LISTEN TO LEARN

BUSINESSMAN AND INVESTOR Mark Cuban, who owns the NBA's Dallas Mavericks and is one of the main investors in ABC's *Shark Tank*, worked at a company called Tronics 2000 right out of college. While there, a man named Larry Menaw gave him some of the best advice he's ever received. Menaw noticed that Cuban was hyper and always on the go. One day before one of their meetings started, Menaw gave Cuban some specific instructions: "Mark, I want you to do one thing for me. Whenever we sit down for a meeting, I want you to take out your pad of paper and pen, and in the upper right-hand corner, write down the word *listen*." To this day, Cuban follows that advice. He writes down the word *listen* before every meeting to remind himself to be quiet and hear what the other people in the room have to say.[61]

---

[61] "The Real Reason Why Mark Cuban Doesn't Believe in Mentorship," YouTube video, posted by Inc., Apr. 8, 2019, https://www.youtube.com/watch?v=ppYrpChucQs.

THE GOLD MINE THAT LIES BETWEEN YOUR EARS

Listening is essential in our 3-second world. We have an incredible amount of information coming at us, so it's easy to become distracted, but focusing and staying present—especially when clients or partners speak—ultimately helps you discover your best Hook Points. When you listen to potential customers carefully, you're more likely to discover their pain points and learn where your skills, products, and services meet their needs.

Taking the time to truly listen can provide you with a gold mine of information that helps you become more valuable. If you ask the right questions, you'll be at an advantage in how you choose to present your products and services. And in meetings, you'll be better equipped to quickly shape your Hook Points and stories to become the solution to your potential customers' problems.

The Sleep Doctor, Michael Breus, reveals that he's absolutely discovered some of his most valuable Hook Points by listening. He's been asked a lot of questions by patients and audience members at the speeches he gives, which have helped him discover the most common pain points around which to create Hook Points and stories. Listening has helped him better frame his messages to show people how he can provide solutions to their most common sleep-related problems.

HOOKS FOR DUMMIES

I mentioned John Kilcullen earlier—the creator of the highly successful *For Dummies* book series. He agrees that a key for success in business is listening to qualified prospects and customers. It's the exact reason why Kilcullen reads many of the feedback cards inside of every *For Dummies* book. When his team released *Quicken for Dummies*, many readers had one common piece of feedback—they wanted a book that would teach them how to manage their money. Receiving this feedback was a defining moment for the brand. It helped Kilcullen and his team realize that they could extend beyond books created for the information-technology industry and release books on personal finance as well.

By listening to their clients' needs, Kilcullen's team expanded a book series about information technology into a brand that covers thousands of topics. Had Kilcullen not listened to his clients' feedback, the brand may not have generated around 2,500 titles with more than 200 million books in print.

Ernest Lupinacci agrees that successful brand extensions can be created by listening to customers. The evolution of the content created by *Life* magazine is a testament to this fact. The most popular section in *Life* was the "People" section, so, in response, the Meredith Corporation created *People* magazine. Then, the most popular section in *People* magazine was the "Style" section; hence, the creation of *InStyle* magazine. After that, they noticed that the most popular section in *InStyle* was the wedding section; therefore, *InStyle Weddings* was born. And last (but certainly not least), the most popular section in *InStyle Weddings* was the celebrity section, so *InStyle: Celebrity Weddings* was created.

Ask for your customers' feedback, take it seriously. You never know, someone might give you a multimillion-dollar idea. But you'll only hear about it if you're asking the right questions (and listening).

TRAINING YOUR EAR TO BE SWIFT

When I talk about listening in person, I'm referring to active listening. This is where you read between the lines and start to truly understand what the person in front of you is saying. It helps you stay present and read people accurately. The information you gather from this practice helps you become more finessed in your delivery of products and services. You start to understand that even if you're talking to three people at the same company—perhaps a CEO, a VP, and a middle manager—you still need to tweak your Hook Points and stories to address the nuanced pain points of each of these parties.

For example, as I touched on earlier in this book, before meeting Taylor Swift, I had to go through a series of meetings to get the opportunity to work with her. I had a licensing deal with MTV, and it was through that connection that I was offered the opportunity to meet her. At the time, I didn't know who Taylor Swift was (because she was just on her way to superstardom), which seems bizarre now, but luckily, as it was early on in my career, I was up for meeting with anyone.

My first meeting was with Swift's record label. Then I had separate meetings with her father, mother, and then finally with Swift. My ability to meet with and listen to each of these people is what ultimately helped me secure the deal. In each interaction, I learned how Swift and her team perceived the world. It enabled me to highlight different aspects of my story to satisfy each party's needs to pass on to the next round.

This process gave me a lot of time to ask questions and to start to truly understand what Swift wanted. I took this information to craft the most compelling Hook Points and stories specific to her needs. I learned that Swift had built her brand herself by fostering a one-to-one connection with her fans. She constantly communicated with them by responding to comments, signing autographs, and taking photos with them. She'd started her internet presence and fan out-reach through Myspace, which she loved because she could control the design of her page with embedded codes.

Now it was time to expand beyond Myspace. She'd spent a fortune on an all-flash website that took two days to update—with the help of a developer. Swift didn't like that she couldn't control the website herself. With the feedback I received from Swift and her family, my team built her an entirely new website in fewer than six hours.

In the meeting, the story I told was, "Taylor, I know you love interacting with your fans and controlling your brand design. We understand that your pain point with your website is that you can't change anything yourself, so we built this system for people like you. You can go in and change any element of this website yourself without having to write code." During the meeting, I also showed her how we could launch new pages and change out the navigation, photos, and backdrop of the entire site to match her latest album in fewer than two seconds. I gave her the mouse during the meeting so she could move things around and revise the site on the spot herself.

In the meetings with Swift's record label, father, and mother, I went in with slightly different variations of the story that specifically served their needs, questions, and concerns. I highlighted the business aspect of the story to the record label and Swift's father, and made Swift's mother feel comfortable about trusting my team. I had to listen to what each of them wanted in order to provide each person on her team with value. Whereas, if I simply went in and pitched my ideas to Swift directly, I may have presented them in a way that wouldn't have met her needs as thoroughly.

The latter is what most people do—they go into meetings, talk a lot, give a presentation, and pitch whatever they're trying to sell. This happens with digital content as well—people generally focus on what they want to say, not on what their audience wants to hear. When I go into a room, most times I don't even bring a presentation. I hardly use demos or PowerPoints anymore because they put you in a position where you can't modify your message to the responses you receive.

Imagine you go into a meeting and find out that the person you're speaking to perceives the situation in a different manner than you anticipated. Or perhaps this person sees the situation differently than someone else within the same company (whom you'll also ultimately have to convince to get the job or sell the product). You could meet with the CEO, who says, "Yes, we love this, but you've got to meet with the VP of marketing because she makes the decisions about this specific service." If that happens, you can't go in and use the exact same talking points as with the CEO—the VP of marketing probably perceives the solutions, pain points, and needs differently—she has distinct roles and responsibilities that alter her perception about what is needed and of value. You need to keep what the CEO said in mind, and also ask the VP of marketing questions to understand what she deems important. Then you can craft your story to help her better see your value.

HOW TO WIN THE GOLD RUSH: THE ART OF ASKING THE RIGHT QUESTIONS

Don't make assumptions or go into meetings with a preconceived idea or pitch, even when you've already met with others at the company. Take a step back, ask questions, and truly listen to what these people have to say. Take the time to understand those on the other side of the table, and how they perceive their problems. Observe their body language, moods, and responses. All of these variables dictate how you package your information so you can better connect with potential clients, partners, and employers.

Don't guess, assuming you know what they want. Use their responses and feedback to craft your stories.

I practice my stories over and over again with different people so that I get really good at telling them. Then, once I'm in the room, I let the other person inform how I change my Hook Point or story. I prepare for meetings by establishing a Hook Point, such as my "Zero to a Million Followers in 30 Days" concept, and then I practice the story with business partners whose opinions I trust.

I conduct this initial practice not only to get better at communicating my Hook Points and stories, but also to get feedback to see if they're working. If you do this, by the time you walk into a meeting, you'll have practiced your Hook Point and story so many times that you can just sit back, listen, and alter your story based on the other person's response.

Enter the room with practiced Hook Points and stories that can be fluid. Get as comfortable as you can with all the information so you can change how you tell your story. Become confident enough to tell it in a different order, leaving out certain parts or adding information in, so you can share what best meets your potential clients' needs. And pay attention to any questions they ask you so that you understand what they deem valuable.

Jim Kane, my father, and former partner of one of the oldest law firms in Chicago (with offices all over the US), agrees that doing research and having background knowledge about a potential client and their needs is critical. Before taking meetings, the marketing department at his firm would conduct research about a potential client's business to see which attorney had the most expertise in the space. Then they would go in with as much preparation as possible so they could let the meeting take on a life of its own.

Aside from addressing the areas of expertise that a potential client is looking for, my dad says that "the most important thing a really good lawyer can do is to listen to the client's response to the presentation." The best lawyers he saw in all his years of practice were the ones who listened and adjusted on the fly to address what potential clients needed.

You can give the best presentation in the world, but it won't secure new business if what you offer doesn't address what clients want. Listen very carefully, and be ready to change your approach. My father adds that oftentimes potential clients don't know what they need until they're asked the right questions.

A Question a Day Keeps the Pain Away

Below are some general questions you can ask when entering a meeting. You'll need to get much more specific based on your industry and potential customers' needs, but these questions offer good starting points:

1. What are your most important goals and objectives?
2. What obstacles are you running into while trying to achieve those goals?
3. What are the pain points that are most frustrating for your organization?
4. What are the biggest pain points you're experiencing in your specific position?

Again, these are very high-level questions, but the answers can help you learn a tremendous amount about your potential clients and their businesses—you will discover their most important obstacles and goals.

I may meet clients who want to lower their cost of acquisition but are struggling to make it happen. And now, because the money spent on paid social media advertising isn't bringing in a return, their executive team doesn't understand the value of paid media. With that information, I can go in and say, "If I run a test that brings down your cost per acquisition, would that be helpful for telling a compelling story to the higher-ups? Could it potentially get you more of a budget to do your job more effectively?"

Essentially, you take the input they're giving you and respond by asking, "If I were able to solve your problem, would it be helpful . . . ?" It's very hard for people to say no to someone who wants to help solve a difficult problem for them. But you can only come up with solutions to your potential clients' problems by asking the right questions and listening. Choosing not to do so forces you to guess, and throw out solutions without really understanding how they perceive the situation (which isn't a good strategy for securing new clients).

SHUT UP! YOU'LL SCARE THE FISH AWAY

A friend of mine told me that American business magnate, producer, and film-studio executive David Geffen is always the quietest person in the room. He doesn't talk much, but when he has something to say, everyone stops and listens.

I've noticed this trend among some of the most impressive and powerful people I've encountered. They don't have the need to speak unless they have something important to say, and they often take the time to think it through before they say it. I distinctly remember when I had my first meeting with Tom Rosenberg, founder and chairman of Lakeshore Entertainment. My father knew that he was an intelligent man and gave me a heads-up that he would have a unique communication style. He told me, "When you go into that meeting with Rosenberg, he may take some very long pauses—it's because he's thinking about what he's going to say next or he's digesting the information." My dad was right. Rosenberg is one of those people who is very vocal when necessary, but many times there's a bit of an uncomfortable silence that leaves you wondering if you were supposed to say something. I quickly learned that this was just his way of listening and processing information.

PRACTICE THE TANGO IN MEETINGS

Keith Ferrazzi, author of the *New York Times* bestselling books *Never Eat Alone* and *Who's Got Your Back*, and founder and CEO of Ferrazzi Greenlight, says that listening is helpful because anytime you want to bring your best self to a situation, you need to care as much as you can about the other people in the meeting. He thinks it's important that others feel like you truly want to make a difference in their lives.

One tool Ferrazzi shares to help you develop a deeper connection with the people you're going to listen to is an imagination exercise. Visualize the person you're about to have a meeting with five years from now. Imagine that at this time he's one of the most important people in your life. If you take the time to see all the ways in which you can help him become successful, then you'll walk into the room with a huge smile and, as Ferrazzi says, "you will create a level of intimacy, connectedness, expectation, and possibility. An authentic, fruitful feeling that this person is part of your 'posse.' If you walk into the room with that energy, you will win." He adds that you should see every interaction as a co-creation. Don't ever go in trying to sell your idea. Go into meetings thinking you're doing the tango. He says, "Sometimes you're dancing forward, and sometimes you're dancing backward, but ultimately it's an interaction that will yield transformational results. As long as you bring power, energy, and attention, the meeting will go well."

LISTEN TO EXPERTS WHO DISAGREE WITH YOU

Billionaire Ray Dalio manages $150 billion in global investments and runs Bridgewater Associates. He shares that one of the strategies that has helped him become rich and successful is listening to smart people who disagree with him. Dalio likes to question experts individually and encourages them to have thoughtful disagreement with each other so he can become better educated and raise his "probability of being right." He doesn't like to assume he's right until he has spoken to many independent thinkers. He advises seeking out "the smartest people who disagree with you the most to stress test your thinking. If they disagree, then the conversation in that disagreement will be enlightening. [It's] the quickest way to get an education."[62]

RECEPTIVITY IS CREATIVITY

Ernest Lupinacci shared that one of his mentors, Tom Carroll (the former CEO of TBWA Worldwide), told him that Lee Clow (the chairman and global director of TBWA) always emphasized that "creativity is receptivity." Creativity is enhanced by the ability to entertain someone else's idea and give it a chance. Lupinacci values listening to others and gets frustrated

---

[62] Tom Huddleston Jr., "Ray Dalio says this tactic helped him from 'hardly any money' to successful billionaire," CNBC make it, Nov. 21, 2019, https://www.cnbc.com/2019/11/21/tactic-helped-bridgewater-asscociates-ray-dalio-become-a-billionaire.html.

when he sees people with narrow-minded points of views or those who are constantly playing the contrarian. For example, he might be in a meeting giving a presentation and use an example like, "Well, you know it's similar to how when you drink coffee . . . ," and then someone interrupts and says, "I don't drink coffee." Or perhaps he's saying, "You know, like in *Stranger Things*, when . . . ," and someone will say, "I've never seen it." Just because this one person doesn't drink coffee and hasn't seen one of the most watched shows on Netflix doesn't make the references obsolete. The person could continue to listen and remain receptive to the larger ideas these details are trying to illustrate even though it doesn't specifically appeal to him or her. Lupinacci says that the smartest people are aware that they're not the one-and-only consumers out there. They think, *It doesn't matter that I personally don't like coffee, or that I've personally never seen the show; I'm going to continue to listen so I can grasp the bigger concept.*

WELCOME TO THE FBI—NOW SHUT UP AND LISTEN

Chris Voss, the former head of FBI international hostage negotiation, explains that active listening is critical in business negotiations. Here are the basics:

1. Listen to what the other person has to say. Don't interrupt, disagree or "evaluate."
2. Make brief acknowledgments by saying "Yes," "Uh-huh," and nodding your head.
3. Repeat back what the other person says, without being awkward, so you can show that you understand their frame of reference.

4. Ask questions to show that you're paying attention and that help move the discussion forward.[63]

I recommend practicing active listening for a week. As you do so, follow the steps below, and keep a journal of your observations:

- Make a point to actively listen to and observe the people around you.
- Try to listen 90 percent of the time.
- Notice how many people around you are truly listening versus how many are simply waiting for their turn to talk.
- Practice staying neutral. Don't react emotionally to other people's responses. Try to understand the other person's point of view (even if you strongly disagree with it).
- Ask thoughtful questions.
- Note how people respond to being asked questions. Do they seem open and excited that you're taking an interest in them?

If you practice active listening and do the exercise above, you'll be amazed by what you discover. Not only will you realize how many people don't take the time to truly listen, but you'll also be surprised by how much more connected you feel to others. You create strong connections by simply focusing your attention on other people instead of trying to explain your personal points of view. If you practice this often and maintain a high level of listening in meetings, you'll have a better chance of winning new business.

---

[63] "Hostage Negotiation Techniques That Will Get You What You Want," Bakadesuyo, https://www.bakadesuyo.com/2013/06/hostage-negotiation/.

LEARN TO READ MINDS LIKE AN ATHLETIC TRAINER

Peter Park is the owner of Platinum Fitness and the author of *Rebound: Regain Strength, Move Effortlessly, Live without Limit—At Any Age*. His clients include billionaires, celebrities, and athletes such as cyclist Lance Armstrong, six-time Major League Baseball All-Star Justin Verlander, and entrepreneur Elon Musk.

Park began his career working as a physical therapy aide at St. Francis Hospital in Santa Barbara. A shy young man, Park was nervous about getting people out of bed to do physical therapy exercises. Many of his patients were disagreeable because they had serious conditions and were in a lot of pain. In fact, some of them would yell and spit at Park.

The job forced Park to get out of his comfort zone. He talked to people from all types of ethnic and socioeconomic backgrounds who perceived the world in many different ways. Over time, he learned how to read all these different types of people and started to better understand body language and behavior, which is especially important when dealing with those who are vulnerable and stressed.

Park went from being from a shy, reserved guy to a person who could interact with anyone. By the time he became a personal trainer, his clients felt like a breeze—for starters, they weren't in as much pain and usually had the desire to work out. And most important, the experience at the hospital made him a fantastic listener, which has been a major factor in his ability to secure and maintain high-level clients.

Use each job you have to become more understanding of others. You never know where the knowledge will take you. Listening to and observing others will make you a better businessperson all around.

SURVIVING SIRIUSXM AND BARRY DILLER, AND THE IMPORTANCE OF MEDITATION

One time I had a meeting with Sirius XM that went horribly wrong. It all started because the company wanted help driving traffic to a new platform they were building. Initially, I had a great conversation with a high-level executive, so they set up a meeting with the developer who was working on the platform.

Unfortunately, the developer wasn't open to hearing how social media presence and advertising could drive traffic to the website. He didn't see the value in what I had to offer and didn't want to invest in it. I kept trying to explain how social media works, how it drives traffic, and how it can provide value—but he kept cutting me off and wouldn't listen.

Eventually, I got up and said, "Well, I can't help you, then. I don't know what you want me to do," and left the room in frustration. I lost the deal because of my decision, which was disappointing. Although I don't think we would have worked well together, I could have handled the situation better. I should've taken a deep breath and worked harder to understand the developer's point of view. I could have been less reactive, and grateful for the meeting, instead of just walking out.

Looking back, I realize that I was very stressed out at the time this happened—I wasn't living as healthy of a life as I am now. When you're stressed and tired, you don't think clearly or handle situations like you would when you're taking good care of yourself. That's one of the reasons why I practice meditation. It's a tool that keeps me balanced and makes me a better listener. It's especially helpful because it slows down the mind and increases awareness, which are useful skills for interviews, meetings, giving speeches, and so on. If you practice meditation regularly, even for just ten minutes a day, you'll have a greater chance of staying present at important events.

You'll also get better at absorbing the information that matters most and remaining calm, regardless of the situation.

Keith Ferrazzi agrees. One time he met with Barry Diller, the creator of the Fox broadcasting company and USA broadcasting, who is now the chairman and senior executive of InterActiveCorp and Expedia Group. Ferrazzi was on the elevator with Diller and became so nervous that he started seeing spots in his eyes. He was very intimidated to meet this media icon. To help himself calm down, Ferrazzi got off the elevator, went into a phone booth, and meditated until the spots in his eyes disappeared. Then he was able to go in and have a productive meeting with Diller.

If you find yourself experiencing a lot of stress and anxiety before big meetings or events, there's a self-hypnosis audio I recommend (created by Steven Gurgevich) called *Hypnotic Rehearsal*. Gurgevich has created a number of self-hypnosis recordings, ranging from 15 to 20 minutes, which cover a variety of topics. Essentially, they're guided meditations where he takes you through the process of rehearsing a meeting and visualizing yourself feeling comfortable in that space. The self-hypnosis guided recording tricks your subconscious into believing you're entering a comfortable situation.

Bringing your best self into a room helps you listen. If you're distracted by anxiety, or are tired from a poor night's sleep, you won't offer your full value. Take care of yourself so you can take care of your clients (which is ultimately another form of taking care of yourself!).

IT'S NOT A FOLLOWER—IT'S A LIVING, BREATHING HUMAN BEING

Shift your thinking from "I'm here to sell or promote my product or service" to "I'm here to deliver value." If you create content without thinking about your audience's desires and needs, you won't succeed. You must know who they are, what they want, and how you can provide them with value.

Naveen Gowda adds that your goal is not only to understand the categorical or topical needs of the audience, but also to understand what the audience needs in terms of content behavior. For example, if a woman is really into coffee without sugar because she believes in living a healthy lifestyle, and you're creating content to reach people like her—be aware of not only her coffee-drinking preferences but also the other lifestyle choices people in her demographic make—and even more important, her expectation for how communication in this category typically appears in her social feed. For example, if she's an average user with healthy lifestyle interests, she will have seen the Facebook page "Goodful." Their videos deliver great ideas for people with very limited downtime—they get to the point really quickly and offer value consistently without it coming off as marketing to the audience. Users receive a holistic experience, and she's probably hungry for that type of content design.

Doing your research is vital. Many observations and inferences can be made from reviewing the content your desired audience is currently watching. Ignoring those clues is the main way Gowda sees content creators fail. Instead of taking the time to make inferences, they try to force their style into the content, or ignore the ecosystem of content altogether.

Try not to make this mistake. If you pay attention and do research, social media can help you succeed—it's a tool that gives you access to a massive amount of people and data at once. As discussed in chapter 3, you can carefully review the analytics of your videos (and other people's videos) to help you better understand your audience's taste. Through conducting a competitive analysis, you can find out why content creators, who reach the people *you'd* like to, perform well. Analyze videos that generate 10,000 shares versus the ones that generate only 100 shares. Through this investigation, you'll learn a wealth of helpful information. You'll better understand the topics your audience is interested in, their needs, the content styles they're gravitating toward, and their pain points.

For research on Facebook, Instagram, YouTube, or Tubular, I advise typing in relevant keywords related to your brand and then searching for which videos have the most views. Dive further into your investigation around the videos that are generating organic reach, and not solely performing well because of advertising dollars. For example, on Facebook you can figure this out by looking at how many shares a video has received versus how many views it's received—typically a strong view-to-share ratio for a video with millions of views is around 1 percent. Here's an example of a video with a strong view-to-share ratio:

This video has 53 million views and 1.5 million shares, which proves that the video generated organic views. If the video had received only thousands of shares and the ratio were lower, I would assume the views were generated through paid advertising, or perhaps they were generated from being cross-posted on another Facebook page with a large following. The more shares a video has generally means the video concept is stronger and more palpable for audiences. Once you find the videos that are being shared the most, dissect why they're performing well. Ask yourself, "What is it about this content and the way they positioned it that works?"

You can also use Google Trends, Reddit, and Google News to do research about the topics and content styles people are searching for and are interested in. After you have a sense of these topics and styles, see if you can craft Hook Points and stories that connect trends with your products or services. Again, if you take the time to do this research, you'll be light-years ahead of those who come up with content ideas from scratch.

When Katie Couric was interviewing celebrities such as DJ Khaled, we would go to Google Trends, as well as Facebook and Instagram, to see which content was trending about him. These searches allowed us to see how other people were positioning headlines and content about Khaled. It gave us clues as to what worked and what didn't, so we could come up with stronger Hook Points. We reviewed the social media posts that were shared at the highest velocity to give us information about Khaled's audience's interests. This research saved us a huge amount of time.

The trending topics you find to inspire your stories don't have to be directly related to your brand. You can connect your product or service to popular topics even if they're seemingly unrelated. It's just a matter of being smart about how you make them relatable.

A successful case of creating content based on a trending topic, which wasn't the brand itself, is Shareability's video campaign for Pizza Hut and Pepsi called "The Dangers of Selfie Sticks." The video is in the form of a goof public-service announcement about the dangers of using selfie sticks. Brownstein's team got the idea from the fact that selfie sticks were a trending topic because they'd just been banned from Disneyland. Pizza Hut was in the process of launching a two-foot-long pizza, so they came up with the concept that you would need a really long selfie stick to take a photo with this new, unusually long pizza. By making that connection in a funny way, and creating a parody of selfies in general, the video went viral on YouTube. It became the most shared ad in the world the month it launched partly due to the relevance of "selfie sticks" in video search at the time.

Digital content strategist Naveen Gowda reminds us that the more you study communication design and consume great content, the better equipped you'll be to create relevant content. You need to listen to the other content creators in your space and become a consumer of the types of content that reach your audience.

Quick Tips and Recap

1. Listening can help you discover Hook Points, stories, and products that provide solutions to your potential customers' most common problems.

2. Ask a lot of questions to figure out what your potential clients truly need. Don't guess, assuming that you know what they want.

3. Don't pitch. Be flexible in how you present your stories, products, and services.

4. Practice your Hook Points and stories with trusted business partners, and measure how they respond.

5. Remember that creativity is enhanced by the ability to listen and entertain other people's ideas.

6. Be cognizant of the fact that active listening helps you win new business.

7. Create content with your audience's desires and needs in mind. Shift your mindset from "I'm here to sell or promote my product or service" to "I'm here to deliver value with my product or service."

8. Use Google News, Google Trends, Reddit, YouTube, Instagram, Tubular, and Facebook to research the topics and content styles that people are searching for and are interested in.

9. Frequently conduct a competitive analysis on trending social media content formats and concepts to save time and create better content.

CHAPTER 7

TAKE EVERYTHING I HAVE— IT'S YOURS FOR FREE: HOW TO ACCELERATE DEMAND FOR YOUR BRAND

VALUE IS AT the core of every successful business. If a product or service doesn't provide value, it shouldn't exist, which is why knowing how to demonstrate value is an essential part of the Hook Point and storytelling process. If you can highlight and package a message properly, you'll capture attention, get into more rooms for interviews, and perform like a rock star in meetings. You'll also have a greater chance of creating more effective content that drives massive reach, and convincing prospects to respond to cold outreach emails.

BREAK THE BOX TO DRIVE DEMAND

Value should be inherent in whatever you're marketing, and oftentimes it's the out-of-the-box concepts related to your product or service that drive the differentiation of your brand against competitors. These unique benefits are not always necessary for your products to function, but they help you stand out, offer something unique, and can become one of the Hook Points that drives massive brand growth. Let's look at some examples of out-of-the-box value that was leveraged for effective Hook Points:

Lady Gaga: The Mother Monster and the LGBTQ Community

For more than a decade, Lady Gaga has leveraged out-of-the-box thinking to truly stand out and become a global superstar. For example, she has advocated for the LGBTQ (lesbian, gay, bisexual, transgender, and queer or questioning) community and has shown her support in truly original ways. In 2009, when she received an award for the song "Poker Face" at Canada's iHeartRadio Much Music Video Awards, she gave thanks "to God and the gays" in her acceptance speech. This may seem like a simple statement, but it was fresh and original in comparison with most speeches of this kind.

Gaga has participated in the National Equality March and the Human Rights Campaign gala, and has protested the military's anti-LGBTQ policy (with her infamous meat dress) to prove her loyalty to this group.[64] Under the moniker "Mother Monster," she's positioned herself to all her "little monsters," aka fans. She says that the term *little monsters* originated from her fear of death, alcohol, and drugs, but it's been a perfect marketing tool to appeal to the outcasts, misfits, LGBTQ community, and other

---

[64] Muri Assuncao, "12 Times Lady Gaga Showed Love for the LGBTQ Community," *Billboard, Sept. 20, 2018,* https://www.billboard.com/articles/news/pride/8475993/lady-gaga-12-times-showed-love-for-lgbtq-community.

marginalized groups. Her communication with her fan base is original and (in some ways) revolutionary.

Gaga has advocated for being different and standing out. She's empowered her fans and has provided them with the tremendous value of feeling strong enough to stand up for who they are. She's built her brand by connecting with people in these groups—she makes them feel like they have someone (in her) who understands and creates music for them.

Helipad at Platinum Fitness

Currently I'm working with Peter Park, the personal trainer and owner of Platinum Fitness, who, as previously mentioned, has trained clients such as Lance Armstrong and Elon Musk. Although he's worked with major celebrities and athletes and often leverages that fact as his Hook Point, he's constantly testing new ways to grab people's attention.

One aspect of Park's Los Angeles–based gym that we've discussed highlighting through social channels is the helipad on top of the building where his gym resides. Park has access to the helipad and has used it in his training sessions and classes. It's a unique, differentiating element of his business because there are very few gyms in the world that have a helipad that you can work out on. We'll take videos and pictures of people working out on the helipad, with the beautiful backdrop of the entire city of Los Angeles, and leverage them in strategic Facebook and Instagram lead-generation advertising campaigns. We think that this Hook Point will drive awareness about Park's new gym because we live in a selfie/social media world. We believe that people will get excited about the opportunity to film themselves working out on a helipad overlooking the city of Los Angeles—the ability to take these pictures is the hook. Then, once people are there, Peter and his trainers will show them the real magic behind why they are some of the best trainers in the world. This will then lead to some people converting into private clients. Additionally, people attending the class will use the content they capture on the helipad as Hook Points for their own personal social channels (showing off the experience to social followers), which will then also serve as the most valuable form of advertising for Peter's gym—word-of-mouth endorsements.

Wrapping Up (the Box)

In the Lady Gaga and Platinum Fitness examples, both of these brands figured out how to combine original Hook Points with something that provides specific value to their target audiences. See how you can do the same by pushing yourself to think outside the box. Do you have something truly unique and original that helps you stand out and tell an interesting story to your customers? (If you're having difficulty coming up with out-of-the-box ideas, I offer private strategy sessions to achieve this goal. If you're interested, email me at bkane@brendanjkane.com.)

WHY WE SHOULD KILL THE ELEVATOR PITCH

To capture people's attention quickly, you can't go into content creation or meetings with your focus on the sale. People love to buy but hate to be sold to—which is why you need to remain focused on providing value. If you fail to do so and stay focused on the sale, the people you're communicating with will feel it, get on edge, and want to shift their attention elsewhere.

This is why I'm not a fan of elevator pitches. The definition of a pitch is: "To present or advertise, especially in a high-pressure way."[65] Essentially, you're almost trying to force someone to buy something. Instead, use the tools I've given you throughout this book to articulate your value proposition. Replace pitching with the use of Hook Points and storytelling.

I want to be clear, however, that of course I understand that your end goal is to sell a product or service—we're all in business to generate revenue. But instead of focusing on *selling* your product or service, focus on leveraging the *value* of your product or service and determining how it solves a specific pain point or problem. There's a huge difference between language that's designed to sell and language that expresses value.

LEVERAGING VALUE TO CONNECT WITH THE A-LIST

While speaking at Web Summit, the world's largest tech event, I secured the opportunity to interview Jon Seifert, worldwide CEO of the marketing, advertising, and public relations firm Ogilvy. When I met him, I asked how many views his best-performing interview of all time received, to which he replied, "Two million views on a CNBC interview." I guaranteed that the interview he did with me would have a larger reach because I would apply my methodologies for the content distribution and testing process that I built while working with Katie Couric. Instead of doing just another press interview, which he probably did dozens of times that day, I added extra value and stood out to him (and Ogilvy's CMO) because I made a bold claim and told a specific story about how I would make it

---

[65] Merriam-Webster, "pitch," 2020, https://www.merriam-webster.com/dictionary/pitch.

happen. Also, because I kept my promise (the interview generated 2.1 million views), it led to my being connected with another high-profile CEO at a major company.

By providing value, you create win-win situations, which helps you help other people. And usually when you truly help people, they want to repay you, which is why providing value is a great tool for acquiring and keeping new business.

HELP WANTED—NO EXPERIENCE REQUIRED!

You don't necessarily need to have a ton of experience to provide value to others—you can do it at all stages of your career. Back when I was starting out as an assistant at the movie studio Lakeshore Entertainment, I was helping with the social media campaign for the movie *Crank*. During this time, I met actor Jason Statham, known for *Snatch*, *Hobbs and Shaw*, *The Transporter*, and many other notable films. He saw the work I was doing and asked if I would come to his house to do a social media strategy session. This request came out of nowhere and felt like a very big deal at the time—especially because I wasn't trying to build a working relationship with Statham. The opportunity simply arose from communicating with him in an open and honest way, and by providing value.

Even as an entry-level assistant, I built trust and credibility with a highly successful movie star. All I had to do was see how I could be of value to him, be helpful, and do a good job. After the strategy session, Statham realized he wanted to prioritize some other projects before committing to the work it takes to keep a social presence afloat. This was back in 2008, so it was early in the social media game, and his focus was elsewhere. Even though the meeting didn't lead to more work, the value I provided still got me in the door for an opportunity that most people only dream about.

HOW TO APPEAR ON *THE DR. OZ SHOW* 35 TIMES

Michael Breus, The Sleep Doctor, shares that a key to securing media opportunities is being a good date. His father used to tell him, "Always be a good date. Be kind and polite whether or not you think there's a romantic connection, because they'll always have a friend." Breus took that advice to heart for his career as well. He promised himself that he'd always do a good job and be kind to everyone he meets because you never know where they'll end up. Applying this advice has worked in Breus's favor. His first appearance on *The Dr. Oz Show* stemmed from a connection with a producer he'd met on another show called *The Doctors*. That producer eventually moved over to *Oz,* and because he'd already seen Breus's work, he trusted him and brought him on the show.

In addition to being a good guest, Breus also provides the added value of offering to consult with any member of the media who has a sleep problem. He believes that this added value also gets him asked back for media appearances. When you help people personally, they're more likely to trust you. They're grateful for your help and want to reciprocate by becoming megaphones for your products or services.

It's important to note that when Breus offers this kind of help, he doesn't expect anything in return. Let me repeat that: *He doesn't expect anything in return.* He simply offers advice because his work is important to him, and he wants people to enjoy improved sleep and better lives. His authentic desire to help is what gives him massive credibility and helps him secure many media appearances.

THE SECRET TO GETTING HIRED FOR A TOP-TIER JOB

My father, Jim Kane, was one of the first lawyers to be hired (without a law degree from an Ivy League or top-tier school) at one of the oldest firms in Chicago. The firm dates back to the Civil War, and historically the majority of attorneys working there had graduated from Ivy League law schools. Clients went to the firm to find the best and brightest lawyers, which was why the school a lawyer graduated from was extremely important. However, in the 1990s, clients started looking not only for lawyers who'd graduated from prestigious law schools, but also for those who could bring value-added representation—they sought out attorneys who could introduce them to individuals and companies who could become potential business partners.

My father had considerable experience before he went into private law practice from working as the former director of real estate for the city of Chicago. During this time, he made considerable contacts and developed relationships with high-powered people in politics and the real estate industry. When he applied to the prestigious firm, where he eventually became partner, he marketed himself as someone who was not only an accomplished attorney, but who also had contacts and working relationships that could benefit the firm in its efforts to expand its client base.

Eventually my dad went on to become involved in the hiring process for new lawyers at the firm. Many applicants came from the top schools in the nation, but he didn't recommend hiring based solely on where someone went to school. He was more interested in their interpersonal skills and how they articulated their views about the legal profession. That gave him the best insight as to how these individuals would communicate and interact with both existing and potential clients. He looked for lawyers with exceptional interpersonal skills and the potential to develop business down the road. While interviewing, he asked questions that helped him understand how candidates' minds worked and whether or not they would be nimble when dealing with existing and potential clients. Most important, my dad knew that candidates could have all the "book smarts" in the world, but it meant nothing if they couldn't communicate effectively and develop relationships that produced new clients and additional revenue for the firm.

Business is founded on relationships—and the ability to create and maintain them is essential. Oftentimes you're appealing to a potential boss or client not only for the value you provide by doing your actual job, but also for the additional value you bring through relationships or skills.

So, take some time to write down your background, additional skills, and experience. I'm sure you'll be pleasantly surprised by how many added benefits you bring to the table. Be sure to highlight these attributes in your Hook Points and stories.

WHY 99 PERCENT OF PEOPLE FAIL WHEN LOOKING FOR JOBS

When trying to secure new business or get hired at a company, 99 percent of people fail because they approach potential employers thinking solely about their own personal needs. They don't think about the fact that managers and decision makers often have several people approaching them every day expecting to receive something from them. Less than 1 percent of the people they talk to think about what the manager or decision maker wants or needs; they forget that these people have their own problems they're attempting to solve.

When you look for a job or speak with potential new clients, go in with the attitude, "How can I be of service to you?" rather than, "Please give me a job." You'll elicit a much better response if you focus on what you can do for them instead of what they can do for you.

HOW TO HACK YOUR WAY INTO ANY JOB

The truth about landing a great job or promotion is that it's less about proving your ability to do the job, and more about building trust and a solid relationship. In fact, at Ernst & Young and Deloitte, employee recommendations account for 45 to 50 percent of hires; and for those who make it to the interview stage, the referred candidates have a 40 percent better chance of being hired than other applicants.

This is because employers hire people they could be friends with. A lot of hiring is done because of someone's attitude, not aptitude. People often see their co-workers more than their wives, kids, and friends. You can be smart, but you also need to be easy to work with every day.

The secret to building trust with anyone is that it's *not* about what they can do for you, it's about the needs you can fulfill for *them*, so think about the needs of the people in the places where you'd like to work. Some common needs include:

- A strong work ethic
- Trustworthiness
- Someone who's fun to be around
- Creative thinking

- Persuasive speaking ability
- Being easy to talk to
- Care and concern for co-workers
- Specialized knowledge (e.g., technology, social networking, accounting, etc.)

Try to think about how you can meet the needs of those you'd like to work with. If you think you have nothing to offer, you're wrong—*everyone* has something to offer. There are all kinds of talents, including something as seemingly simple as the ability to listen and share a passion for common interests. Figure out what you're good at, and use that as a starting point to form strong connections.

FULFILLING-NEEDS EXERCISE

Take ten minutes to write down a list of all the things you're good at. This should include both business and personal skills:

- Business examples: writing, public speaking, strategy, content creation, analytics, math, accounting, etc.
- Personal examples: surfing, great with dogs, golfing, making people laugh, etc.

Keep these skills in mind when talking with potential employers or clients. Think strategically about how these skills can help you create strong connections, and keep them in the back of your mind at interviews. Be mindful not to leverage irrelevant skill sets if they're not of value to those on the other side of the table (e.g., if an individual is serious, don't constantly try to crack jokes; or if you're applying for a writing position, don't talk about the fact that you're great at calculus—unless you're working for a media company that has a math focus. If you can provide true value to those around you, you'll eventually secure your dream job.

THE SECRET TO HAPPINESS (WORK EDITION)

People lose the opportunity to work with great employees and service providers by not recognizing the value in those they want to hire. If you have something of value, and a potential client or employer tries to negotiate you down or doesn't recognize what you're worth, it's probably not the right fit. Yes, clients and employers pay you, but money isn't everything. If a company doesn't make you feel appreciated, they're not providing *you* with enough value and you should walk away.

Personally, I don't work simply for the paycheck. I work for clients who appreciate the value I offer. If they don't appreciate it, then although they can meet my financial needs, they aren't worth working with because they can't fulfill my psychological and emotional needs. This is important to keep in mind when you're the one hiring. If you appreciate the people you hire, you'll have a better chance of attracting A-list talent.

STOP KIDDING YOURSELF—*EVERY* INDUSTRY IS THE SERVICE INDUSTRY

Erick Brownstein of Shareability was once told, "If you want to feel satisfied and happy in your life, be of service." He's taken this principle and spread it across the various facets of his life. He believes that in business meetings, you win the room by focusing on being of service. If you genuinely want to help others, you go further. In fact, he's gone into meetings with midlevel executives and told them that if they work with Shareability, a primary goal of his will be to see them get promoted, which has actually happened several times.

Brownstein also believes in giving away his best ideas and insights. He recommends a book by Patrick Lencioni called *Getting Naked*, which is a business fable about a consulting company that generates a lot of business. The company doesn't go into meetings with a big deck or presentation—they informally talk with potential clients. They ask a lot of questions, give away ideas, and approach the meeting with the mindset, "We're already working together." Essentially, the fable shows how the consultants win business through their genuine desire to be helpful.

DON'T PLAY THE VICTIM

You can deliver the same message in many different ways. When packaging information in business, focus on sharing the benefits those you're speaking with will receive. That way you avoid coming across as self-serving. I once hired a contractor who didn't understand how to package information in terms of providing value to his clients. This person would only present information from his point of view, explaining how situations were beneficial to *him*. He would go so far as to talk about what a rough time he was going through financially to try to make his clients feel sorry for him, in order to get more business. This is *not* a good strategy—you don't want anyone doing business with you because they feel sorry for you. You want to make your intelligence, capability, product, or service so good that others *can't* stop working with you.

Eventually, I cut ties with this contractor, but at one point while he was working for me, he told me that he wanted to raise his rates so he could hire more people and sign up for platforms that would "make his job easier." The language he used in his pitch was not effective. This proposal was solely focused on what *he* needed and wanted. Had he been in the practice of focusing on his clients' needs, he could have proposed the same plan in a way that made me feel that I was getting more out of his service by paying more. He could have said, "I'm upgrading my service to make it more effective. You will benefit because of X, Y, and Z, but in order to deliver at this higher level, I need to raise my rates to cover the necessary expenses that allow me to offer this higher level of service." If he'd presented the information in this way, I would have been far more receptive to the idea.

So don't play the victim, don't try to get people to feel sorry for you, and don't be self-serving. Instead, play up your strengths, and always put yourself in the other person's shoes. We all want to work with individuals who provide us with value.

I LOVE HOMEWORK! HOW TO PREPARE FOR CRITICAL MEETINGS

John Kilcullen, creator of the *For Dummies* book series, recommends doing your due diligence before you meet with people. If you do your homework, you can provide potential clients with more value. Figure out if you have any common connections, and do research on their markets. People pay for timely solutions to unrecognized needs. If you can spot those needs, you can paint a picture of what they're missing and price your products or services at a higher rate. Additionally, Kilcullen recommends having conversations with the company's customers and employees to find any inside pearls of wisdom that may help you provide value.

HOW TO STAND OUT WITH BILLIONAIRES

According to the Bureau of Labor Statistics, there were approximately 338,000 personal trainers in the US in 2018,[66] so the fact that Peter Park, the owner of Platinum Fitness, has differentiated himself and become such a successful trainer at the highest levels is remarkable. He thinks that his passion and love for training is a huge part of his value proposition. People see that he lives for his job, and this passion helps him stand out. He won't stop until he sees a client improve, no matter if it's a professional athlete, a billionaire, or a person who's just starting to train for the first time.

Focus on your areas of passion. People will pick up on your energy, and it will provide them with value—we all want to feel ignited and enthusiastic! Clients and customers enjoy being around people who are happy and positive.

HOW MORTON'S SALT AND TSA MAKE SEXY, BREAKTHROUGH CONTENT

It's critically important for customers to feel connected to your brand. If you can connect with your viewers, whether that be through emotion, humor, surprise, excitement, or education, you're more likely to get audiences to engage with you and share your content at a higher rate.

---

[66] "Fitness Trainers and Instructors," U.S. Bureau of Labor Statistics, Sept. 4, 2019, https://www.bls.gov/ooh/personal-care-and-service/fitness-trainers-and-instructors.htm.

Mike Jurkovac, Emmy Award–winning director/producer at TheBridge. co, has worked with the Black Eyed Peas since 2001. He explains that when he first met these musicians, he was not only impressed by the positive messages in their songs but also by frontman will.i.am's ability to connect with all types of audiences. When he performed in Brazil, he wore the soccer team's jersey. When he performed in Mexico, he held up the country's national flag. It's obvious that will.i.am is a genius when it comes to engaging with people and discovering things that excite each individual culture.

Some people think that their products or brands are difficult to make exciting—Jurkovac would argue that any brand has the capacity to create a connection with consumers. He cites Morton Salt as an example of a brand that has some incredibly engaging content even though salt wouldn't necessarily be considered a "sexy" subject.

One time Morton Salt created a video with a band called OK Go. The hook is that the beginning of the video shows a complete moment that is 4.2 seconds long, and after it ends, it's revealed that this 4.2-second part of the video is actually a sped-up version of a longer piece of content that was about four minutes long, which plays in its entirety right after the 4.2-second intro. The content worked in both the four-second format and the four-minute-long version. (You can watch the *OK Go—The One Moment* official video here: www.brendanjkane.com/okgo.) Because the video was sponsored by Morton Salt, it connects the brand with a very hip band and an interesting concept that got people excited—therefore, making this brand of salt seem cool.

Another brand that has been able to make content engaging against the odds is the Transportation Security Administration (TSA). They have an incredible Instagram account, which you can see here: https://www.instagram.com/tsa/?hl=en. This account shares unique and funny stories about all the crazy items that people try to bring through airport security, including maple syrup, slingshots, and a ninja-throwing star. TSA takes pictures of these items and accompanies them with funny captions to warn people not to bring these things to the airport. The account currently has more than a million followers. Jurkovac adds that no one would think that TSA could make breakthrough content, but they do.

This is a testament to the fact that as long as you create unique content that delivers relevant truths to viewers, you can be successful. If you make people feel a connection with your brand, consumers will choose your products and services over others.

DON'T TIE YOUR YOGURT BRAND TO A MAN'S DECEASED WIFE: THE IMPORTANCE OF BRANDED UTILITY

Ernest Lupinacci, of Ernest Industries, explains that he really liked Google's Super Bowl commercial "Loretta," which you can watch here: www .brendanjkane.com/loretta. "Loretta" is about a man who has clearly lost his wife but is able to reconnect with her through pictures that Google Assistant finds for him. Lupinacci believes that the ad speaks to the fact that "oftentimes our memories outlive the people, places, or things that we remember." Lupinacci loves that the ad is not using "borrowed interest," meaning it doesn't attempt to merely entertain viewers with a reference to popular culture. For example, this is not a commercial that strains to link remembering a deceased love one with yogurt (which would not make much sense to most people). Instead, Google's ad has an authentic reason to engage in a conversation about love, loss, memory, and nostalgia.

Focusing on branded utility, or how your products and services are useful and meaningful to your customers, should be one of your main focuses when coming up with Hook Points and telling stories. It helps you provide more value and accelerates demand for your brand. As Lupinacci likes to say, "Brand is the reward you get for keeping the promises you've made." So, use marketing to establish the promises you make, and demonstrate how you've kept those promises.

HOW TO BUILD A MULTIMILLION-DOLLAR T-SHIRT BRAND

My friend Zech Francis created a very successful T-shirt line called Society that got into a huge retail chain called Buckle. I asked him how he made his product line stand out. He explained that his office was located within the largest T-shirt print factory in North America, which allowed him to design, print, and ship new T-shirt designs to the Buckle executives overnight. The speed at which he could address requests really impressed the Buckle team. Executives could get on the phone, ask him to change any aspect of his designs, and receive the shipment with new samples the very next day—which is unheard of in the fashion world. This high level of service made Francis more appealing to work with. In fact, after everything he learned from Society, in 2018 he launched another brand with Buckle called Dibs. Dibs experienced the fastest brand growth in Buckle's 50-year retail history—it went from zero dollars in revenue to seven figures in sales in less than 45 days.

Figure out how you can provide value with your products or services. Think about the extra value you can offer to make your brand stand out.

DEATH TO COLD OUTREACH; LONG LIVE COLD OUTREACH

Sometimes the best way to understand how to do something is to understand how *not* to do it, so let's start there. Following are some examples of poor cold outreach. These examples do not focus on what the other person needs or on providing them with value. They're all written from the standpoint of what the sender needs.

This person tries to disguise this message as providing value, but it's only self-serving:

The first sentence in the next example is all about what *he* wants. I already have engineers; he has no clue about my business because he hasn't taken the time to do the research. This is obviously stock content:

How is this valuable to me? I'm not in health care. Again, they did no research on me:

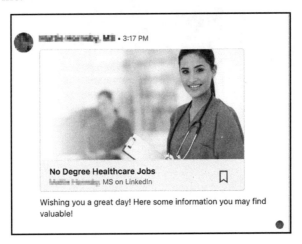

"Greetings Potential Investor" is a horrible introduction. I have no clue who this guy is, and he's already pitching me on investing? I stopped reading after I saw this line:

Why would I go to this meeting? Where's the incentive for me?

I don't even play golf:

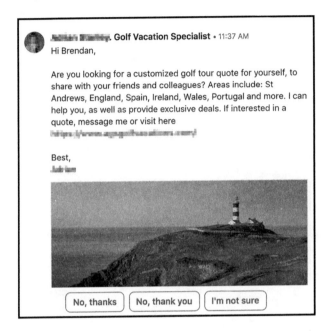

As you can see in all of the examples above, these people haven't done the research on their prospects. They haven't thought about the person or the business they're reaching out to. They've only thought about themselves and how *they* can receive value. Please don't do this. Rather, do your research, and figure out how to offer value to whomever you're reaching out to.

To secure new business, it's better to try and learn what others are up to and offer ideas specifically tailored to their needs. It would be more beneficial if these people approached me and said, "Hey, your company's really cool. I'd love to learn more about it and see if there's a way I can generate business for you. What are you guys up to?" If they showed interest in my company and had a specific way to drive growth, it would help build a relationship that could potentially lead to us working together.

Again, don't use LinkedIn or email as a tool to harass your contacts—you won't get good results. Instead, be strategic—think about how you can use these tools to connect, build relationships, and provide value.

An example of an effective cold outreach email that I received on LinkedIn was:

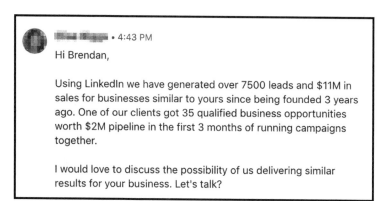

This company gave me tangible evidence of the success they had with other clients and appears to be focused on how they can help me achieve similar results. This email got me to respond.

Through the use of cold outreach, I've personally closed deals with Disney, Xbox, and Fox, which generated more than $15 million in business. I simply used the tools I've shared with you throughout this book to send effective messages to the right people.

The approach I take is to think about how I can provide the most value to the contacts I'm reaching out to. I think about their pain points and how I can help solve them. I don't focus on *selling* my service, but instead on how I can provide *value* with my service. It may seem like a small distinction, but it makes all the impact in the world.

When I sent a cold outreach message to an executive who worked at Disney, which led to a sizable business partnership, I wrote about *her* value and all the amazing work *she* was doing. I also added that I could save her a bunch of money on YouTube advertising and significantly increase performance on all the campaigns Disney was running. The email I sent was completely positioned on helping Disney achieve more success.

Here's an example of how it was structured:

Hi, [person's name],

I first want to say congrats on all of your success at [company name]. What you were able to achieve with [cite a specific project, product, or campaign] is truly remarkable.

Because you're an expert in the digital field, I wanted to let you know about a new tech platform we've launched that provides exact data on what all of your competitors are spending on social channels, along with insights on their past performance. It also provides deep data on which videos visitors view before and after watching a competitor's video, as well as on which social platforms they viewed the video.

The intriguing part of the platform is that all of this data can then be mined and used to increase the quality score of your own videos, which in return drops the cost per view of your own campaigns and increases the organic virality of the video. The best part of the platform is that it is 100 percent transparent and can save you up to [insert impressive statistic] on your paid media campaigns, while also increasing your performance by [insert impressive statistic].

We're currently using this new technology with [list client names]. Because you're always on the cutting edge of digital, I wanted to forward this info along, as I thought it might be helpful. I would be happy to introduce you to my company's CEO if you're interested in learning more.

Best,

Brendan Kane

Again, this email focuses on providing this executive with value. I highlight her achievements and explain how my product can help her achieve more. I offer to make her job easier and show her the value of using the service. Also, I add further value by offering to introduce her directly to the CEO (my role at the time was as an adviser to the company).

Now, variations of that email didn't secure new business with everyone I sent it to, which at the time was around 20 people. And prior to this batch, I'd tested different variations of messages like this one to see which tweaks could increase performance. If I'd received no responses from the message above after sending it to 20 people, I would have modified it before sending it to the next 20. But luckily, the one person from the one company who did respond helped generate millions of dollars in business. Spending the time to craft and send these cold outreach messages was obviously worth my time—all I had to do was think about the pain points and needs of the person on the other side of the table.

In-boxes are constantly filled with spam, which is why it's critically important to have a strong Hook Point and a strong value proposition. It's the only way to differentiate yourself so that the person you want to reach actually opens the email in the first place.

ROCK CLIMBING, SNOWBOARDING,
AND ADVENTURES IN CONTENT MARKETING

Latham Arneson, former vice president of digital marketing at Paramount Pictures, reminds us that information is by far one of the best and most important pieces of content marketing. It's human nature to want to learn new things—if you provide people with the value of acquiring knowledge, they may also want to buy the product you're selling.

Arneson loves the "experience letters" that outdoor clothing brand Patagonia publishes in their magazines. He gets to learn about new adventures that motivate him to plan trips into the wilderness. He also learns how people use Patagonia's products during the adventures, which makes him want to buy their clothing in preparation for his own.

You can provide knowledge around *any* product or service. A tax adviser could educate potential clients with tips on the best ways to manage their money throughout the year—the YouTube channel ClearValue Tax is a great reference. A yoga teacher could send out a newsletter with the specific benefits of various yoga poses or meditation practices. Ultimately, any type of business can use content marketing to create a relationship with potential and current customers.

GIVE AWAY YOUR BEST STUFF

Too many businesses operate out of the scarcity mindset that if they put out content for free, people won't want to pay for their products and services, when actually, the opposite is true—the more valuable the content you put out there, the more people will want to hire you or buy your product or service. You prove your value by letting people *experience* it. Entrepreneur Gary Vaynerchuk, for example, provides a lot of valuable information for free. In fact, he's built his entire brand by doing so. And the majority of free content he shares has substance—one time he gave away an 88-page document outlining his content strategy, for which he easily could have charged $1,500.

I'm not suggesting that you give everything away for free, but you do need to understand the stage of communication you're in with your audience. If it's early on in the process, you need to focus on building trust. You can't ask for money right away; you need to provide value first.

In the retail environment, people give away free products all the time. The whole purpose of giving out samples is to drive commerce by getting people to try products and fall in love with them. It's one of the reasons why companies like makeup subscription service IPSY are so successful. IPSY has a good Hook Point for both consumers and brands. The Hook Point for customers is that they get to try the latest hair, makeup, skincare, and fragrance products that come in the mail each month, while the Hook Point for brands is that they get their products into the hands of a large array of potential consumers, many of whom will ultimately turn into customers. This model provides a lot of value to all parties involved.

Even when giving speeches, Michael Breus, The Sleep Doctor, gives away valuable information that he hopes will be shared with others. At the end of the presentations during his speeches, he always says, "Hey, everybody, if you'd like a copy of my slides, text me your email address." This opens a door because people send him their email addresses, and then he sends them a Dropbox folder with slides in a PDF format. The slides include his bio, headshot, the different lectures he gives, the VIP services he provides, and a handout with general sleep guidelines and recommendations. This handout is valuable information that's easy to remember and share with others. By providing this value, Breus has received a number of new clients and opportunities.

The smartest companies give away a lot of their best stuff. If you truly help people, they'll come back and figure out a way to spend money with you. You gain their trust and open the door to a long-lasting relationship.

THE SECRET TO GENERATING FOUR BILLION VIEWS

Erick Brownstein of Shareability reminds us that in our new 3-second digital world, there's an unbelievable amount of content being distributed at all times. He thinks that now, more than ever, people need to realize that engagement metrics are much more important than views. He emphasizes, "Anybody can buy millions of views!" You have to create something that people want to engage with, share, and discuss with others, and it's essential that you think about what your viewers want.

Digital content strategist Naveen Gowda always tells his content producers to imagine a person who's just arrived to work and who's scrolling through their social feeds at 9:00 a.m. Then, he urges them to ask themselves, "What does that person need? What does my audience deem valuable, and what are their biggest pain points?" You can't effectively articulate value until you know your core audience and customers. Perhaps these people need five-minute breaks or a pick-me-up during the day. At that moment they're not searching for your brand's messaging; they're looking for something a little more creative (like the types of content ideas and formats noted in chapter 3).

Entrepreneur Roland Frasier and Jay Shetty (a content creator who creates viral wisdom videos that have garnered more than four billion views and who has over 24-plus million followers globally[67]), had a conversation on Frasier's podcast, *Business Lunch*. Since Shetty is one of the most viewed people on the internet internationally, Frasier asked him about shareability and the five themes that help content go viral. Shetty shared that the five themes are: adventure, comedy, emotion, inspiration, and surprise. He pointed out that virality is in direct correlation to how often a video is shared, and that people share a video not because it makes them think, but because it makes them feel. If you provide people with value by making them feel surprised, happy, amused, or inspired to do something new, they're more likely to share your video, and it will have a better chance of going viral.

Shetty believes that he has some of the most viewed videos on Facebook for three reasons:

1. The concepts are developed from real-life experience. Shetty comes up with video concepts from actual experiences or conversations he's had with others. The idea for one of his most shared videos came from a conversation with a 35-year-old who felt that it was too late to take risks and try new things in his life. Shetty recognized that this is a common feeling and decided to make a video to debunk this myth.

2. Shetty uses scientific studies to back up his concepts. He wants to present ideas that are credible and verifiable, so he always adds in data to support his messages.

3. He uses poetic and simplistic language to explain his concepts. Shetty points out that we remember lyrics more than prose.

---

[67] Jay Shetty, "My Story," 2020, https://jayshetty.me/.

Speaking poetically and with a cadence allows people to remember your videos and quote them to their friends.

(You can listen to the full discussion here: https://podcasts.apple.com/us/podcast/business-lunch/id1442654104?i=1000438001431.)

You can gauge how well your content is performing by observing people's responses to it—look at the comments they're making and how often they're sharing the content. This information is really great feedback about how much value you're providing. You can test different concepts, learn what provides the most value, and allow this information to inform your content strategy, both online and off.

LIONS, TIGERS, MANSIONS, AND LAMBORGHINIS—OH MY!

Expert copywriter Craig Clemens urges you to deliver value right away when developing digital content. Make yourself a source for unique information that people can't get anywhere else and that helps them lead better lives. It's all about having a differentiator that draws people in, provides them with value, and keeps them coming back for more.

It's one thing to stop people from scrolling, but if you want them to keep coming back to your page, you need to provide them with something valuable. Clemens cites Tai Lopez as an example of a creator who does this successfully. Lopez holds a lot of capital in the social media advertising space. He hooks people with pictures and videos of his Lamborghini and mansion. That is his Hook Point, but the value he provides is what keeps people around. He shares videos with the Hook Point, "You must read these books!" Then he teaches lessons from the books that people can use right away to grow their businesses or income. One of Lopez's catch phrases is: "Knowledge is better than college." It's super easy to remember and leads people to actions they can start implementing right away.

Give your audience actionable bites of information that can quickly improve their lives, and they'll keep coming back to receive them. Also, try to make them feel like a part of your brand family or your own personal following. That way they'll keep consuming your content and tell their friends about it. Remember, the more value you give, the more value you get.

Quick Tips and Recap

1. If a product or service doesn't provide value, it shouldn't exist.

2. If you focus on providing unique value to others, you will stand out and capture attention.

3. You can win new business through your genuine desire and ability to be helpful.

4. People pay for timely solutions to unrecognized needs. If you can spot those needs, you can paint a picture of what they're missing and price your products or services at a higher rate.

5. Business is founded upon relationships, so the ability to create and maintain them is important.

6. Connect with your audiences through emotion, humor, surprise, excitement, or education, and they'll be more likely to share your content at a higher rate.

7. Focusing on branded utility, or how your products and services are useful and meaningful to your customers, should be one of your main goals when coming up with Hook Points and telling stories.

8. Be strategic about how you use LinkedIn and cold outreach emails—connect, build relationships, and provide value rather than sell, sell, sell.

9. Use content marketing to develop your relationship with potential and current customers.

10. Deliver value right away in your online content—make yourself a source for unique information that people can't get anywhere else and that helps them lead better lives.

11. Five themes that make content shareable and help it go viral are: adventure, comedy, emotion, inspiration, and surprise.

12. Jay Shetty believes that his videos are among the most viewed on Facebook because his concepts are developed from real-life experiences, he uses scientific studies to support his concepts, and he explains them with poetic and simplistic language.

13. The more value you give, the more value you get.

CHAPTER 8

FROM HOOK TO SCALE: THE SECRET TO $1.6 BILLION IN 48 MONTHS

ONCE YOU'VE BUILT an effective business and marketing strategy that uses clear Hook Points and stories, you'll most likely reach a point where you want to scale. Providing your customers with value will inevitably help you grow, but oftentimes the hardest part is getting in front of the right audiences with potential customers. Going to where traffic already exists, finding Super Connectors (which I'll explain later on in this chapter), leveraging referrals, and combining online and offline marketing efforts are surefire ways to help you scale, and this is exactly what we'll cover in this chapter.

DON'T START FROM SCRATCH! GO WHERE THE TRAFFIC ALREADY EXISTS

Many of the smartest and most successful companies have grown at a rapid rate because they knew how to capitalize on audiences that were already built. For example, YouTube sold their company to Google for $1.65

billion in less than two years by harnessing Myspace's traffic.[68] At the time, Myspace didn't have a video player built in to their platform. YouTube recognized this fact and was one of the first companies to create a video embed code that was compatible with Myspace. Myspace users took YouTube's embed codes and put them on their profiles. Whether it was a music video, a movie trailer, or their own user-generated content, when their social connections saw the videos on their friends' profiles, they wanted to follow suit. When users clicked on a video, they were sent to YouTube's website, where they could upload their own videos or grab an embed code to put on their Myspace profile. The fact that YouTube harnessed Myspace's built-in audience and traffic helped the business scale rapidly, and the growth made them attractive to Google. Instagram leveraged a similar model, building a user base quickly off of Facebook's traffic.

Another good example is the existing traffic I harnessed by building relationships with bloggers. Back when I worked at the movie studio Lakeshore Entertainment, I observed that film bloggers had a lot of power (and traffic) that we could harness for our marketing campaigns. At the time, many of the studios weren't treating bloggers with the same respect as other media outlets, such as *Entertainment Tonight* or traditional newspapers. However, I saw the untapped opportunity in working with bloggers—their websites were receiving a lot of traffic, and they had the ability to market Lakeshore's movies to thousands of film buffs. With this in mind, I reached out to foster relationships with them.

---

[68] Matt Marshall, "They did it! YouTube bought by Google for $1.65B in less than two years," *Venture Beat, Oct. 9, 2006,* https://venturebeat.com/2006/10/09/they-did-it -youtube-gets-bought-by-gooogle-for-165b-in-less-than-two-years/.

To provide value to these bloggers, Lakeshore hosted parties where bloggers could interact with movie stars and industry people. One of the most successful parties was sponsored by Lakeshore at Comic-Con and was called "The Wrath of Con." Movie bloggers had been hosting the party for a couple years, but it was still small, with only around 50 attendees. At the time, Lakeshore had a small independent movie called *Pathology* that we didn't have a big budget to promote. To get the bloggers to help us promote the film, we gave them money to throw a bigger party and invited the stars of the film: Milo Ventimiglia (currently on the TV series *This Is Us*) and Alyssa Milano. That year the party grew a ton, and with larger sponsors every year, it eventually turned into one of the biggest parties at Comic-Con.

Investing in the party helped build relationships with the bloggers because they were given access to stars and people they wanted to write exclusive content about (which has now become a common practice in the film industry). From then on, they were more inclined to market Lakeshore's films on their blogs, which put them in front of the eyeballs of many potential moviegoers, quickly and cheaply. It was a win-win situation for both sides.

You can do something similar in *your* industry. Think about where viable traffic exists to promote your products and services. Once you uncover a few places, if appropriate, think about how you can provide value to these traffic drivers.

You can also harness traffic from the more general places where everyone is going. Entrepreneur Gary Vaynerchuk says, "The new NBC, ABC, and Fox are Facebook, Instagram, and Snapchat." People's eyeballs are there, so those are the best places to buy media and to get in front of potential customers.

Expert copywriter Craig Clemens also recommends diversifying and testing various traffic sources. In addition to social media sites, his company often tests traffic from HuffPost, TMZ, and other news sites. However, Clemens cautions that because everyone's eyeballs are generally in the same place, it's easier to find people than it is to grab their attention, which is why the use of a really strong Hook Point is so important.

A SCALABLE TRAFFIC SOURCE TO TEST YOUR HOOK POINTS

Social media advertising platforms provide traffic at scale that allows you to test and learn quickly. You can test to find which Hook Points provide success for awareness, lead generation, email list building, e-commerce conversions, and follower growth. You will quickly know the quality of your message by how effective it is at drawing people in and getting them to click on your content.

HOW I LEVERAGED EXISTING TRAFFIC TO GENERATE UPWARD OF 200,000-PLUS NEW INSTAGRAM FOLLOWERS IN A MONTH

I used existing traffic sources to grow my Instagram page to one million followers at a very rapid pace. I generated upward of 200,000-plus followers in a single month and sometimes upward of 75,000-plus followers in a single day. My Instagram growth strategy was to distribute content out onto other Instagram accounts that had significant follower bases to get in front of their audiences and drive traffic back to my page. I tested content extensively to see which Hook Points were strong enough to drive viewers back to my channel so I could get them to opt in and follow the account.

To ensure the content was strong enough—prior to promoting it at scale on various pages—I used one of my partner's accounts, which has more than four million followers. I would test various Hook Points and content formats to see which ones most effectively grabbed people's attention and caused them to go to my account and click the "Follow" button. I would measure the response to determine the effectiveness of each piece of content and test until I found the strongest variation. Then, once I was sure it was working, I'd distribute the winning variation of content on between seven and ten different partner accounts, each of whom had millions of followers.

(For more information on this process, check out my Rapid Audience Growth Course: https://www.rapidaudiencegrowth.com/.)

GET ONSTAGE! HOW SPEAKING ENGAGEMENTS DRIVE BUSINESS

The Sleep Doctor, Michael Breus, does a lot of speaking gigs. He does them not only because they're lucrative, but also because every time he gives a lecture (in front of hundreds and in some cases thousands of people), it's an opportunity to garner new business that might come in the form of an endorsement deal, a future speech, or a new patient. Breus structures his lectures so that people in the audience identify with the services he provides. In his lecture "The Exhausted Executive," he gives tips, hacks, and inside information all framed in two or three case studies that allow the majority of audience members to feel represented.

For example, he may have a case study about John, who's 45 years old and reports feeling a high level of exhaustion every morning. He drinks a little alcohol, has been gaining weight, and doesn't exercise as much as he'd like. Currently, he wakes up three to four times a night. Breus creates these types of profiles or avatars through which he can display information. If audience members identify with the case studies, they're more likely to ask questions during the Q&A sessions he does at the end of his talks, which represent his true opportunity for sales.

During these Q&A sessions, audience members generally ask two types of questions—personal questions or curiosity questions. When someone asks him a personal question, Breus will generally respond, "Do me a favor and meet with me afterward, because I'd like to talk with you about that privately." If he gets four or five of those types of questions, he has four or five potential new clients.

MEET YOUR GATEKEEPERS

Breus was interviewed 241 times in 2018. Some months he was doing up to 20 interviews. He secured the majority of these interviews by sending out a journalists-only newsletter each month to all those in the media who'd interviewed him in the past. In the newsletter he sends research about sleep, and pitches Hook Points for their articles or TV shows. After ten years of list building, he has access to more than 650 journalists in every major media outlet in the world. He doesn't need a publicist, because he goes straight to the source. He's built solid relationships with those who can help him the most.

SUPER CONNECTORS

To scale your business in the offline world, you need to look for what I call Super Connectors—people who are well connected to those whom you want to do business with. (Yes, I'm aware that there's a book called *Superconnector*, and my definition is a bit different, but this is the best term for what I want to teach you.) You go to Super Connectors because they have relationships with people who are typically hard to access.

You need to find the people in your industry who have the power to connect you with potential partners, high-paying clients, traffic sources, or customers. If you're just starting out in your career, or are simply not a skilled networker, Super Connectors are amazing assets. One well-respected person can make dozens of introductions. I personally use this strategy because I am naturally an introvert—it's great for anyone who dreads the idea of having to constantly go out and meet new people. One really important Super Connector for me was the MTV executive I did licensing deals with for my technology platforms. He opened the door to opportunities with Taylor Swift, *Vice* magazine, Snoop Dogg, Michael Strahan, and more (discussed in detail in chapter 1).

SUPER CONNECTORS CAN IMPROVE YOUR PRODUCTS

John Kilcullen, the creator of the *For Dummies* book series, thinks that a major part of the success of this series can be attributed to the talented writers who were brought on by Waterside Productions literary agent Bill Gladstone (who also happens to be *my* agent). Kilcullen said that finding great writers was essential, and Gladstone had access to a lot of them. He became the gatekeeper and broker for finding writers who were not only excellent explainers but who also had a comedic sensibility.

Gladstone, however, was not the only Super Connector who helped the series thrive. Kilcullen had met Eric Tyson playing basketball on a street in San Francisco, and he would eventually become the author of *Personal Finance for Dummies*. They got to know each other through casual conversation, and then Kilcullen brought him in to talk to his colleagues and employees. Tyson happened to be teaching a class for UC Berkeley's Extension program about personal finance, so they asked him to write the book. Later on, they discovered that Tyson had a relationship with investor Charles Schwab, who ended up writing the foreword.

Kilcullen feels that the series grew through the presence of great collaborators. It wasn't built by just one person—they had a great team. You never know who may end up becoming instrumental to your business's development, so be open, kind, and take the time to listen to everyone you meet. They may open doors for referrals or for new ways to build traffic.

THE TRUE VALUE OF A CELEBRITY FOR YOUR BRAND

Alex Livian is the cofounder of LMS Inc., a modern-day distribution company that builds brands online. LMS uses the most advanced paid-media growth strategies, with a heavy focus on building brands with high-profile influencers. One of LMS's most impressive clients is soccer player Cristiano Ronaldo, and his underwear brand, CR7, for whom they're the exclusive distributors in North America. Ronaldo currently has the largest Instagram following on the platform, with more than 205 million followers. This is more than Kim Kardashian, Taylor Swift, The Rock, and Ariana Grande have! Due to his mass-market appeal, Livian has leveraged Ronaldo's existing brand instead of creating one from scratch, which has helped him scale rapidly.

Livian chose to distribute Ronaldo's CR7 brand because of the preestablished trust the soccer player has built with his fans. If, instead, Livian had started a line from scratch, he would have had to push harder to make the brand known in the public eye. When you work with an existing brand, you fast-track the marketing process because of the relationships the influencer has already built.

Although the pros outweigh the cons, Livian says there are some potential disadvantages to working with celebrities. You need to choose those whom you trust because there's always the risk that they can form a negative image in the public eye, which can in turn hurt your brand and sales. Livian cites how when celebrities are involved in a scandal or are looked down upon in the public eye, brands that are associated with them often have to back away to avoid putting the brand's reputation in jeopardy as well.

Also, when you attach your brand to one person, you increase the risk of having your image spoiled by that person's actions, so choose wisely. Luckily, Ronaldo has been a safe choice for Livian. In addition to being considered a god in the soccer community, Ronaldo has proven his mass-market appeal through his massive social following. Tapping into this loyal following has significantly lowered Livian's cost per acquisition of new customers.

When you partner with big influencers or celebrities, you also need to make sure they have an authentic connection with your product. If they don't, it won't help your marketing tactics. For example, Livian says that when he sees Shaq in a Buick commercial, he thinks, *The guy can't even fit in the car, and yet he's the spokesman for the car . . . it doesn't make sense.* Whereas when he sees George Clooney in a Casamigos tequila commercial, he feels that it works because Clooney has a suave personality that resonates with viewers, so the Casamigos brand matches his persona. The pairing makes sense. If you can pair with the right people, whom people trust, they will likely have faith in your product immediately.

If done right, working with celebrities can be a great way to scale your business quickly. It lowers your cost per acquisition and can fast-track the marketing process. You just have to make sure you choose wisely when attaching your company and product to someone else's name.

THE POWER OF REFERRALS AND HOW TO LEVERAGE THEM TO GROW YOUR BUSINESS

Peter Park, the owner of Platinum Fitness, hardly does any traditional marketing for his business. To date, all his clients, including his celebrity and billionaire clients, have come via word-of-mouth advertising. Park explains that many of his clients (especially those that are all-star athletes or CEOs) value their privacy and don't want the general public to know what they're up to. To protect and maintain trust with his clients, Park is cautious about how he uses social media and other newer forms of advertising. Park and I have become friends, and now, every time we talk, I learn about a new celebrity client I had no idea he trained. It organically comes up in casual conversation, and he never boasts or brags, which is another reason why top A-listers love him.

Park has some big referral sources for his business, including Dr. Chris Renna (another Super Connector), who is one of the top doctors in the world. Dr. Renna, along with three or four other physicians, send Park a lot of clients. To the people these doctors refer, they usually say, "If you want to get in shape, Peter's the best. He's really professional. You can learn more about his philosophy in his book." And because these doctors are some of the world's top medical professionals, their patients trust them and therefore inherently trust Park.

Park's referrals also come from the results he obtains for his clients. You gain new clients by living up to your word and delivering on your promises to your current clients. When Park helps people lose 30 pounds or strengthens their backs so they can pick up their kids for the first time in years, he's changed their lives. That joy and gratitude turns into testimonials, and those testimonials turn into referrals.

My father, Jim Kane, explains that the majority of new business at his former law firm (one of the oldest and most respected in Chicago) also came from referrals. Attorneys had to go out and find new clients, and many of them would join organizations related to their field of expertise so they could network. Connections were key.

My dad had an advantage because he'd worked for a former mayor of Chicago and a former governor of Illinois. Mayors and governors are always involved in major transactions within their municipalities or states, so gaining their confidence in his ability gave my father leads on potential clients. You can never underestimate the importance of relationships in developing new business.

Having relationships with important people related to your industry can help you scale, so try to gain the trust of one or two Super Connectors so they can refer business to you. If you focus your effort and energy on the right people, you'll scale faster.

CAUTION: STEADY SCALE AHEAD

When doctors refer people to Peter Park, they cite *him* as the expert and not his business, Platinum Fitness. But this has created a problem for Park.

He has too many clients and can't take on all of them himself, which is why he has built a world-class team to help him. Unfortunately, though, when referrals hear Park's name, they don't necessarily want to work with a member of his team—they want to work with him personally—limiting the success and scalability of his company.

I've been working with Park to reposition his message. Now, when someone gives him a referral, he expresses the value of his entire team. I've coached him to change his story to emphasize the fact that he works with a *team of specialists*, all of whom focus on a specific area. If someone is struggling with back issues, there's an expert on his team for that; if it's a knee issue, another person handles that area of expertise. Organizing his team in this way helps shift the Hook Point from "Park is the best in the world" to "Park's *team* is the best in the world," which will help his business scale more efficiently.

Think about how *you* are positioning yourself when you create your Hook Points and stories. Make sure they're scalable for the long-term future of your business. Thinking ahead will help you grow more efficiently.

TARGET BEYOND YOUR DEMOGRAPHIC

When leveraging paid advertising, the most common strategy is to hyper-target your advertising content to the specific niche audience that is most likely to purchase your products or services. When it comes to organic social media, however, many times it's smart to focus on a content strategy that goes extremely broad, which will eventually connect you to your niche audience.

When digital content strategist Naveen Gowda was designing social content at First Media, his team was going after huge wins. So instead of simply targeting fans of DIY craft projects, for example, they worked on designing their content for a much broader audience. They did so because of how the algorithms work (as explained in detail in chapter 3). Reaching a broader audience allowed their videos to generally gain between 30 million and 100 million views. In that way, they didn't only hit their core audience, but they also captured new audience members who wouldn't have seen their content otherwise.

The high level of interest in these videos allowed First Media to evolve the structure of the brand, expanding their audience beyond babies and millennial moms to millennial women and other verticals. Reaching a wider audience gave the business new possibilities. In two and a half years, they went from being a digital team of only three people to one of more than 55 people who were generating approximately three billion views a month.

When first launching social paid advertising campaigns, I generally recommend targeting a *wide* audience and letting the data reveal your *true* audience. I discuss the social media-targeting process in detail in my first book, *One Million Followers* (www.onemillionfollowers.com), which you can read more about; but for now, just know that there may be audiences you never dreamed would be interested in your product, and you can use social platforms to test and discover your ideal customers.

THE REVERSE OF 1,000 TRUE FANS

In Kevin Kelly's book, *1000 True Fans*, he outlines the idea that you only need 1,000 true fans who will pay you $100 each to gain $100,000 a year. He recommends building this audience slowly over time so that you're certain these people will buy your products or services. Although I respect the concept and think there's value in it, I want to explain why I take a different approach.

I started out in the entertainment industry, where reaching an audience of 1,000 people is way too small to provide a return on investment. If I walked into a meeting with a concept that would only reach 1,000, or even 10,000, people, I'd be fired. I had to show up with ideas for reaching millions of people in the shortest possible amount of time.

As a result, my mind has been trained to think big when it comes to potential audience size. When promoting a movie (other than a sequel), you have to build a brand in less than a few months. Those brands cannot survive on a mere 5,000 or even 10,000 people. You have to reach 20, 30, 50, or 100 *million* people in a very short period of time.

My background in the entertainment industry trained me to quickly reach huge amounts of potential consumers in very short time frames. I think that knowing how to do so provides people from any industry with a unique opportunity. Whether you're an author, a writer, a chef, or an athlete, knowing how to reach the masses helps.

Recently, I looked at the social media accounts of the world's top chefs. Many of the really big ones, even Wolfgang Puck, have fewer than 215,000 Instagram followers (at the time of writing this chapter). For Instagram, this is not a huge number, but it's a large number for the culinary world. Imagine a chef with 300,000 to 350,000 followers—this person would stand out in that niche industry. People who are outliers because of their large audience sizes attract attention. They can leverage a larger-than-average audience size to gain new opportunities, brand deals, appearances on podcasts, and spots on television shows.

Again, there's tremendous value in having 1,000 true fans; it's a great accomplishment that can help your business. But by having the largest possible exposure, you're more likely to find your 1,000 true fans quicker in addition to larger offline opportunities. I grew one million followers in 30 days so I could go as wide and as loud as possible. I knew that not all one million would be true, dedicated fans who would buy something from me; that wasn't the point. The point was leveraging the hook (zero to one million followers in 30 days) to get onto podcasts, speaking stages, and television shows; and to build strategic partnerships that would give me even more exposure, accelerating my path to 1,000 true fans—and even more.

I urge you, too, to think as big as possible. What kind of opportunities would be life changing for your career? How can you use your audience size to expose yourself to potential change makers? In other words, go as big and loud as possible so you can grab the attention of more of the right people who can make impactful changes in your career trajectory.

SCALE BY COMBINING ONLINE AND OFFLINE EFFORTS

There are many ways to merge your online and offline presence to further fuel brand awareness, drive massive growth, and create meaningful opportunities. If you effectively combine your offline and online presences, which I explain below, you can truly scale and create a long-lasting brand:

Social Numbers for Offline Validation

Anyone trying to release content recognizes that a large social following, if authentic, is a validation metric. It causes people to pay attention to you. People will more likely want to look at your content if masses of others are already doing so. It's human nature.

Build your audience as widely and quickly as possible so you can use it as a validation and credibility metric. This will help you stand out, because only a small percentage of people can achieve it. That in itself will become a Hook Point for you. It might not be the hook you lead with—that hook is likely related to what you actually do in your business. But whether you're a doctor, an author, an actor, or a writer, a large social following will cause people to pay attention to you and absorb your core messages.

How I Turned My Social Audience into Offline Opportunities

As you know, I generated one million Facebook followers in 30 days and then figured out how to reach one million Instagram followers in a very short period of time. A lot of people find that fascinating, and it helps me stand out. I've used the hook of that achievement, which took place online as a story I've told offline. It has helped me fuel attention, awareness, education, and inspiration.

As you're probably aware, building a large following presents revenue-generating opportunities through brand partnerships and influencer deals, and also builds business relationships with your brand. Social platforms' advertising capabilities can also be leveraged to generate leads for potential clients and to directly sell your products and services online at scale. But what I find even more interesting than the online opportunities these platforms provide is the fact that once people begin engaging with your content, or buying your products and services online, you can take that momentum and transfer it to significant opportunities offline.

You can take your online following and use it as a leverage point to get strategic partnerships, deals, and to get people to take you more seriously. One clear example is actress Sophie Turner (best known for her role as

Sansa Stark on the HBO series *Game of Thrones*), who admits that she was once chosen for a role over another actress she considers "far better" because Turner has a larger social following.[69]

Personally, I leveraged the story about my accomplishments online to secure a literary agent, which allowed me to acquire a publishing deal. Suddenly, I had a physical product in the offline world that was created because of what I did in the online world. Then I went back to the online world and used my social platforms to sell my book. From there, I leveraged the Hook Point of my large social following—and the fact that I wrote a book about it—to secure speaking engagements on stages around the world. I spoke at prestigious events hosted by IKEA, Mindvalley, and Web Summit (which has an audience of more than 70,000 people).

The fact that I had a good Hook Point, a published book, and several speaking engagements under my belt gave me the opportunity to appear on well-known podcasts with large followings around the world. This exposed me to even more audiences, and I reached still more people with my message. Then, this led to opportunities to appear in media outlets such as Fox Business, SiriusXM, KTLA, Yahoo! Finance, and more, which gave me even more clout and exposed my brand to still more people.

Do you see how each step both online and offline created a snowball effect to continue the growth of my brand? I took the story of my large social audience and established myself in other offline mediums, which you can also do. Whether you have 1,000,000 or 10,000 followers, don't limit yourself to thinking about that following in terms of direct revenue

---

[69] John Lynch, "'Game of Thrones' star Sophie Turner says she beat out a 'far better actress' for a job because she has millions of social followers," *Business Insider, Aug. 2, 2017,* https://www.businessinsider.com/game-of-thrones-star-sophie-turner-says-she-got-role -due-to-social-media-following-2017-8.

or brand deals. People will take you more seriously because of your social credibility, so leverage it. You can widen your opportunities to obtain strategic partnerships and deals offline, which will likely lead to larger deals and revenue potential than if you were to solely focus online.

Take an Offline Brand and Grow It Online

This process can also work in reverse. One recent example is the work I'm doing with Michael Breus, The Sleep Doctor. As mentioned previously, Breus has built a tremendous offline brand. He's spoken at many events and has appeared on many television shows, including *The Oprah Winfrey Show*, the *Today* show, and *The Dr. Oz Show*. However, despite this tremendous exposure and success, he hasn't had a similar level of growth online.

As noted earlier, at speaking events, Breus collects email addresses to find potential clients at the end of each talk. However, after years on the speaking circuit, he's only acquired a few thousand emails. When we met, I shared that in the online space, that number of email addresses can be acquired in just one or two days. We're currently working to take his Hook Points and all the data he's collected offline to fuel his growth online. This will allow his online and offline exposure to work together to grow his brand and business.

You can also take your best-performing offline Hook Points and push them to people online. You can reach hundreds of thousands of potential customers online within days, and if they resonate with your content, they'll provide you with their names and email addresses. For example, one of The Sleep Doctor's Hook Points that we discussed earlier is, "What is the perfect time to have sex before going to bed?" Breus can make a video that answers this question and push it to more than a million people through the social-testing strategies I outlined in my first book, *One Million Followers*. By offering this engaging content for free, he will acquire thousands of names and email addresses. From there, he can leverage this new email distribution list amassed online for further revenue opportunities (e.g., online courses, sponsorships, book promotions, and workshops).

This is just one example of what can happen when you learn how to make online and offline exposure work together. Instead of solely focusing on building your business offline or growing online, look at how these two engines can fuel each other. Leverage your growth in both spaces cohesively to drive massive growth.

Test Your Stories Offline

My goal in achieving one million followers was to allow me to have offline conversations. Although I could have immediately leveraged the following for brand deals and other revenue opportunities, I felt that the digital space was already very crowded, with lots of influencers. I wanted to have a stronger hook. I wanted to differentiate myself and felt that leveraging the following more strategically for offline opportunities would drive more potential growth and scale for my brand.

With that said, recently I've looked into hiring someone to obtain brand deals for me to see how I can specifically leverage them online. Again, you can make money directly from your following, and some influencers make millions of dollars through their online interactions. If that's your goal, I hope you do the same. However, I urge you to look at the broader picture. It's really exciting that you can take what you build online and amplify your message, grow your brand, and create unique opportunities for scale, both offline and online.

Mine Podcasts for Big Opportunities

My appearance on the podcast *Finding Mastery: High Performance Psychology with Michael Gervais* presents another example of combining offline opportunities with online awareness. This highly successful podcast has a large audience, so my appearance allowed me to close a significant amount of revenue—executives at several large companies who listen to the podcast reached out to hire me.

To acquire these new clients, I used the process of combining online and offline efforts. I leveraged the book (an offline item) and the Hook Point of gaining one million followers (an online strategy) during a meeting that came through an introduction from a friend (an offline interaction) to get on the podcast (online), which got me work (offline) through exposure to a large audience (online)—some of whom reached out to work with me (both online and offline). Okay, that's a mouthful—I hope you're not too confused. But the point is that combining online and offline efforts works! Can you start to see how the online and offline worlds meet, interact with, and support each other? In this example, offline and online interactions are constantly being leveraged back and forth to enhance one another and create opportunities. It all starts with having an interesting Hook Point and story that you can leverage across different mediums. That way you can diversify your audience and grow your brand recognition.

HOW TO LAND YOUR FIRST PODCAST APPEARANCE

You can take several approaches to appear on your first podcast. One way is to hire a publicist. Publicists generate and manage publicity, and in addition to finding podcasts, they can find radio, television, and print opportunities. But make sure to do your research. Choose someone who won't lock you into a long-term contract (you want to test out this person to see if he or she can actually deliver), whom you enjoy working with, and who understands your brand.

Another way to get on a podcast is to hire a company that specializes in finding podcast opportunities for potential interviewees. A company called Interview Valet focuses on podcast interview marketing. They can help place you on podcasts that are a good match. They'll also help you prepare for the interview and promote it on social media.[70] In my experience, however, companies such as these usually only place you on podcasts with audiences ranging from 1,000 to 40,000 downloads per episode rather than the top shows generating 100,000-plus downloads per episode. However, it's a great place to start.

(If you're looking for an introduction to Interview Valet, please email me at bkane@brendanjkane.com.)

Referrals from colleagues and friends have helped me land appearances on top-rated podcasts. Strategic introductions are always the easiest and best sources to leverage—not to mention, they're usually free. But if you don't yet have those types of relationships, you can either focus on identifying Super Connectors to help you, or on building a large audience to leverage for new potential connections and partnerships.

This brings us to the next way to gain podcast appearances—you can leverage a large social following to appear on podcasts or to build your own podcast. Podcasts need audiences. If you have a large social following, people will want to interview you to grow and expand their own networks.

Alternatively, you can create a podcast by attracting guests who want to be exposed to your following. Jay Shetty started out as a viral content

---

[70] Interview Valet, "About Us," 2020, https://interviewvalet.com/about-us/.

creator and leveraged his success to build a very successful podcast called *On Purpose with Jay Shetty*. He's had guests such as entrepreneur Gary Vaynerchuk; personal-transformation pioneer and integrative-medicine doctor Deepak Chopra; Grammy Award–winning singer Alicia Keys; Jordan Belfort, the author of *The Wolf of Wall Street*; reality TV star Khloe Kardashian; award-winning actresses Kate Bosworth (best known for *Superman Returns* and *Blue Crush*) and Eva Longoria (best known for her work on the TV series *Desperate Housewives*); and clothing designer Kenneth Cole. Inviting these people on his podcast has given Shetty clout and increases his ability to reach new audiences. He also makes strategic connections with the guests who may benefit him in the future. In turn, the guests, regardless of how large an audience they may already have, can pick up new fans as well.

The combination of having one million followers and the hook that I built it in, in less than 30 days, has landed me on a plethora of podcasts. When hosts see that I have one million followers, they realize that my social credibility warrants asking me to speak on their shows. They view it as beneficial for their growth on top of it being a great story that their audiences can engage with.

Once you've been on a few podcasts, other podcast hosts will start seeking you out. People who've heard me on podcasts reach out via LinkedIn with other podcast-appearance opportunities two or three times a week. Being on a few podcasts can lead to a snowball effect if you maximize every appearance and do a great job. When people hear how amazing you are, they'll begin to contact you.

When starting out, I recommend taking every podcast opportunity you can get. Regardless of the size of the podcast, I usually say yes to any appearance opportunity that comes my way—I'm open to the exposure each one provides. Even if I'm only talking to a hundred people, I think it's worth it. These appearances usually take only 20 or 30 minutes of my time and give me the chance to practice for bigger opportunities.

LANDING YOUR FIRST SPEAKING GIG

Before I tried to obtain a speaking gig, I hired a speaking coach. I take speaking very seriously and didn't want to go into it lightly. I'd seen the difference between trained and untrained speakers. Some think that charisma is enough, but successful speakers structure their speeches. They apply a methodology that makes them keynote worthy. Because I aspired to speak at the highest levels, I wanted to become an expert.

(If you'd like an introduction to my speaking coach, email me at bkane@ brendanjkane.com.)

When I felt confident, I started telling all my friends and colleagues that I was looking for speaking opportunities. A business partner introduced me to a few people who work in event planning. From that meeting, I was introduced to IKEA and had the opportunity to speak and run a workshop with IKEA's creative global team in Sweden.

As is the case with podcasts, a snowball effect comes into play. The more speaking gigs you do—and perform well at—the more referrals you'll receive. If people see that you deliver a good speech, they'll want to hire you to speak at their events. In addition, many audience members may be potential clients/customers.

At your first speaking gig, connect with the other speakers in the green room. These people are always a great resource for referrals for other speaking opportunities. For example, I met Michael Breus, The Sleep Doctor, at a speaking event, and now he refers me to additional events.

Again, referrals are always the best and easiest way to find new opportunities, but you can also hire a manager. I signed with a manager who represents me to scale the number of paid speaking gigs I do in a year. Not everyone is in the position to secure a manager, but you can always do cold outreach yourself. Make a list of the people in your field who are paid to speak. Go to their websites and take a look at events where they're speaking, and the dates. Then pitch yourself to the events on that list.

You probably won't get paid for your first speaking event—unless you're a big celebrity, already have a well-known brand, or are an expert in something very specific. Most likely you'll start out speaking at events for free, which will then eventually lead to paid opportunities. In my case, the gig at IKEA was paid, but again, it came through a strategic introduction. However, even after that, when I was just starting out, I spoke at many unpaid events to build up my credibility and speaking reel.

To acquire more speaking opportunities, I also leverage the fact that I stand out because of my large social audience. I let event planners know that I can promote their events to my audience. Event planners always want to hear this; it's valuable to them.

At Web Summit, I took my digital advertising expertise a step further to provide value. With more than 70,000 attendees, Web Summit is one of the largest tech conferences in the world. When I met the event organizers, I'd done some research to find out how many people had viewed their top video, which had around one million views at the time. I told them I could beat that amount of views and then leveraged my advertising strategies outlined in *One Million Followers* to produce a video from the event that generated more than 1.2 million views.

This campaign for Web Summit allowed me to stand out from a credibility standpoint. The event organizers were extremely happy about the results because I provided value that no other speaker had previously chosen to provide. Doing so helped *me*, as well. I have since leveraged the case study about what I did for Web Summit to obtain other paid speaking opportunities. This case study shows event organizers what I can bring to the equation. Providing this value has given me the opportunity to speak all over the world. Even as I write this, I'm speaking at an event in Portugal.

APPEARING ON YOUR FIRST TELEVISION SHOW

I ended up on my first TV show through a relationship I'd cultivated for about ten years with a friend who has a show on Fox Business. I didn't foster that relationship because I wanted to get on this woman's show, nor did I ever think I would end up there, but that's how it happened.

All my other TV appearances have come through a publicist. Television has not been my main focus, but again, it's a matter of looking at the connections you already have, providing unique value, and leveraging your social audience. TV producers want people who already have audiences because they believe this will translate into more viewership. The amount of people tuning in matters. Leveraging your social validation and credibility will help you stand out and will increase your chances of landing on TV, which in turn will help your business scale.

Quick Tips and Recap

1. Don't try to create traffic for your products, services, and content from scratch—go where the traffic already exists.
2. Social media advertising platforms are a great scalable traffic source that allows you to test and learn at scale.

3. You can use existing traffic sources to grow your social following at a very rapid pace. I generated upward of 200,000-plus followers in a single month, and sometimes upward of 75,000-plus followers in a single day.

4. To scale your business in the offline world, you need to look for Super Connectors—people who are well connected to those you want to do business with.

5. Working with the *right* celebrities can fast-track your marketing process.

6. You never know who may end up becoming instrumental to your business's development, so be kind, open, and take the time to listen to everyone you meet.

7. Referrals and word-of-mouth advertising are some of the best and most effective ways to market your business.

8. Make sure your Hook Points are scalable for the long-term future of your business.

9. Go as big and as loud as possible so you can grab the attention of the right people who can make impactful changes in your career trajectory.

10. If you effectively combine your offline and online presences, you can scale more quickly and create a long-lasting brand.

CHAPTER 9

STANDING OUT AS WORLD CLASS, AND HOW TO GET SCARLETT JOHANSSON TO EAT HOT WINGS WITH YOU . . .

Now THAT YOU understand how to create Hook Points, tell compelling stories, build trust and credibility, listen, provide value, and scale your business, you're ready to attract prominent clients, close bigger deals, and survive high-level situations. The key to building and maintaining an impressive client roster is knowing how to make decisions that keep you top of mind and that help you stand out as world class, in seconds.

SELENA GOMEZ AND JIMMY FALLON CRY
WHILE EATING SPICY WINGS (*HOT ONES*)

You don't have to invent a new product or service to attract top-tier clientele—you just need to find innovative ways to package your products and/or services to make them more attractive. *Hot Ones*, created by

Christopher Schonberger, is a web series where celebrities are interviewed by host Sean Evans while eating a platter of increasingly spicy chicken wings. The Hook Point that draws people to this show is that the biggest celebrities eat the hottest wings in the world and have insane reactions to how hot they are during the interview. These wings are so hot that some guests have cried, others have thrown up, and comedian Bobby Lee even shat himself.[71] The show's tagline is: "The show with hot questions, and even hotter wings." Guests are asked a question after each chicken wing they eat, and if they're able to eat all ten of the wings, they get to promote the project they're working on at the time. Guests who fail to eat the wings are also afforded the opportunity to promote their projects . . . but they're added to the show's "Hall of Shame."

Hot Ones has featured major celebrity guests such as Scarlett Johansson, Shaq, Seth Meyers, John Mayer, Kevin Hart, and Natalie Portman; and there was even a live version of the show with Selena Gomez on *The Tonight Show Starring Jimmy Fallon*. Schonberger attracted this clientele by coming up with a novelty factor that made interviews more fun and unique. The Hook Point allowed him to stand out and attract world-class guests in a very crowded space.

Think about how *you* can take seemingly common products or services and give them a spin that makes them stand out. If you find ways to be innovative, it may help you more quickly attract the kinds of clients you've been dreaming about.

---

[71] Robert Anthony, "Bobby Lee Eats Hot Wings and Poops His Pants," *Elite Daily*, Oct. 27, 2016, https://www.elitedaily.com/envision/food/spicy-wings-eaten-guy-poops -pants/1673578.

OBTAINING AND MAINTAINING WORLD-CLASS CLIENTS

Top-tier clients can be difficult to reach, but if you have something of value to offer and you go about it in the correct way, they *are* obtainable. Many people are often impressed that I've worked with Taylor Swift, but what they don't realize is that it's not as difficult as often presumed to get a client like her. To reach someone of that stature, you just need an efficient strategy. I applied the strategy of reaching out to a Super Connector (outlined in the last chapter). If you want access to someone like Swift, you don't go to her directly. You have to reach out through the trusted circle around her and provide value to an individual within it. As I mentioned earlier, when I met Swift's manager, father, and mother, I provided them with value so I could attain the ultimate goal of working with *her*. If I'd gone straight to Swift, it wouldn't have worked because most likely she wouldn't have taken a meeting with someone without a trusted referral.

HELLO, CELEBRITY, DO YOU TRUST ME?

Once you're in the sphere of the high-profile people you want to work with, you need to focus on developing trust. Celebrities, CEOs, and billionaires often put up their guards to protect themselves from the many people who try to use them for their own personal gain. You'll stand out if you have a genuine conversation with them without trying to make a sale. If you simply listen and offer solutions to their problems and growth obstacles, they'll be more likely to want to work with you. The choice to provide valuable information and insights will put you light-years ahead of others who approach high-profile people.

Michael Breus adds that a lot of billionaires, millionaires, and celebrities work off of social credibility—not how many Facebook or Instagram followers you have, but the level of prestige in the articles you've written and your media appearances. He recommends that you maintain an up-to-date bio of yourself with your media coverage included so you can prove your social credibility quickly. Breus then leverages this credibility to perform cold outreach in order to connect with celebrities. For example, he'll look for news stories about celebrities who aren't sleeping well and contact them to offer assistance.

Breus usually writes something along the lines of, "Hey I'm a sleep specialist, and I'm not far away. I think I might know what's going on with you. I'd love to help you out at no charge." Nine times out of ten, the person will take the time to look him up and meet with him based on his proven track record. The best part is that once Breus has helped the person heal, he or she often talks about the great work Breus does, which generates even more business.

With billionaires, however, he moves a bit more slowly (albeit steadily). You never want to come across as though you're after high-profile people's money, so if Breus sees that a billionaire has a sleep-related issue, he won't reach out, saying, "Hey, let me fix your problem." Instead, to build rapport, he may send the person a couple of articles in which he's been featured that address the individual's specific problem. That's why being interviewed in newspapers, magazines, or journals that wealthy people read, such as *The Robb Report*, *Business Insider*, or the *Wall Street Journal*, is so helpful for lead generation—it helps establish credibility fast.

If people aren't reporting on the types of issues that you cover with your products or services, think about where celebrities and billionaires hang out and how you can get in front of them. For example, Breus works with the Young Presidents' Organization. A business has to gross more than $10 million a year to be invited into this club. When Breus gives a speech to these types of groups, he's putting himself directly in front of the population he wants to reach. Joining a country club or giving a lecture at an exclusive club helps you network, build new relationships, and garner business. These relationships also lead to referrals, which, in the long run, is the best strategy for reaching high-profile individuals.

So, develop strategies for reaching out to prominent people. Build trust with their inner circle, and put yourself in situations where you'll be seen by those you want to work with. If you're good at what you do, and honestly try to provide solutions with your products and services, you'll go far.

WHAT KEEPS A CEO UP AT NIGHT?

To prepare for a meeting with clients at a high level, Erick Brownstein of Shareability will ask himself, "What keeps the CEO up at night?" He's found that this is what successful consultants who work with huge companies think about—they try to discover the kinds of problems that CEOs want to fix. When in rooms with leaders of organizations, Brownstein will often ask, "As the leader of this company, what are your biggest priorities?" as well as "What are your biggest concerns?"

After some experience engaging with people at this level, Brownstein realizes that his CEO clients are probably not thinking, *How many views is our next viral video going to get?* but rather, *The world has gone digital, and we haven't. How can we be a significant player in this new world?* A CEO's concerns are extraordinarily different from those of directors of brand marketing who have set budgets and metrics by which they're measured. You need to take a very different approach when pitching yourself to each of these parties.

Recently, Brownstein was on a call with the chairman of a massive global conglomerate driving nearly $50 billion in revenue. To secure that meeting, Brownstein's Hook Point was: "I understand that you're focused on your company's involvement in raising awareness about climate change and the role that corporations play. We're working with the DiCaprio Foundation and several other big players who are also focused on that issue. I'd love to talk about how we could combine resources to have a bigger impact." The Hook Point above is very different from the one Brownstein would have used with a manager of one of the nearly 100 brands that this company owns. It's also much longer of a Hook Point than he would have used for promoting to the masses. (The Hook Point in this longer format works because it's targeted to one specific person and is being delivered directly.)

Communication must be tailored to each case. If Brownstein were speaking to a venture-backed start-up with a small budget, he'd communicate the lowest-cost option for his services that still provide real value. Information would be presented in a very different way than it would be to an established corporation with a multimillion-dollar budget that wants to undergo a digital transformation.

It all goes back to understanding your audience and their needs. Make sure you know whom you're targeting, put yourself in their shoes, and ask the right questions. This will help you provide the best service for each type of client.

OPRAH WINFREY STARTS EVERY MEETING
WITH THESE THREE QUESTIONS

Here are the three questions Oprah Winfrey asks: "What is our intention for this meeting?" "What's important?" and "What matters?" Brendon Burchard, the author of *High Performance Habits: How Extraordinary People Become That Way*, explains that Winfrey uses these questions to help everyone in the room get on the same page.

The questions above help us understand how A-listers think; we see that they're focused and don't want to waste time. So think about these questions before your next important meeting, and let them help you prepare.

THE KEY TO SURVIVAL AT THE HIGHEST LEVELS

It's important to deliver on what you promise because it helps you maintain trust and credibility. If, however, for some reason you can't deliver, make sure you can articulate why. Strong communication between you and your clients is essential. Understand what your clients' communication styles are, what type of information they like to receive, and how they like to receive that information. Some clients want an update via phone where you check in once a day, once a week, or once a month. Others prefer a very detailed report with progress updates sent by email. You can also use the Process Communication Model, outlined in chapter 4, to help you match your clients' or prospects' communication styles.

Additionally, figuring out how to communicate can help you deal with tough-to-crack clients. For example, actor Kevin Costner wasn't interested in working with a trainer, but his wife encouraged him to meet with Platinum Fitness owner Peter Park. It was one of the first times Park felt he might fail with a client. Costner wasn't excited about having to be at the gym, and Park was working hard to find a Hook Point to motivate him. Eventually, Park realized that Costner had a deep love of baseball. When the actor came into the gym, he would see Park training a lot of professional baseball players, and he would light up. They started talking about baseball, and Costner would get enthused by how much knowledge Park had about his beloved sport. That was the hook that broke the barrier and got Costner interested in Park's experience and training. Finding this connection helped them communicate. From baseball they moved on to talking about their kids, and they've had a great relationship ever since.

As soon as I acquire celebrity clients—or any clients, for that matter—I figure out who they are as people, how they like to communicate, what they like and don't like, and what their business-related issues are. Then I pull all that information together and figure out a way to maintain effective communication and a strong connection with them.

Our personal lives and businesses revolve around communication. Every conflict and war is a result of poor communication in some sense. So, do whatever you can to become the best possible communicator you can be in order to create success and harmony.

YOUR JACKET DOESN'T FIT; GET IT TAILORED

Peter Park often competes with himself to see how quickly he can figure out what type of exercise program a new client may need. These days he can very quickly read if people are Type A and need a super-strict, challenging, ketogenic workout, or if they require a more relaxed approach. Park is able to go in, figure out the best solution, and deliver within the first session.

He notes that some personal trainers do the same cookie-cutter workouts with all their clients, which doesn't work—this often leads to huge client-retention issues. Instead, they should experiment and find the best approach for each client.

One size does not usually fit all, which is why the process of testing and learning applies to any business. If you want to acquire first-rate clients, be adaptable, read each person as an individual, and meet his or her needs so you can provide top-notch service to all.

KILLING IT WITH CONFIDENCE

When working with well-known clients, a lot of people psych themselves out—they get nervous and lose their confidence. But even when Peter Park is at Elon Musk's house, he knows that the entrepreneur is just another guy. Once he starts watching Musk move, Park gets into his flow and sees that people are just people, regardless of their stature.

Park wasn't always this levelheaded. When he worked with his first major clients, such as Lance Armstrong, he would get very nervous. It's taken time and experience for him to develop 100 percent confidence. Now, when he walks into a room, he knows that he's good at what he does, and his mental attitude is, "I'm going to go in and show this guy that he can't live without me." His clients desire health and fitness, and he knows he can help them achieve their goals.

It's normal to feel insecure when first putting yourself in top-level environments where you deal with the most successful people in the world. To better manage unproductive nerves, stay present in the moment and remain focused on the work.

THE SKILLFUL ART OF BOUNDARIES

Sometimes celebrity clients are tough to work with. They can require a lot of extra attention, which often makes having a lot of them on your roster impractical. You have to set boundaries for yourself and be sure not to overextend for specific clients, especially if they'll be a detriment to the rest of your business and your other clients.

Recently, I had discussions with a celebrity client who really wanted to work with me. Based on the initial conversations with this person's team, I knew he would be difficult to work with. I ended up putting a huge price tag on my services because I didn't really want to take him on. And if I were going to do it, I wanted enough financial compensation that it would be worth dealing with these potential difficulties. By throwing out this huge price for my services, the deal didn't go through (which, again, was essentially why I did it).

To provide world-class service, avoid difficult and draining people. Personally, I don't want to deal with that type of energy. I have private clients who pay me a lot of money, and I need to focus a lot of attention on them to ensure they're successful, so I'm cautious about those I decide to work with. I always vet people to make sure they're the right fit before accepting them as new clients.

Don't go after people just because they have a lot of money or because they're big names. Put up boundaries for you and your business so you can maintain trust and credibility with the clients who matter. Make sure you choose the right clients, whom you can have healthy relationships with. Doing so will put you in the best position to provide stellar service.

WHEN WEAKNESS = SUCCESS

Know your strengths and find people who can cover for you in weak areas. It's critically important to have a clear understanding of what you do and do not excel in. With this awareness, you can double down on what you're good at and use your energy more efficiently.

A lot of people think the contrary is true—they feel that they need to focus on their weak areas to fill in the gaps. If it's an area or skill that's crucial to your success, then go ahead and work on improving it. Otherwise, I advise focusing on your expertise. In other words, if you're gifted with communication and language skills, don't focus on math and writing code.

THE MOST SUCCESSFUL PEOPLE KNOW NOTHING

The most successful people are humble. They know that they don't know everything, so they stay hungry for knowledge. Ignorant people, on the other hand, believe they already know everything, so they ultimately stop learning . . . and fail. I find that whether these people are competitors or those in a related field, I'm constantly learning from others. I enjoy talking with people about their pricing structures, business models, and marketing strategies—I love to understand how they approach different facets of their work. Then I dissect what I learn and figure out how to apply this information to improve my business model.

Recently, I met author and CEO Nathan Latka, a very smart and successful entrepreneur who's the author of the *Wall Street Journal* bestseller *How to Be a Capitalist Without Any Capital: The Four Rules You Must Break to Get Rich.* I had the pleasure of having breakfast with him while he broke down his business strategies. One of the things that resonated with me was that when he first started out, he would only present million-dollar deals to potential clients and partners. He knew that most of those deals would be turned down, but it taught him to feel comfortable asking for large dollar amounts. I found this to be a really smart way to approach the business mindset—you quickly learn how to change your self-perception about what you're worth as well as how to demonstrate your perceived value to others.

By conversing with smart and savvy businesspeople, you learn how they approach business. You don't have to follow suit necessarily, but you can take that information, digest it, and then determine if and how you'd like to use it. You don't have to reinvent the wheel. Let other people's success guide you in creating yours.

(If you're interested in having me coach or advise you personally, email me at bkane@brendanjkane.com, or visit brendanjkane.com/work-with -brendan.)

Quick Tips and Recap

1. The key to building and maintaining an impressive client roster is knowing how to make decisions that keep you top of mind.
2. If you want access to celebrities, CEOs, or billionaires, don't approach them directly. Go through the trusted circle around them, and provide value to each individual within it.

3. Before meetings with CEOs, ask yourself, "What keeps them up at night?"

4. When in rooms with leaders of organizations, ask: "As the leader of this company, what are your biggest priorities?" as well as "What are your biggest concerns?"

5. If you want first-rate clients, be adaptable, read each person as an individual, and meet their needs so you can provide top-notch service to all.

6. If you feel insecure around high-level people, remember to stay present and focus on the work.

7. Know your strengths, and hire people who can cover for you in your weaker areas.

8. You don't have to reinvent the wheel. Learn from other people's success, and let it guide you in creating yours.

CHAPTER 10

YOUR HOOK POINT IS DEAD; LONG LIVE THE HOOK POINT

As we've discussed throughout this book, Hook Points are designed to help you stand out and thrive in the 3-second world. Once you've identified and perfected the Hook Point process, you need to build a solid brand foundation to support the growth that comes from the attention your Hook Points bring. If your brand is solid, you'll be better able to harness the power of the attention you'll receive from effective Hook Points.

You also have to be willing to revise, test, and innovate your hooks continually (especially when attaining success). What works today may not work in a year, a month, or even a week from now. This is because of several factors that contribute to what I call "hook fatigue," which I cover at the end of this chapter. Engaging in this process is what leads to long-term success.

WHO ARE YOU?

When Nate Morley, founder of Works Collective, and one of the top brand strategists in the United States, works with a brand to reach the next level, he helps them answer these fundamental questions about who they are:

- What is our purpose?
- Why do we exist?
- What do we want to say?
- Who do we want to say it to?
- How are we different?
- What do we value?
- How do we behave?
- How are we different from other people in the space?

Morley explains that when brands answer these questions, they learn who they are and develop a distinct point of view. He believes that lasting growth, strength, and success do not come from knowing what you *do*, but from knowing who you *are* as a brand; if you solely talk about what you do, you make yourself more vulnerable to competitors and don't allow yourself to connect with people in a long-term, meaningful way. Morley states, "The best brands in the world use their marketing efforts to tell people who they are; and what they do, make, or offer becomes an expression or proof of who they are."

Morley states, however, that for companies who are just starting out, there are situations where they need to talk about what they do before they can talk about who they are. For example, photo book printing company Chatbooks (which Morley advises) started their marketing efforts by saying, "Print $6 photo books from your Instagram account." This message served to get the company up and running—initial users needed to know what Chatbooks did, but eventually they had to change this message as the company evolved and as competitors arrived to the space.

Morley posits, "Imagine if Chatbooks was still using the same messaging two years from their inception, and another company came along and said,

'Print $5 photo books from your Instagram account.' That would put Chatbooks in a very vulnerable position. This is inevitable in any space. At some point a brand has to transform from talking about what they do to talking about who [they are] to keep their customers loyal."

Talking about who you are creates longevity. To help Chatbooks evolve from "Print $6 photo books from your Instagram account," Morley asked the founders why they started the company and why they wanted to sell photo books. By answering these fundamental questions, the founders learned that "who they were" and "why they did it" was tied to their desire to strengthen family connections. After discovering this, Morley developed the messaging: "Hold On to What Matters." Chatbooks is a great way to allow people to hold on to what is meaningful to them—the memories, the people, the experiences, and so on—in a completely new way. And there's a double meaning, in that customers can not only hold on to their memories, but they can also hold the physical photo book in their hands.

Morley explains, "Chatbooks evolved from a $6 photobook printing company to a 'Hold On to What Matters' company, and eventually they even evolved a little further—currently they talk about strengthening families." Morley says that science proves that having photos of your family ready and available creates bonds with kids, parents, grandparents, and cousins; it actually makes family ties stronger. Chatbooks has become a company that helps strengthen families, which can be expressed in a variety of ways. Morley's guidance around the difference between "what we do" and "who we are" helped the brand evolve.

So take the time to discover who you are. It will help your company grow and achieve lasting longevity. Your customers are loyal to who you are, not what you do. It may take time to discover who you are, but you won't regret asking yourself these fundamental questions.

IT ISN'T EASY, BUT IT'S SIMPLE

Many people find that coming up with great Hook Points and stories is hard. Copywriter Ernest Lupinacci says that the truth is, while it may be hard, it's also simple. He points out that writing a movie, climbing Mount Everest, and completing a triathlon are in no way easy tasks, but they're all actually quite simple—there are a few clear steps one needs to take in order to achieve each goal—the kicker is that completing those steps is difficult. For example, to finish the Ironman Triathlon, you simply need to swim 2.4 miles, bike 112 miles, and run 26.2 miles. When Lupinacci explains this to people, they usually react by saying, "That sounds hard." To which he replies, "I didn't say it was easy, I said it was *simple*."

Lupinacci continues, "Finding a Hook Point that stops people in their tracks is simple. We all know what it sounds like—something likened to the 1969 newspaper headline: "'3:56 am: man steps on to the moon.'"[72] Recognizing a great Hook Point after the fact is easy, and the steps to creating one are simple, but actually finding a hook for your business or brand is hard. That's why you need to work at it every day and keep the Hook Point Framework in your mind. As with any endeavor, it takes repetition to become a master. Luckily, I've had the advantage of practicing this process every day for the past 15 years.

(So, if you or your business would like help from my team in creating Hook Points, please visit: www.hookpoint.com/agency and fill out the brief questionnaire telling us about your business and goals.)

---

[72] Anthony Tucker, "3 56 am: man steps on to the moon," *The Guardian, Jul. 21, 1969,* https://www.theguardian.com/theguardian/from-the-archive-blog/2011/jun/01/newspapers -national-newspapers.

RUN YOUR BRAND LIKE MARVEL RUNS ITS STUDIO

Doug Scott, former president of Ogilvy Entertainment and current president of Big Block, believes that because we live in a world of "moments," where digital and social media make everything move at a faster pace, brands often lose sight of building long-term consumer relationships, and instead focus on short-term campaign communications. He explains that although a lot of sales efforts are now direct to consumer, brands need to continue to build their cultural relevance. Oftentimes people are in transit or taking breaks from their regular activities, and during this downtime they scroll through social media until something hooks them. Today, there are many micro-touchpoints where you can market and sell to consumers quickly. But to actually succeed in turning the attention you capture in these short windows into actual sales, you need to build strong relationships with your customers and have consistency in your narratives across various platforms.

Remember that brands are storytellers, no different from Marvel Studios. Scott thinks that Kevin Feige, the president of Marvel Studios, has done an amazing job of transmedia storytelling, saying, "Marvel and Disney have built a meta-verse that lives across various mediums, which is critically important to help people connect with their characters and stories. So, if it's a strategic tool for Marvel, why would a global brand think it's not important for them to ensure their messaging remains consistent and clear across the various platforms in which they tell their stories?"

You can't just capture someone's attention on social media and abandon the relationship or show something catchy that's incongruent with the rest of your content. Your brand needs to be structured like a movie studio. Scott explains that products ladder up into master brand positioning just like movies within a franchise property. They drive the return on investment and the quarterly earnings of your "studio," and it should be clear that your "plush toys" and "theme-park experiences" are part of your intellectual property and not someone else's. The toys are likened to your products, and the theme park is likened to your physical store or social media content, where people can engage with and experience what you make.

Essentially, every touchpoint must be connected, which is achieved by understanding the role the particular medium plays in your overall narrative. Scott believes that whether a person is leaning back after a long day and watching 30-second TV spots, coming across content in their social streams, or receiving emails, the brand's narrative needs to be consistent and relevant because that's what earns permission and trust, leading to consumers' limited time and attention.

Using the tools provided in this book can help you create a strong brand narrative, so remember to develop Hook Points and stories that are authentic and provide value to your audience.

FIND YOUR *MONEYBALL* SOLUTION

Ernest Lupinacci explains that a major plot point in the movie *Moneyball* is how for years, the scouts would pore over tons of statistics to determine whether or not players would be good draft picks. In the movie, Jonah Hill's character realizes that there is ultimately only one data point that matters, which is if players can get on first base. This is because if they can't do so, they can't score runs. So as implausible as it sounds, if players can consistently get on first, it mitigates every negative statistic they might lay claim to—and vice versa, even if players are very good at playing certain positions and boast all sorts of records, this won't actually help the team if they can't get to first base consistently.

Using this analogy, Lupinacci tries to find *Moneyball* solutions for all his clients. For business strategy and advertising, the *Moneyball* solution is the principle that helps a company understand why they make the decisions they do. For instance, Lupinacci posits that Apple's success is rooted in the belief system that "if you want to be successful, you don't have to think harder or more intelligently; you just have to think *different*." This "think different" principle is the *Moneyball* solution that theoretically helps Apple make all of their decisions.

"Why did Apple come up with the idea of opening up their own branded retail stores? Couldn't they have just sold their products at Best Buy?" The response is, "No, because they had to think different." And if someone asked, "Why does Apple invest so much energy and money on their design and packaging? Once people open the boxes, don't they just throw them away?" The response, again driven by the *Moneyball* solution is, "Yeah, but they thought different."

Another example of a company that has historically benefited from embracing their *Moneyball* solution is FedEx. Lupinacci asks, "You know how in order to be successful in business, there are certain things that absolutely, positively, have to arrive somewhere overnight?" To which most people would reply, "Yeah, I do know that." "And you know how a lot of people aren't working 40-hour workweeks anymore, they work 80-hour workweeks, so at the end of each day there's a lot of stuff people need to send across the country and it absolutely has to be there overnight?" To which, again, most people would reply, "Yes." "Well, FedEx is the solution to that problem."

One could argue that over the course of the evolution of their business, every single thing FedEx did was to ensure the packages they were trusted with would absolutely, positively, arrive when and where they promised. When FedEx makes a decision to buy extra trucks, it's because this helps them keep their promise. When they decided to buy Kinko's, it's because this acquisition helped make it easier for them to get more types of things to where they had to be when they needed to be there. Every decision FedEx makes is in service to this one guiding *Moneyball* principle.

In my opinion, this same analogy of the *Moneyball* solution can be applied to the importance of your Hook Point. Having a great Hook Point is the first step in your *Moneyball* solution because it is literally what gets you on first base with your customers. Without it, you can't get anyone's attention in order to score more runs with them. Hook Points help you earn consumers' time and attention so you can tell them about the stories and beliefs that drive your business.

EMPATHY IS THE GREATEST DRIVER OF INNOVATION

Lupinacci says that when trying to come up with new ideas for Hook Points and stories, you should keep in mind that "empathy is the greatest driver of innovation." As a business, you're trying to solve people's problems, and oftentimes the most important ones you can solve for your customers are mutually exclusive from your products. For example, Lupinacci explains that the main problem Nike always sought to help address is that while many people aspire to be athletic, not everyone felt fit enough or confident enough to go to the gym, take a class, or play a sport. Nike's solution is to consistently encourage us all to "Just Do It" anyway. The brilliance of this message is that you don't even need to buy their products—you just need to get out there and do whatever it is that you want to do.

Lupinacci adds that most of us walk (or sit) around with our personal problems rattling about in our heads, so if—along with your Hook Points, stories, or products—you can ask, "How can I be of assistance to you?" instead of "Do you want to try our new XYZ?" you will better connect with your consumers. Using empathy to anticipate and understand your customers' needs helps you structure your campaigns and products with meaningfully innovative solutions. Using empathy helps you go further and faster, and also helps you come up with better Hook Points.

INCLUSION FOR SUCCESS

John Kilcullen, the creator of the *For Dummies* book series, explains that we typically hire people who are similar or familiar to us. He recommends breaking away from this cycle and your norm. Through inclusion and diversity of thought, geography, and point of view, you'll arrive at greater truths and receive breakthrough insights more quickly.

He also advises creating an environment of *eustress* in your business and on your teams. Eustress is moderate psychological stress that's beneficial for the person experiencing it. Creating this type of environment makes people feel like they're thriving. They think, *Wow, this is taking a lot of hours and it's hard work, but I feel challenged, pushed, and invigorated.* Be cautious, however, to find the balance between an environment where people feel overly stressed, in fight-or-flight mode, and one where they feel truly passionate about their challenges.

THE HOOK POINT MARATHON

Endurance, follow-through, and the willingness to learn are at the core of most people's success. You can only fail if you give up. Maintain a strong work ethic, and surround yourself with people who inspire and support you—and steer away from those who tear you down and who don't believe in your dreams.

As you work toward your goals, also remember to stay clear about who you are and why you do what you do. Align your Hook Points with your personal ideals, provide value through your stories, be true to yourself, and again, don't give up. The more you practice the principles in this book, the more you'll learn, which will help you stand out quickly in the 3-second world in which you find yourself.

HOOK FATIGUE: EVEN WHEN YOU SUCCEED, TRY, TRY AGAIN

A time will come when you find a Hook Point that helps you stand out and scale your brand. When this happens, you'll probably think that your work is done—but think again—the truth is, your work in applying the Hook Point Framework to your business has just begun. Hooks need to be revised, tested, and innovated constantly. What works today may not work a year, a month, or even a week from now. This is because of several factors that contribute to what I call "hook fatigue."

The first cause of hook fatigue is attributed to the truth in the old adage "Imitation is the sincerest form of flattery." If you come up with an innovative Hook Point, it's inevitable that someone will eventually copy your concept. When this happens, take it as a compliment and go back to the drawing board, because your hook is about to become less effective.

Unfortunately, even if the other company does a bad job of copying your hook, it still makes it less unique.

Earlier we discussed how other brands started copying the Toms Shoes "one for one" Hook Point. This was a brilliant hook that worked very well, but when other brands started implementing the concept into their campaigns, it became less unique and therefore less effective. The same can be said about Netflix's original hook. Initially, Netflix beat out the competition, especially Blockbuster, by launching their streaming service. Today, Hulu, Amazon, Disney, and Showtime all have their own streaming services. The competition has forced Netflix to be innovative, which is why they're projected to spend $17 billion on content creation alone in 2020.[73] Currently, compelling Netflix original content, such as *Stranger Things* and *The Umbrella Academy*, is Netflix's hook.

The second reason you need to constantly evolve your Hook Points is because regardless of whether or not other brands copy them, over time, hooks lose their appeal. As soon as people become too familiar with your hooks, you're forced to innovate. The decision makers at Disneyland and Disney World are well aware of this fact, which is why they've invested $1 billion to build Star Wars: Galaxy's Edge (the *Star Wars*–themed area inside Disneyland and Disney World that I mentioned in chapter 1).[74] Disney knows that to keep their revenue high, they need a constant influx of

---

[73] Todd Spangler, "Netflix Projected to Spend More Than $17 Billion on Content in 2020," *Variety, Jan. 16, 2020,* https://variety.com/2020/digital/news/netflix-2020-content-spending-17-billion-1203469237/.

[74] Frank Pallotta, "Disney spared no expense in building Star Wars: Galaxy's Edge," CNN Business, May, 30, 2019, https://www.cnn.com/2019/05/29/media/star-wars-land-galaxys-edge-opening/index.html.

visitors coming to their parks. Again, I'm not suggesting that no one would ever go back to these entertainment venues if the company never launched a new ride again—I'm simply explaining that if Disney wants to maintain their share of the market and attention in this 3-second world we now live in, they have to stay relevant and create new hooks that keep people coming back for more.

A NEW HOOK POINT EVERY WEEK?

The frequency with which you need to generate new Hook Points is unique for each brand and business. Some brands can wait as long as every couple of years, while others will need to create new hooks on a daily basis. For example, when I was working with Katie Couric, we conducted interviews every few days and created new Hook Points to drive people to her content, which was released nearly every day. Compared to Netflix, Nike and many of the other larger brands don't have to come up with hooks at that frequency. Also, keep a close eye on your competition, because what they do will affect the frequency with which you need to create new hooks as well. Above all, regardless of your industry and the size of your brand, I advise you to constantly have your next Hook Point in the back of your mind. In our micro-attention culture, having compelling hooks at your disposal is one of the best ways to ensure you stand out and retain/gain market share.

However, with that said, I do have one word of caution—make sure you evolve and develop your hooks in a way that doesn't confuse your consumers. Nike and Netflix are in a position where they can have hundreds, potentially thousands of hooks, and it won't confuse their consumers because people are so familiar with those brands—they have a solid foundation and brand voice that they don't stray from when they come up with new hooks. Other lesser-known brands don't have that luxury. They may need to start by focusing on one or two hooks for a duration of six months to a year to build a solid foundation—and before they start to reach hook fatigue—which is when they will need to work on finding new Hook Points.

THE HOOK POINT FIVE-STEP CREATION PROCESS IS YOUR LIFE RAFT

Having an understanding of hooks and working through the Hook Point Five-Step Creation Process *often* will help any company. If you build the use of this framework into your overall business strategy, you'll have a one-up on competitors. Revising and examining your hooks on an ongoing basis gives you power. Even Craig Clemens, whose copywriting has sold more than $1 billion in products, still tests and writes copy for Golden Hippo's landing pages. He says, "I still write hooks, headlines, and copy because it keeps me fresh. Testing out new ideas helps me stay innovative and run a more successful company."

I want you to walk away knowing that the Hook Point Framework—and everything you've learned in this book—are tools that you should use again and again. Most likely you won't create the best hook the first time around, and even if you do hit the jackpot right away, your successful hook will eventually decline. To triumph in the long term, hooks need to be constantly created, tested, and revised. Some of the smartest people I know have achieved remarkable results through continual testing and evolution of themselves and their brands.

Be aware that what works today may not work tomorrow, six months, or a year from now. To make sure you stay relevant and top of mind with potential consumers, instill the Hook Point Framework, and the "test, learn, and evolve" way of thinking to your approach to business. It will help you create the best Hook Points; and give your brand, products, and services a better chance at long-term success. These concepts help you survive when the competition strikes, the economy takes a dip, there's an industry-wide issue, or when other obstacles come your way. Innovation keeps you strong and helps you stay in the forefront of the 3-second marketplace.

Quick Tips and Recap

1. Build a solid brand foundation to support and sustain the growth that comes from the attention your Hook Points capture.

2. Take the time to answer the fundamental questions shared in this chapter about who you are as a brand. It will lead to lasting growth, success, and strength.

3. Finding a hook for your business or brand is difficult, which is why you need to work at it every day and keep the Hook Point Framework in mind.

4. Brands are storytellers—no different from Marvel Studios—so treat your brand as though it is a movie studio, and keep your messaging consistent and clear across various platforms.

5. Hook Points help you earn consumers' time and attention so you can tell them about the stories and beliefs that drive your business.

6. Use empathy to understand your customers' needs so you can structure your campaigns with meaningfully innovative solutions.

7. Hooks need to be revised, tested, and innovated constantly.

8. In our micro-attention culture, having compelling hooks at your disposal is one of the best ways to ensure that you stand out and retain/gain market share.

9. If you build the use of the Hook Point Framework into your overall business strategy, you'll have a one-up on competitors. Revising and examining your hooks on an ongoing basis gives you power to survive when the competition strikes, the economy takes a dip, there's an industry-wide issue, or when other obstacles come your way.

10. Instill the "test, learn, and evolve" way of thinking into your approach to business.

11. Innovation keeps you strong and helps you stay in the forefront of the 3-second marketplace.

ACKNOWLEDGMENTS

First, I want to thank my literary agent, Bill Gladstone, the best agent in the world, without whom this book would not be possible. Bill, it still astonishes me that someone with your stature, having represented more than $5 billion worth of book sales, has taken the time to pilot this project and my career as an author. Thank you for your continuing support, and I look forward to working with you on future books.

Thank you, Latham Arneson, for being such a wonderful friend. I enjoyed our meaningful conversations about how to achieve maximum results for all of the movies we worked on at Paramount Pictures, and I'm glad we're continuing to have great conversations. I'm so grateful you were able to contribute to this book.

To Michael Breus, thank you for your friendship and guidance over the years. I look forward to continuing to work together to have a positive impact on the world.

Erick Brownstein, I'm eternally grateful for all the guidance and insight you've provided over the years. What you and your team do at Shareability is extraordinary, and your perspective is always valuable.

Thank you, Craig Clemens, for your friendship. Learning from you has been a true pleasure, and I enjoy spending time with both you and your wife, Sara Anne Stewart. I appreciate everything you've done for me, all of the knowledge you've shared, and I look forward to years of friendship to come.

Keith Ferrazzi, thank you for being such a great friend, mentor, and collaborator. I look forward to working together more closely in the future.

To Naveen Gowda, thanks for being such an incredible creator and collaborator. You've taught me so much about content creation, mindset, and approaching content in a way that can reach tens of millions, if not hundreds of millions, of people. I look forward to our continued partnership and to watching how your expertise has a tremendous impact on other people's social media business goals.

As always, thank you, Mike Jurkovac, for your creative partnership, guidance, and support over the years. I'm enthused to continue working with you on future projects.

Jim Kane, thanks so much for the support and mentorship over the years, both as a father and as a businessperson. I truly appreciate the countless hours you've spent reviewing agreements since the earliest stages of my entrepreneurial career. And, of course, thank you for sharing your wisdom in this book. I know that it will have a significant impact on people's lives, similar to the way it has had an impact on my life.

To John Kilcullen, thank you so much for sharing your experience with everyone out there reading this book. It's going to provide tremendous value, and I greatly appreciate your insight, from which I have learned so much.

Thank you, Jeff King. Your teachings about the Process Communication Model (PCM) have transformed my life. I'm grateful for all your support and guidance. I love our conversations about communication and how it not only impacts business, content, and social media, but also our daily lives. PCM and your presence in my life have been greatly significant.

To Vishen Lakhiani, thank you so much for taking the time to write the foreword and for championing my work. I hope we continue to collaborate for many years and work together to leave the world a better place for all the "Eves."

Alex Livian, thank you so much for participating in this book. It's been a true pleasure getting to know you as a friend and also as a business collaborator. You have a tremendous amount of wisdom and knowledge that I know is going to transform the world in a positive way.

To Ernest Lupinacci, thank you so much for taking the time to share your knowledge and wisdom with not only myself, but with the world. Even though we've only known each other for a short period of time, I really look forward to continuing conversations and finding different ways to collaborate.

Thank you, Nate Morley, for the knowledge you provided not only in this book but in every conversation we've ever had. Your experience and knowledge in branding are unmatched. You always find innovative ways to make an impact.

Peter Park, thank you for all of your mentorship and for helping me with my health and wellness over the past few years. You've made a tremendous impact on my life, both personally and professionally. I'm grateful you were willing to share your experiences and stories in this book. I know they will impact a lot of people's lives.

Thank you so much, Doug Scott, for your contributions to this book. Your wisdom will help people all over the world, and I truly appreciate that you took the time to share it.

To the team at Waterside Productions, thank you for your dedication to this book and for preparing it to go to market. A sincere thanks to all the team, and especially to Bill and Gayle Gladstone, Jill Kramer, Kenneth Kales, and Josh Freel.

Thank you to the brilliant members of my team. Our growth would not be possible without your continual hard work and dedication. A special salute to Faye Chuasukonthip, Strahil Hadzhiev, Patricia Handschiegel, Javier Vital, and Gary White.

Last, but certainly not least, Tara Rose Gladstone, thank you for all of your dedication, effort, and support in creating this book. Your knowledge and hard work have made this possible. I appreciate our collaborations and look forward to continuing to work together on future projects.

ABOUT THE AUTHOR

BRENDAN KANE is an out-of-the-box thinker for Fortune 500 corporations, brands, and celebrities. He thrives on helping his clients systematically engage new audiences that reward relevant content, products, and services with their attention and purchases. His greatest strength lies in unlocking value by transforming complexity into simplicity through tools and methods that amplify growth and enable execution.

Having started his career at Lakeshore Entertainment, Brendan oversaw all aspects of the company's interactive media strategy. He worked on 16 films that generated a worldwide gross of $685 million and also pioneered the first-ever influencer campaign to effectively promote *Crank* starring Jason Statham.

Brendan went on to build social media applications and digital platforms for celebrity clients such as Taylor Swift, Rihanna, supermodel Adriana Lima, and pro skateboarder Ryan Sheckler. He also served as vice president of digital for Paramount Pictures and helped scale one of the largest social optimization firms in the world; worked with brands such as Disney, Fox, NBC, Netflix, Xbox, and LinkedIn; as well as many notable Fortune 100 companies.

Most recently, Brendan is known for generating one million followers in over 100 countries in less than 30 days. He went on to publish the best-selling book *One Million Followers*, which breaks down how he achieved such a feat.

brendanjkane.com

WE CAN HELP

As I mentioned earlier, my team and I have been perfecting the Hook Point system for more than 15 years. We know from experience how much time it takes to get the perfect Hook Point for a business. So that's why I wanted to create a way that I can make myself and my team of creatives available to you and your brand to help you develop your Hook Points.

The Hook Points we develop for our private clients drive:

- Large-scale revenue growth
- Significant deals and partnerships (e.g., publishing deals and high-paying licensing deals)
- Winning marketing campaigns
- Successful rebranding
- Any other specific business goal

The investment for us to create a done-for-you Hook Point is significant; however, the results we achieve for our clients are exponential, and the return on investment is massive.

If you're interested in hiring us to develop a Hook Point for you, visit www.hookpoint.com/agency, and fill out the brief questionnaire telling us about your business and goals.